Corporate Whistleblowing Regulation

Sulette Lombard · Vivienne Brand ·
Janet Austin
Editors

Corporate Whistleblowing Regulation

Theory, Practice, and Design

Springer

Editors
Sulette Lombard
Flinders University
Bedford Park, SA, Australia

Vivienne Brand
Flinders University
Bedford Park, SA, Australia

Janet Austin
University of New Brunswick
Fredericton, NB, Canada

ISBN 978-981-15-0258-3 ISBN 978-981-15-0259-0 (eBook)
https://doi.org/10.1007/978-981-15-0259-0

This Springer imprint is published by the registered company Springer Nature Singapore Pte Ltd.
The registered company address is: 152 Beach Road, #21-01/04 Gateway East, Singapore 189721, Singapore

Foreword

A number of recent high-profile corruption scandals have demonstrated the positive impact of employees speaking out to expose wrongdoing. Whistleblowers are becoming an increasingly important part of corporate compliance, of national law enforcement and of international efforts against corruption. In response, several countries, including Australia, have passed laws to better protect whistleblowers over the last decade.

Company policies are also beginning to reflect the value of whistleblowers to corporate governance and risk management. Most whistleblowers choose to report misconduct internally within their organisations, as opposed to reporting straight to law enforcement agencies. The facilitation and protection of whistleblowing should be a central pillar to corporate internal controls and ethics and compliance programmes, and be mainstreamed in corporate culture. Such practices can help to strengthen trust with the public, detect misconduct, and avoid fines, scandals and the kind of reputational damage that can weigh on a company's long-term performance.

Despite these positive shifts, whistleblowing in both the public and private sectors remains a dangerous activity across the globe. Contributing factors include power differences between organisations and individual employees, legal uncertainty over protection, poor reporting mechanisms and cultural barriers. From a law enforcement perspective, discrepancies between whistleblower protection standards at the national and international levels also pose a significant obstacle to detecting, preventing and punishing misconduct.

The OECD has long recognised the importance of whistleblowing, and has established a number of intergovernmental whistleblower protection instruments around its multilateral Anti-Bribery Convention, such as the OECD's 2009 Recommendation on Further Combating Foreign Bribery. After 20 years of monitoring countries' compliance with the convention and associated provisions, it is clear that whistleblower protection frameworks in many countries are lacking. Currently, only two per cent of foreign bribery schemes resulting in sanctions were detected by whistleblowers—which is well below expectations given the advantage employees have in detecting wrongdoing.

Corporate Whistleblowing Regulation—Theory, Practice, and Design speaks to these trends and the challenges that surround them. It compares a range of measures taken across jurisdictions to encourage corporate whistleblowing, and delves into important questions about financial incentives and rewards. It also explores the complex relationship between whistleblowing and corporate compliance, provides insights into the design of comprehensive corporate whistleblowing systems and underlines the benefits for business. These are important considerations because such systems can have grave implications for those who decide to speak out in the face of misconduct, and for those responsible for protecting them.

As attitudes towards whistleblowing change, so does the international policy landscape around it. In 2019, the European Union adopted far-reaching legislation for the legal protection of whistleblowers across its member states, while G20 leaders endorsed new High-Level Principles Effective Protection of Whistleblowers at their summit in Osaka. The ISO is developing an industry standard for whistleblowing, while the OECD's current review of its Recommendation on Further Combating Foreign Bribery includes reconsideration of whistleblower provisions.

All of these developments are helping to drive much needed harmonisation of whistleblowing standards. Against such a promising backdrop, *Corporate Whistleblowing Regulation—Theory, Practice, and Design* makes a timely contribution to national and international discussions, and serves as a valuable reference point for policymakers, businesses and civil society alike.

Greg Medcraft
Director, Directorate for Financial
and Enterprise Affairs
Organisation for Economic Co-operation
and Development
Paris, France

Acknowledgements

The idea for this book had its germination in a range of corporate whistleblowing research activity over a period of years, as regulatory attention to whistleblowing issues continued to gain momentum. At the point at which it became clear that whistleblowing had become a key concern for many corporate regulators across a range of jurisdictions, we perceived the need for a compilation of discussions addressing this fast-evolving area of corporate regulation and practice. We are grateful to the authors of chapters in this book for their ready acceptance of our invitation to participate. Their enthusiasm for the topic of whistleblowing, and their wide-ranging review of issues relevant to contemporary whistleblowing practice in corporations, further confirmed our perception that corporate whistleblowing was an idea whose time had come.

In preparing a book across continents, jurisdictions and time zones, we have been immensely assisted by the responsiveness and professionalism of the contributing authors. The editors would like to express their sincere thanks to each of the contributors for their willingness to participate in this project—the valuable perspectives that they offer from different areas of expertise and practice, as well as punctual delivery of contributions, are greatly appreciated. In the background, we have received excellent ongoing support from Springer, who immediately recognised the value of a book of this kind when initially approached, and we are very grateful. A heartfelt thank you also to Leigh-Ellen Dunstan, Chee Ng and Patrick Delaney for the significant time commitment and amount of work that they put in to get the manuscript ready for submission.

We anticipate that whistleblowing will continue to grow in significance as a regulatory tool and hope that this book will contribute to the debate that will accompany that growth.

July 2019

Sulette Lombard
Vivienne Brand
Janet Austin

Introduction

Corporate governance is arguably entering a new phase internationally, with increasing pressure on corporations to account for their impact on all stakeholders and to justify their social licence to operate. In this environment, regulators are frequently searching for new tools to make regulation more effective, both to improve their enforcement outcomes and to compliment efforts by corporations to enhance corporate culture and transparency.

Corporate Whistleblowing

Against this background, encouraging corporate whistleblowing is emerging as an important regulatory mechanism. Miceli and Near's describe whistleblowing as 'organization members' disclosure of illegal, immoral or illegitimate practices under the control of their employers, to parties who may be able to effect action'.[1] The 'parties who may be able to effect action' could be reached through internal reporting and compliance mechanisms, or externally, for example, by way of reporting to a regulator. Corporate whistleblowing is becoming regarded as a very useful way in which to expose wrongdoing and, at the same time, promote good governance in the corporate sector.[2] Previously underutilised, fostering such

[1] Miceli M. P. and Near J. P., 'Characteristics of Organizational Climate and Perceived Wrongdoing Associated with Whistle-Blowing Decisions' (1985) 38 *Personnel Psychology* 525, at 525.

[2] Brand V. and Lombard S., 'Good Governance Practice in Relation to Corporate Whistleblowing' (2015) 67 *Governance Directions* 10, 10; Near J. P. and Dworkin T. M., 'Responses to Legislative Changes: Corporate Whistleblowing Policies' (1998) 17 *Journal of Business Ethics* 1551; Hassink H., De Vries M. and Bollen L., 'A Content Analysis of Whistleblowing Policies of Leading European Companies' (2007) 75 *Journal of Business Ethics* 25, 26; Ebersole D., 'Blowing the Whistle on the Dodd-Frank Whistleblower Provisions' (2011) 6 *Ohio State entrepreneurial Business Law Journal* 123, 137; Lee G. and Fargher N., 'Companies' Use of Whistle-Blowing to Detect Fraud: An Examination of corporate Whistle-Blowing Policies' (2013) 114 *Journal of Business Ethics* 283, 285.

whistleblowing is now starting to gain widespread acceptance by regulators and corporations.

One of the rationales for encouraging corporate whistleblowing appears to be that due to the nature of the corporation, those inside the organisation are often best placed to detect and disclose wrongful conduct, or make sure it is disclosed earlier than would have been the case otherwise, thus reducing the potential harm that would result.[3] From this perspective, it seems obvious that whistleblowing should be encouraged. However, there are numerous reasons why insiders with information about wrongdoing in an organisation may feel reluctant to come forward and the significant disincentives faced by corporate whistleblowers are well documented.[4] There is also substantial debate as to the optimum way to encourage this practice. This makes a review of the regulatory and practical implications of this important device particularly timely.

An important element of any programme to encourage whistleblowing seems to be the protection of whistleblowers against retaliation.[5] The inclusion of such whistleblower protection measures in whistleblowing regulatory frameworks in many jurisdictions across the world seems to indicate almost universal support for this idea.[6]

---

[3] Vega M. A., 'Beyond Incentives: Making Corporate Whistleblowing Moral in the New Era of Dodd-Frank Bounty Hunting' (2012) *Connecticut Law Review* 483, 489; Rapp GC, 'Four Signal Movements in Whistleblower Law: 1983–2013' 30 *Hofstra Labor & Employment Law Journal* 389, 389; Kovacic W. E., 'Private Monitoring and Antitrust Enforcement: Paying Informants to Reveal Cartels' (2000–2001) 69 *George Washington Law Review* 766, 774; Pascoe J. and Welsh M., 'Whistleblowing Ethics and Corporate Culture: Theory and Practice in Australia' (2011) 40 *Common Law World Review* 144, 145; Brand V., Lombard S. and Fitzpatrick J., 'Bounty Hunters, Whistleblowers and a New Regulatory Paradigm' (2013) 41 *Australian Business Law Journal* 292, 292–293.

[4] Lipton F. D. *Whistleblowers: Incentives, Disincentives, and Protection Strategies* (Wiley, 2012), 1–2; Rapp GC, 'Beyond Protection: Invigorating Incentives for Sarbanes-Oxley Corporate and Securities Fraud Whistleblowers' (2009) 87 *Boston University Law Review* 91, 95–96; Pascoe J., 'Corporate Sector Whistleblowing in Australia: Ethics and Corporate Culture' (2009) 27 *Company and Securities Law Journal* 524, 528.

[5] Beller L., 'Whistleblower Protection Legislation of the East and West: Can It Really Reduce Corporate Fraud and Improve Corporate Governance? A Study of the Successes and Failures of Whistleblower Protection Legislation in the US and China' (2011) 873 *New York University Journal of Law and Business* 873, 876; Labriola L., 'Paying Too Dearly for a Whistle: Properly Protecting Internal Whistleblowers' (2017) 85 *Fordham Law Review* 2839, 2841–2842; Lipton F. D. *Whistleblowers: Incentives, Disincentives, and Protection Strategies* (Wiley, 2012), 179; Mavrakis N. and Legg M., 'The Dodd-Frank Act Whistleblower Reforms Put Bounty on Corporate Non-compliance: Ramifications and Lessons for Australia' (2012) 40 *Australian Business Law Review* 26, 41–42.

[6] Lipton F. D. *Whistleblowers: Incentives, Disincentives, and Protection Strategies* (Wiley, 2012), 179 indicates that about 50 countries across the world, including Australia, Canada, the United Kingdom, the USA, South Africa, etc have adopted some form of national law to protect whistleblowers. The recent proposed EU directive on whistleblowers is likely to expand the number of countries as it requires protection from retaliation provisions in the laws of countries in the EU by 2021, see Proposed Directive of the EU Parliament and of the Council on the protection of persons reporting on breaches of Union law (Proposal of 23 April 2018—Com/2018/218 Final —2018/0106).

However, regulators in the United States and Canada (Ontario) have gone one step further—both jurisdictions electing to adopt a corporate whistleblowing financial incentive scheme to complement and enhance measures to protect whistleblowers from retaliation.[7] Australia's Parliament considered financial incentives to encourage whistleblowing during a recent legislative reform process, but similar to the UK, rejected the notion,[8] instead adopting a 'compensation' scheme for whistleblowers who have suffered detriment as a result of having blown the whistle.[9] The jurisdictional divide in respect of adoption (or not) of a financial incentive scheme to encourage whistleblowing is also reflected in academic debate, with some commentators advocating for adoption of such schemes[10] and others strongly opposed to the idea.[11]

These diverse approaches, as to how to best foster corporate whistleblowing in different jurisdictions, are generating ongoing academic interest. Yet the value of these measures is not only interesting from an academic perspective—it is critically important from a practical perspective. Regulators involved in administrating and enforcing laws; legal practitioners who represent whistleblowers and the whistleblowers themselves need to be aware of the various protection measures and the possible availability of a financial incentive. Company directors and legal practitioners who advise corporate clients also need to be aware of the rules and protections surrounding corporate whistleblowers with a view to adjusting their

[7] In the USA this is achieved through the *Dodd-Frank Wall Street Reform and Consumer Protection Act* § 1, 124 Stat 1376 (2010), particularly s 21F, while the Ontario Securities Commission is operating the whistleblowing financial reward scheme on the basis of OSC Policy 15-610 *Whistleblower Program*, adopted under the *Securities Act (Ontario)*, RSO 1990, c S.5.

[8] The UK Financial Conduct Authority (FCA) and the Bank of England Prudential Regulation Authority (PRA) rejected the introduction of financial incentives for whistleblowers in a 2014 report on the basis of lack of empirical evidence demonstrating its success; moral hazards; offence it could cause to public opinion, etc.

[9] *Treasury Laws Amendment (Enhancing Whistleblower Protections) Act 2019* (Cth), ss 1317AD–1317AH provide for a broader compensation remedy, including a reverse onus of proof (s 1317AD (2B)).

[10] Arnold M. T., 'It's "Déjà vu" All Over Again: Using Bounty Hunters to Leverage Gatekeeper Duties, (2010) 45 *Tulsa Law Review* 419; Brand V., Lombard S. and Fitzpatrick J., 'Bounty Hunters, Whistleblowers and a New Regulatory Paradigm' (2013) 41 *Australian Business Law Review* 292, Rapp GC, 'Mutiny by the Bounties—The Attempt to Reform Wall Street by the New Whistleblower Provisions of the Dodd-Frank Act' (2012) 73 *Brigham Young University Law Review* 73.

[11] Berger L., Perreault S. and Wainberg J., 'Hijacking the Moral Imperative: How Financial Incentives Can Discourage Whistleblower Reporting' (2017) 36 *Auditing: A Journal of Practice and Theory* 1; Ebersole D., 'Blowing the Whistle on the Dodd-Frank Whistleblower Provisions' (2011) 6 *Ohio State Entrepreneurial Business Law Journal* 123; Lee J., 'Corporate Corruption and the New Gold Mine' (2011–2012) 77 *Brooklyn Law Review* 303; Mavrakis N. and Legg M., 'The Dodd-Frank Act Whistleblower Reforms Put Bounty on Corporate Non-compliance: Ramifications and Lessons for Australia' (2012) 40 *Australian Business Law Review* 26.

behaviour in light of the possibility of an enhanced expectation that a whistleblower may disclose information about wrongdoing within the company.

This book is designed to advance and develop the discourse on corporate whistleblowing by adopting a cross-jurisdictional approach to consider regulatory measures aimed at ensuring effective corporate whistleblowing systems. It addresses aspects such as the way in which whistleblowing is encouraged, whether it be by protection of the whistleblower from retaliation or some form of financial incentive. It studies the arguments in favour of and against the adoption of financial incentive schemes, as well as the potential implications of adoption of such schemes, from ethical-theoretical, regulatory and practical perspectives. A comparative analysis is valuable for a number of reasons, not the least of which is that it presents an opportunity to compare and contrast the approach and success of the various law reform measures. Furthermore, it has also become apparent that whistleblowers from jurisdictions other than the one in which a whistleblowing financial incentive is provided for having attempted to access that type of benefit,[12] sometimes successfully, indicating the necessity to maintain a degree of familiarity with international developments in this area of law.

Organisation and Contributions

The book draws together authors from different jurisdictions—Canada, Australia and the USA—who, through their exposure and experiences in this area of law, be it as practitioners or academics, offer valuable and interesting insights. To varying degrees, the authors consider the corporate whistleblowing regimes within these countries as well as the United Kingdom. This cross-jurisdictional approach creates an opportunity to assess how measures to enhance corporate whistleblowing work and how they may be contributing to improved corporate governance. Furthermore, for those in other countries considering reforms to their own whistleblowing regulatory frameworks, these insights may assist in determining the best approach.

The book is divided into three parts as follows:

Part I provides the context for the rest of the book and has relevance across jurisdictions. It provides insight in relation to the theoretical, political and structural issues associated with corporate whistleblower regulations and laws. Sulette Lombard (Australia) provides a cross-jurisdictional overview of key elements of private sector whistleblowing frameworks in the USA, Canada and Australia, to demonstrate how the broader legislative context could potentially influence the way in which whistleblowing frameworks operate in various jurisdictions (Chap. 1). Vivienne Brand (Australia) explores the ethical dilemmas created by

[12] In its 2017 Annual Report to Congress: Whistleblower Program, the USA Securities Exchange Commission indicates that since the inception of the whistleblower program, the Commission has received whistleblower tips from individuals in 114 countries outside the USA, the highest number of 'foreign' tips coming from the United Kingdom, Canada and Australia.

whistleblowing rewards (Chap. 2)—an issue that needed to be addressed wherever this was considered as part of the framework of whistleblower protection and regulation. Janet Austin (Canada) analyses and compares the reasons and politics behind why particular regulators in different jurisdictions decided in favour of or against the adoption of a whistleblowing rewards scheme (Chap. 3).

Part II focuses on the relationship between whistleblowing regulation and corporate governance. Ken Jull (Canada) investigates the link between whistleblowing and compliance theory, particularly where whistleblowing rewards are offered (Chap. 4). Sulette Lombard and Vivienne Brand (Australia) explore the relationship between internal whistleblowing frameworks and good corporate governance and discuss the ways in which external regulation attempts to ensure development of such internal channels of disclosure (Chap. 5). In the last chapter of Part II, Rosemary Teele Langford (Australia) analyses the relationship between corporate whistleblowing and directors' duties (Chap. 6).

Part III provides valuable practical perspectives and useful guidance for those who may be directly affected by the implementation of corporate whistleblowing regulation from two authors who have significant real-world experience in this area. Daniel J. Hurson (USA) approaches practical questions from the perspective of cases that he has been involved in representing whistleblowers seeking a reward—providing useful pointers about what it takes to be a successful whistleblower (Chap. 7). Greg Golding (Australia), also from a very practical perspective based on his area of specialisation, provides useful insights into the approach that directors should be taking in light of new trends and developments in relation to regulatory reform around corporate whistleblowing (Chap. 8).

Comment

The chapters in this book reflect upon the significant changes that have taken place in relation to corporate whistleblowing regulation over approximately the last decade until mid-2019 as the world economy has emerged from the Global Financial Crisis (GFC) to a period of relative stability. Nevertheless, despite this stability, the GFC prompted governments, regulators and corporations to reflect upon how best to strengthen corporate governance practices and how to ensure effective enforcement of securities and corporate regulations. The fostering of corporate whistleblowing has emerged as one significant way in which to advance these goals.

Given the speed of the development of corporate whistleblowing regulation over the past decade around the globe, and the interest in introducing whistleblower regulations in a number of jurisdictions, undoubtedly the law in this area will continue to evolve. More specifically, over the next few years the impact on corporate governance practices and regulator's enforcement outcomes of the reforms in the areas of both increased protection for corporate whistleblowers from retaliation and as financial incentives schemes is likely to emerge. This may spur calls for further changes to laws, regulations and practices. This push and pull of regulation may continue for some time but ultimately we are hopeful that what will emerge will be a system of corporate whistleblowing regulation which motivates corporations to avoid engaging in misconduct and results in a corporate culture which allows whistleblowers to speak out without fear of reprisal.

July 2019

Sulette Lombard
Vivienne Brand
Janet Austin

Contents

Editors and Contributors

About the Editors

Sulette Lombard is a corporate and insolvency law academic at Flinders University, Australia. She has taught and researched in an array of corporate and insolvency law areas, in both South Africa and Australia, including corporate governance and regulatory theory, and the role and position of corporate whistle-blowing in that context. She is an active member of the Australian Law Council's Corporations Committee, as well as the Insolvency and Restructuring Committee, and has been invited to appear before Australian parliamentary inquiries in relation to whistleblowing on multiple occasions.

Vivienne Brand is a legal academic with an early career in private commercial legal practice. She researches in corporate law, whistleblowing and business ethics, the area in which she undertook her doctoral studies. She has published widely on these topics within Australia and also internationally and has appeared by invitation before Federal parliamentary inquiries on whistleblowing and related topics. Vivienne is an active member of the Business Law Section of the Law Council of Australia's Corporations Committee and Foreign Corrupt Practices Working Party and has participated in the Council's submissions on whistleblowing matters.

Janet Austin is an Associate Professor in the Faculty of Law, University of New Brunswick, Canada. She previously lectured at the University of New South Wales, Sydney, Australia and spent many years as a Senior Prosecutor at Australia's Federal Prosecution Service, the Commonwealth Director of Public Prosecutions, where she conducted significant prosecutions for securities fraud. During her career she also practiced as a lawyer for Australia's corporate and securities regulator, the Australian Securities and Investments Commission and for private commercial law firms. She obtained her Ph.D. from Osgoode Law School, York University, Canada and has published many journal articles and book chapters in relation to white-collar crime and its detection, investigation and prosecution.

Contributors

Janet Austin Faculty of Law, University of New Brunswick, Fredericton, Canada

Vivienne Brand College of Business, Government and Law, Flinders University, Adelaide, Australia

Greg Golding Ashurst, Sydney, NSW, Australia

Daniel J. Hurson The Law Offices of Daniel J. Hurson, Annapolis, MD, USA

Ken Jull Gardiner Roberts LLP, Toronto, Canada

Rosemary Teele Langford Melbourne Law School, University of Melbourne, Carlton, VIC, Australia

Sulette Lombard College of Business, Government and Law, Flinders University, Adelaide, Australia

Part I
Corporate Whistleblowing Context in Australia, Canada and USA

Chapter 1
Regulatory Policies and Practices to Optimize Corporate Whistleblowing: A Comparative Analysis

Sulette Lombard

Abstract Measures to encourage corporate whistleblowing and reap subsequent regulatory benefits of increased whistleblowing activity have been a focus point in a number of jurisdictions. However, none of these measures will be able to achieve optimum success in encouraging corporate whistleblowing if corporate whistleblowers are not able to access them in a practical, meaningful way. It is also important to recognise that every element of a whistleblowing framework forms part of a bigger whole, and that individual elements and their impact can only be properly understood where the context of their operation is appreciated. For these reasons, this chapter aims to provide a broad, comparative overview of measures encouraging whistleblowing—including, for example, financial incentives for whistleblowers—that were adopted in the USA, Canada, and Australia, as well as the regulatory background against which they operate. It therefore also considers whether the corporate whistleblowing framework as a whole, as well as local institutional arrangements, is able to support these measures appropriately in order to encourage corporate whistleblowing.

Keywords Whistleblowing · Corporate whistleblowing · Whistleblowing regulation · Whistleblowing policy · Dodd-Frank Act · Whistleblowing Canada · Whistleblowing Australia · Whistleblowing USA

1.1 Introduction

It has been said that '[w]histleblowing is…an important means of ensuring the transparency and integrity of global markets'[1] and that '[t]he emergence of the whistleblower as an institution is one of the most significant developments in corporate governance in the last fifty years'.[2] The ability of whistleblowing to expose delinquent conduct that might not otherwise be detected, or be detected much later, is

[1]Dworkin (2007, p. 1758).
[2]Vega (2012–2013, p. 485).

S. Lombard (✉)
Flinders University, Bedford Park, Australia
e-mail: sulette.lombard@flinders.edu.au

S. Lombard et al. (eds.), *Corporate Whistleblowing Regulation*,
https://doi.org/10.1007/978-981-15-0259-0_1

therefore not only useful in a *public* context, but is also a very useful tool in bringing to light *corporate* wrongdoing and in prosecuting it—especially since the nature of the corporate entity makes it relatively easy to 'hide' information and wrongful conduct.

The importance of an effective whistleblowing regulatory framework in ensuring these 'whistleblowing benefits' appears to be recognised by the regulators or legislators in a number of jurisdictions. The Australian Parliament has indicated, for example, that

> Australia and many other countries have statutory whistleblower regimes with legally enforceable protections for people who make disclosures. These regimes recognise the critical role whistleblowing can play in the early detection and prosecution of misconduct in the businesses and the avoidance or evasion of tax liabilities.[3]

Similar sentiments are expressed by the Ontario Securities Commission, which indicates that whistleblowing is relevant in 'furtherance of the Commission's mandate to provide protection to investors from unfair, improper or fraudulent practices and to foster fair and efficient capital markets and confidence in capital markets'.[4]

However, it is clearly true that whistleblowing will only be able to fulfill these valuable functions where the regulatory framework is effective in facilitating and encouraging disclosure of information by insiders. Aspects that are relevant in this context are, for example, the ease with which whistleblowing regulation could be navigated; the scope of application of the particular whistleblowing regulation; and the means that are used to encourage insiders with information to come forward. It is also critical to avoid unnecessary impediments that would prevent potential whistleblowers from making protected disclosures. In this context, structures that support the making of disclosures, or structures that facilitate accessing protection and remedies, could play an important role.

The purpose of this chapter is to provide an overview of some corporate whistleblowing regulatory frameworks and to assess how effective they appear to be in supporting and facilitating corporate whistleblowing. This comparison will provide a useful reference point for some of the chapters to follow. For the purposes of this chapter, a broad overview of the primary corporate whistleblowing regulations in Australia, Canada and the USA will be provided with reference to aspects such as the source of private sector whistleblowing regulation; the scope of application of the relevant regulations; the mechanisms that are used to encourage whistleblowers to disclose wrongdoing; as well as the way in which broader supporting structures and frameworks facilitate whistleblowing.

---

[3]The Parliament of the Commonwealth of Australia, Explanatory Memorandum to Treasury Laws Amendment (Enhancing Whistleblower Protections) Bill, [1.4].

[4]OSC Policy 15-601 *Whistleblower Program* Part 1 (hereinafter *OSC Whistleblower Policy*).

1.2 Source of Corporate Whistleblowing Regulation and Regulatory Alignment

The importance of clear and accessible whistleblowing regulation seems obvious—a potential whistleblower necessarily has to be aware of protection and remedies that are available should they decide to blow the whistle, and also of requirements that apply in order to access the protection and remedies. There are different models for adopting such whistleblowing regulations, and a broad distinction can be made between a fragmented approach—in terms of which whistleblowing regulation is scattered across different pieces of legislation, or an 'umbrella' type approach—where whistleblowing regulation is contained in a distinct piece of legislation. In this respect, organisations such as Transparency International suggest that dedicated, stand-alone legislation is preferable to a piecemeal or sectoral approach, 'in order to ensure clarity and seamless application of the whistleblower framework'.[5] The jurisdictions discussed in this chapter adopted different approaches.

The Australian whistleblowing framework indicates a clear distinction between public interest disclosures and disclosures in the private/corporate sector. Whistleblowing in the public sector is regulated by a separate Act—the *Public Interest Disclosure Act 2012* (Cth). Australia is also the very recent recipient of new corporate whistleblowing regulation, with the Australian Parliament passing the *Treasury Laws Amendment (Enhancing Whistleblower Protections) Bill 2018* (Cth) (Whistleblower Bill) on 19 February 2019, which came into force on 1 July 2019. The new Australian whistleblower legislation consolidates whistleblower protection for the corporate and financial sector[6]—as well as provides for a whistleblower protection regime in respect of disclosures in relation to breaches of tax laws[7]—through amendments to the *Corporations Act 2001* (Cth) and the *Taxation Administration Act 1953* (Cth).[8] The need for law reform in this area was based on wide-ranging criticism of the Australian corporate whistleblowing regime at the time[9] around matters such as gaps in protection (as only contraventions of the *Corporations Act 2001* (Cth) were included under protected disclosures), the 'confusing web' of protections it created, inadequacy of protections, and a general piecemeal approach in respect of private sector whistleblowing regulation.[10] Australian whistleblowing regulation,

---

[5]Transparency International (2018, p. 66).

[6]For example, in respect of legislation such as the *Banking Act 1959* (Cth), the *Insurance Act 1973* (Cth), the *Life Insurance Act 1995* (Cth) and the *Superannuation Industry (Supervision) Act 1993* (Cth).

[7]Such as the *Taxation Administration Act 1953* (Cth).

[8]The Parliament of the Commonwealth of Australia, Explanatory Memorandum to Treasury Laws Amendment (Enhancing Whistleblower Protections) Bill, [1.21].

[9]See e.g. Brand et al. (2013, pp. 294–295), Lombard and Brand (2014, pp. 354–358). Also see Commonwealth of Australia, Treasury Options Paper: *Improving Protections for Corporate Whistleblowers* (October 2009).

[10]The Parliament of the Commonwealth of Australia, Explanatory Memorandum to Treasury Laws Amendment (Enhancing Whistleblower Protections) Bill, [1.6]–[1.9].

being divided between the public and corporate sector, clearly does not conform to the idea of a broad umbrella regulatory approach as advocated by organisations such as Transparency International. That said, the movement towards unified private sector whistleblowing regulation is definitely a step in the right direction.

In Canada—unlike public sector disclosures that are protected at a federal level in terms of the *Public Servants Disclosure Protection Act*,[11] as well as at provincial level in most provinces[12]—private sector 'whistleblowing' disclosures enjoy no general civil protection, either at federal level, or provincial level in Canada. The Canadian *Criminal Code*[13] does provide whistleblower protection to the extent that it is an offence for an employer to take reprisal action against a whistleblower-employee. However, this legislation does not provide for any civil remedies. Corporate whistleblowing regulation and policies are focused to a large extent on securities fraud and misconduct, and are currently dealt with at a provincial level, with each province providing for its own regulations and a regulatory body.[14] The most prominent securities regulator, the Ontario Securities Commission (OSC), adopted its OSC Policy 15-601 *Whistleblower Program* under the *Ontario Securities Act*,[15] with a view to 'encourage individuals to report information on serious securities- or derivatives-related misconduct' in 2016.[16] Quebec's securities regulator, the Autorité des marchés financiers (AMF), launched its whistleblowing program in June 2016. In 2018 Alberta followed suit, launching a Whistleblower Program through amendments to its *Securities Act*,[17] subsequently followed by the release of the Alberta Securities Act Policy 15-602 *Whistleblower Program*. The Canadian approach is therefore even more fragmented than the Australian model—not only between public and private sector disclosures,

---

[11]SC 2005, c. 46.

[12]E.g., the *Public Interest Disclosure (Whistleblower Protection) Act* (SA 2012, c. P-39.5) in Alberta; the *Public Interest Disclosure (Whistleblower Protection) Act* (CCSM, c. P217) in Manitoba; the *Public Interest Disclosure Act* (RSNB 2012, c. 112) in New Brunswick; the *Public Interest Disclosure and Whistleblower Protection Act* (SNL 2014, c. P-37.2) in Newfoundland and Labrador; the *Public Interest Disclosure of Wrongdoing Act* (SNS 2010, c. 42) in Nova Scotia; the *Public Service of Ontario Act* (SO 2006, c. 35) in Ontario; the *Public Interest Disclosure and Whistleblower Protection Act* (SPEI 2017, c.11) in Prince Edward Island; the *Act to Facilitate the Disclosure of Wrongdoings Relating to Public Bodies* (CQLR, c. D11-1.1) in Quebec; the *Public Interest Disclosure Act* (SS 2011, c. P-38.1) in Saskatchewan; the *Public Interest Disclosure of Wrongdoing Act* (SY 2014, c. 19) in Yukon. British Columbia is a notable exception.

[13]RSC 1985, c. C-46, s. 425.1.

[14]However, the coming into existence of a Pan-Canadian National Securities Regulator became more likely with the Canadian Supreme Court recently (November 2018) indicating that a proposed national cooperative for the regulation of the capital markets would be constitutional. See *Re Pan-Canadian Securities Regulation* 2018 SCC 48.

[15]R.S.O. 1990, c. S.5 (hereinafter *Ontario Securities Act*).

[16]In 2018 Alberta followed suit, launching its Whistleblower Program through amendments to its *Securities Act*, R.S.A 2000, c. S.5 (hereinafter *Alberta Securities Act*), subsequently followed by the release of the Alberta Securities Act Policy 15-602 *Whistleblower Program*. Other examples of prominent corporate securities legislation include the Quebec *Securities Act*, 1982, c. 48; 2001, c. 38, and the British Columbia *Securities Act*, R.S.B.C. 1996, c. 418.

[17]R.S.A. 2000, c. S.5 (hereinafter *Alberta Securities Act*).

but also insofar as there is little evidence of moving towards a comprehensive corporate whistleblowing regulatory instrument or policy, with 'corporate' whistleblowing regulation being largely confined to regulations dealing with securities violations. Matters are further complicated as a result of the fragmentation between regulation at federal and provincial levels.

Similar to Australia and Canada, the USA provides for a public sector whistleblowing Act in the form of the *Whistleblower Protection Act 1989*. Private sector whistleblowing regulation in the USA, however, is very fragmented, with a plethora of whistleblowing regulatory instruments available. This is the case even should the discussion be restricted to consideration of only 'corporate' whistleblowing regulation. One of the primary 'corporate' whistleblowing regulatory instruments in the USA is the *Dodd-Frank Wall Street Reform and Consumer Protection Act*,[18] enacted in 2010. Section 922 of the *Dodd-Frank Act* provides for a new s 21F to the USA *Securities and Exchange Act of 1934*,[19] entitled 'Securities Whistleblower Incentives and Protection'. The USA Securities and Exchange Commission (SEC) proposed Regulation 21F,[20] containing a number of relevant whistleblowing rules, in November 2010, in order to implement s 21F. Whistleblowing provisions under the *Dodd-Frank Act* are essentially confined to securities regulatory matters.

The other critical instrument insofar as whistleblowing regulation is concerned is the *Sarbanes-Oxley Act*,[21] which was enacted in 2002. The *Sarbanes-Oxley Act* was passed in response to a series of corporate scandals that occurred during the 2000s, including Enron, WorldCom, and so on,[22] and primarily deals with violation of securities laws and improper accounting practices.

The way in which whistleblowing protection is regulated through securities laws and securities regulatory bodies in both the USA and Canada makes it clear that the purpose of that 'corporate' whistleblower regulatory framework is very much aimed at securities laws enforcement. The benefit of the method in the USA and Canada is, of course, a targeted approach in respect of enforcement of securities laws, and subsequent efficiencies created by the focus on a single aspect. Regulatory alignment here could also ensure development of an organizational entity with expertise in handling securities regulation whistleblowing matters.

However, in spite of the clear 'corporate' focus of the *Sarbanes-Oxley Act*, complaints in terms of one of its whistleblowing protection provisions (section 806) are administered by the Department of Labor's Occupational Safety and Health Administration (OSHA). On the face of it, it is useful to have an administrative agency with

---

[18] *Dodd-Frank Wall Street Reform and Consumer Protection Act* Pub. L. No. 111-203, 124 Stat 1376, 1871 (2010) (codified at 15 USC) (hereinafter *Dodd-Frank Act*).

[19] Pub. L. 73-291, 48 Stat 881 (hereinafter referred to as *Securities Exchange Act*).

[20] 17 CFR § 240.21F. See Securities and Exchange Commission, 17 CFR Parts 240 and 249 [Release No 34-64545; File No S7-33-10] RIN 3235-AK78 *Implementation of the Whistleblower Provisions of Section 21F of the Securities Exchange Act of 1934* for detailed commentary on the content of the rules.

[21] *Sarbanes-Oxley Act of 2002* Pub. L. No. 107-204, 116 Stat. 745 (hereinafter *Sarbanes-Oxley Act*).

[22] Rubinstein (2007, p. 638). Also see Fanto (2007, p. 518).

'a record of helping workers penalized for voicing concerns'[23] handling whistleblowing complaints. Also, it appears sensible in some ways that it should be a Department of Labour agency, in light of the emphasis on protection of whistleblower *employees* in many regulatory instruments. However, giving this function to an entity such as OSHA is not without its problems—it has been noted that OSHA lacks the necessary authority, in that '[i]t has no subpoena power; [i]t can't force companies to turn over documents or require witnesses to testify; [i]t can't place anyone under oath'.[24] In addition, OSHA is not very experienced or knowledgeable in this field.[25] This is understandable in light of OSHA's wide mandate, having to enforce more than twenty whistleblower statutes, covering violations over a broad spectrum of regulation, including workplace safety and health, airline, commercial motor carrier, consumer product, environmental, financial reform, food safety, health insurance reform, motor vehicle safety, nuclear, pipeline, public transportation agency, railroad, maritime, and securities laws.[26]

Although some have called for enforcement of this part of the *Sarbanes-Oxley Act* to be moved to the SEC, since SOX whistleblowers are reporting on violations of securities laws and accounting practices,[27] no changes have been made in this regard.

It is clear that private sector whistleblowers in Canada and the USA in particular are likely to be confronted with a patchwork of potential whistleblowing protection regulations—depending on the nature of the wrongdoing, or even the type of remedy that is sought—as well as, potentially, having to deal with different 'administrators' of the whistleblowing regulations. This could make it challenging for a would-be whistleblower to find their path in gathering information about their obligations, rights, protection and remedies. It is not surprising, therefore, that the Canadian whistleblowing regulatory framework has been described as offering limited protection to whistleblowers in general, due to it being 'a patchwork of legislation, at the federal and provincial levels'[28] and also for being 'uncertain, unclear and deficient'; a 'mishmash of legal rules',[29] and its effectiveness as being 'questionable'.[30] Similar sentiments could be expressed in terms of the patchwork of whistleblowing regulation that exists in the USA.

In that respect, a model closer to the Australian model of providing more 'general' private sector whistleblowing regulation is preferable for the advantage of relative

---

[23] Solomon (2004).

[24] Ibid.

[25] Earle and Madek (2004, p. 3). Also see Solomon (2004), who raises the concern of OSHA officials, typically trained in investigating health and safety issues, now having to 'understand sophisticated financial stratagems'.

[26] According to information available on the United States Department of Labor, Occupational Safety and Health Administration, The Whistleblower Protection Programs website, available at https://www.whistleblowers.gov/.

[27] Earle and Madek (2004, pp. 3, 52).

[28] Marin-Bariteau and Newman (2018, pp. 4, 12).

[29] Ibid., p. 7.

[30] McEvoy (2016, p. 53).

ease of navigation and clarity that it offers. However, it is important to recognise that the 'regulatory alignment' in Australia may allow for this to a much larger extent than is the case in the USA and Canada. As both the SEC in the USA and the OSC in Canada are regulatory bodies that are concerned with securities regulation, it is understandable that the focus of whistleblowing regulation that will be administered by these bodies would have a securities laws regulatory focus. This is very different from the context in Australia, where the corporate regulator, the Australian Securities and Investments Commission (ASIC), has very broad regulatory powers as a corporate and market regulator. As such, it will be more feasible for a body such as ASIC to administer whistleblowing regulations aimed at corporate and market misconduct in a much broader sense, compared to the position of the SEC or the OSC, where the primary and exclusive responsibility of the regulatory body is securities regulation.

1.3 Scope of Application of Corporate Whistleblowing Regulation

1.3.1 Who Are Covered by the Whistleblowing Regulation?

It has been said in the whistleblowing context that '[e]mployees clearly have the best access to information'[31] and that '[f]ew, if any frauds can be committed without the knowledge and often support of several employees'.[32] Employees therefore appear to be in a prime position to expose wrongful conduct in a corporation. It is consequently not surprising that this potential 'source' of inside information is given wide recognition in whistleblower protection regulation.

In the Australian context, employees are included in the category of 'eligible whistleblower'. However, under recent reforms this category has been expanded significantly to also include others, such as officers of the entity, an individual who supplies services or goods to the entity, an employee of such a person, as well as relatives of such a person, whether they are currently in that position, or have been in that position in the past.[33]

Section 806 of the *Sarbanes-Oxley Act* provides protection particularly to *employees*, where the employees report on, or otherwise assist in disclosure of specific allegations of misconduct in relation to securities fraud, fraudulent accounting practices and other conduct that defrauds shareholders.[34] The provision, titled 'Civil action to protect against retaliation in fraud cases' reads as follows:

> No company with a class of securities registered under section of the Securities Exchange Act of 1934…or that is required to file reports under section 15(d) of the Securities Exchange

[31] Dyck et al. (2010, p. 2240).

[32] Ibid.

[33] *Corporations Act 2001* (Cth), s 1317AAA.

[34] *Sarbanes-Oxley Act* s 806.

> Act of 1934…or any officer, employee, contractor, subcontractor, or agent of such company or nationally recognized statistical rating organization, may discharged, demote, suspend, threaten, harass, or in any other manner discriminate against an employee in the terms and conditions of employment because of any lawful act done by the employee…[35]

The USA Supreme Court recognised the ambiguity in the language of the statute in relation to the definition of the protected class: is it merely employees of the public company that will enjoy protection under the Act, or also employees of the other bodies mentioned in the provision? It was held by majority, that based on the text of the provision

> the mischief to which Congress was responding, and earlier legislation that Congress drew, that the provision shelters employees of private contractors and subcontractors, just as it shelters employees of the public company served by the contractors and subcontractors.[36]

The anti-retaliation measure provided for in terms of the *Dodd-Frank Act* states that

> No employer may discharge, demote, suspend, threaten, harass, directly or indirectly, or in any other manner discriminate against, a whistleblower in the terms and conditions of employment because of any lawful act done by the whistleblower –
>
> (i) in providing information to the Commission in accordance with this section;
>
> (ii) in initiating, testifying in, or assisting in any investigation or judicial or administrative action of the Commission based upon or related to such information; or
>
> (iii) in making disclosures that are required or protected under the Sarbanes-Oxley Act of 2002…the Securities Exchange Act of 1934…and any other law, rules or regulation subject to the jurisdiction of the Commission.[37]

This provision appears to be framed more broadly compared to its counterpart in the *Sarbanes-Oxley Act*, as it expressly applies to all employers. However, read with the term 'whistleblower' as defined in terms of s 21F(a)(6) of the *Securities Exchange Act*,[38] namely

> [a]ny individual who provides, or 2 or more individuals acting jointly who *provide, information relating to a violation of the securities laws to the Commission*,[39] in a manner established, by rule or regulation, by the Commission

the restrictions of the protection become apparent. This was amply illustrated in the USA Supreme Court case of *Digital Realty Trust Inc v Somers*,[40] in which case the Court held that individuals who only reported internally, and not to the SEC, are, per definition, not whistleblowers, and therefore not protected by the anti-retaliation provisions of the Dodd-Frank Act. This significantly restricts the protection afforded by the anti-retaliation provisions, and also has a detrimental impact on the notion that

[35] Ibid.

[36] *Lawson v FMR LLC* No. 12-3 571 US (March 4, 2014), at 2.

[37] *Securities Exchange Act*, s 21F, as provided for in terms of the *Dodd-Frank Act*, s 922.

[38] As inserted in terms of the *Dodd-Frank Act*, s 922.

[39] Own emphasis.

[40] *Digital Realty Trust, Inc v Somers* 583 US (2018).

internal reporting channels should be used first, in order to provide an opportunity to the company to address matters internally.[41]

The *OSC Whistleblower Policy* defines 'whistleblower' as 'an individual, or two or more individuals acting jointly, who voluntarily provide(s) original information relating to a violation of Ontario securities law that has occurred, is ongoing or is about to occur' and who provides the information as per the requirements described in terms of the *OSC Whistleblower Policy*.[42] Even though no exclusion from the protections and awards under the *OSC Whistleblower Policy* is immediately apparent from the definition of 'whistleblower' as such, an extensive list of exclusions to the category of whistleblowers eligible for an award makes it clear that the application of the Policy is not necessarily as broad as it might appear at first glance. Exclusions apply, for example, to those whistleblowers who refuse a request for additional information without good reason, in-house counsel, directors and officers of the entity which employs the whistleblower, Chief Compliance Officers of the entity that employs the whistleblower, and so on.[43] Protection against reprisals is limited to the employment context, as regulation only prohibits reprisals by an *employer* against an *employee*.[44]

In order to encourage whistleblowing to the maximum extent possible, it would seem clear that the category of 'protected whistleblowers' should be framed as broadly as possible. There is no apparent reason to exclude non-employees from potential whistleblowing protection, where their knowledge of wrongdoing may be equally useful, and they may similarly suffer detrimental consequences for disclosing the wrongdoing. For example, an independent contractor who has a reasonable belief to suspect fraud may lose an important business relationship where they disclose the wrongdoing. In circumstances like those, they may be more likely to come forward with information about wrongdoing where there is opportunity to be compensated for the loss that they suffered as a result of having disclosed the information.

1.3.2 What Type of Whistleblowing Activity Is Covered by the Whistleblowing Regulations?

The most obvious type of conduct that whistleblowers typically engage in that would expose them to potential retaliatory action and victimisation and that would therefore require protection of some sort, is disclosure or reporting of wrongdoing in their organisation. This is in line with the typical definition of whistleblowing as described by Miceli and Near, namely 'organization members' *disclosure* of illegal, immoral, or illegitimate practices under the control of their employers, to parties who may be able to effect action'.[45]

---

[41] See discussion in Sect. 1.3.4.2.

[42] *OSC Whistleblower Policy*, Part 1.

[43] *OSC Whistleblower Policy*, s 15.1.

[44] *Ontario Securities Act*, R.S.O. 1990, c. S.5, s 121.5; also see *OSC Whistleblower Policy*, s 13.

[45] Miceli and Near (1985, p. 525) (emphasis added).

However, this is not the only conduct that may cause a whistleblower to be harmed. Other actions on the part of a whistleblower that are equally deserving of protection are recognised in terms of, for example, the *Sarbanes-Oxley Act*, which provides that employees are protected insofar as they 'file, cause to be filed, testify, participate in, or otherwise assist in a proceeding filed or about to be filed…relating to an alleged violation…'.[46] The extended recognition of 'whistleblowing conduct' is useful, as it is equally possible for insiders who participate in exposing wrongdoing or in an action to address the wrongdoing to suffer the consequences of their involvement, as it is for the person who makes the disclosure to the appropriate recipient. As such, a broad range of 'whistleblowing activity' should be recognised in terms of whistleblowing regulations, in order to provide maximum protection to insiders involved in disclosing, investigating and supporting actions in regard to corporate wrongdoing.

A similar approach is adopted in Ontario, in that protection against retaliation is provided to employees who, for example, sought advice about providing information, expressed an intention to provide information,[47] or cooperated, testified or assisted with an investigation by the Commission, or expressed an intention to do so, in relation to the information provided.[48]

The Australian approach is much more limited in this regard, and in spite of a recommendation that whistleblowing protection be extended to those proposing to make a disclosure, those who could make disclosure but do not propose to do so, or those who may be suspected of making, proposing to make, or be capable of making a disclosure—even if they do not make a disclosure[49]—it appears that protection will be afforded in line with the usual definition of whistleblowing, namely, actual disclosure of information about wrongdoing.[50]

Providing protection against retaliation and victimisation for participation in a broader range of whistleblowing activity may not be that contentious. However, it could become more challenging to frame regulations in this way where whistleblowers are competing for the reward of a whistleblowing bounty.[51]

---

[46] *Sarbanes-Oxley Act*, s 1514A(a)(2).

[47] *Ontario Securities Act*, s 121.5(1)(a).

[48] *Ontario Securities Act*, s 121.5(1)(b).

[49] Parliamentary Joint Committee on Corporations and Financial Services *Whistleblower Protections* (September 2017), Recommendation 6.30, at 70.

[50] The protections afforded to whistleblowers are clearly formulated around the 'disclosure' of information. See *Corporations Act 2001* (Cth), s 1317AA, titled '*Disclosures* qualifying for protection under this Part' (emphasis added).

[51] See Sect. 1.4.2 for further discussion in this regard.

1.3.3 What Type of Wrongdoing Is Covered by the Whistleblowing Regulations?

Corporate whistleblowing regulation in all three jurisdictions confines protection under the relevant legislation to disclosure of information about particular types of wrongs.

Australian corporate whistleblowing protections have previously been criticized for, among other reasons, their restricted application, in that only disclosures in relation to contraventions of the *Corporations Act 2001* (Cth) would qualify as protected disclosures.[52] Disclosure of any other type of wrongdoing would not qualify. The range of conduct that could be the subject of a protected disclosure has been broadened significantly under the new private sector whistleblowing regulations to include information about misconduct or an improper state of affairs in relation to the entity or organisation, conduct that could cause danger to the public or financial system, contravention of any law administered by ASIC or Australian Prudential Regulation Authority (APRA), as well as an offence against any other law of the Commonwealth that is punishable by imprisonment for a period of at least 12 months.[53]

The emphasis in Canada is on contravention of securities laws, as is the case with the whistleblowing provisions in the *Dodd-Frank Act*. This is not surprising in light of the clear structural alignment with securities legislation and securities regulatory bodies, as discussed above.[54]

The *Sarbanes-Oxley Act* contains two provisions that aim to protect whistleblowers against retaliation. One of these, section 1107, applies to whistleblowers who provide information about *any* federal offence. This provision has been described as having ‘the potential to become the most important of all the SOX provisions because it could develop into a general whistleblower statute’.[55] However, it is important to note that s 1107 does not provide for a civil remedy, and instead imposes criminal liability where an employer takes retaliatory action against a whistleblower employee. The other, section 806, does allow for civil remedies, but has a more limited application in that it only provides protection for disclosures about securities violations or conduct relating to fraud against shareholders.[56]

From the perspective of an insider who detected wrongdoing in an organization, this means that they might have to ‘classify’ the nature of the wrongdoing first in order to determine whether there is whistleblowing remedy available, or whether there might be a financial reward available, and also to determine under which instrument it might be available. This could prove to be challenging to the whistleblower, who would potentially have no other option but to obtain legal advice in order to navigate the maze that could be the whistleblowing regulations. Ideally, and in order

[52]Lombard and Brand (2014, pp. 354–358).

[53]*Corporations Act 2001* (Cth), s 1317AA(4) and s 1317AA(5) (Disclosable matters).

[54]See Sect. 1.2.

[55]Dworkin (2007, p. 1764).

[56]*Sarbanes-Oxley Act*, s 806(a)(1).

to encourage whistleblowing as much as possible, whistleblowers should be entitled to whistleblower remedies irrespective of the *type* of wrong that they are reporting on. This is something that is likely more achievable when a comprehensive, stand-alone corporate whistleblowing regulatory framework with broad coverage is developed, rather than by piecemeal adoption of whistleblowing protective measures.

1.3.4 Whom Can Disclosures Be Made To?

1.3.4.1 General

Whistleblowing regulation generally requires that the disclosure of information about wrongdoing should be made to a particular body or person in order for the whistleblower to enjoy the benefits of, or the protection provided by, the relevant whistleblowing legislation.

In Australia, for example, a disclosure will qualify for protection under the Act if it is made to a regulatory body, for example ASIC, APRA or another relevant Commonwealth authority,[57] or an *eligible recipient*.[58] Eligible recipients are internal to the organisation and include, for example, an officer or senior manager of the corporation, an auditor or a member of an audit team in respect of the corporation, an actuary of the corporation, or a person authorised by the corporation to receive disclosures.[59] A disclosure to a legal practitioner for the purposes of obtaining legal advice or legal representation will also be protected.[60] Whistleblowers who wish to enjoy the benefits of the whistleblower regulations would have to make the disclosure to a recipient identified in the Act in order to do so.

In limited circumstances, the whistleblower could potentially also make a disclosure to a member of Parliament, or a journalist. This option is available in the case of a *public interest disclosure* or an *emergency disclosure*.[61] However, in both these instances, the disclosure would only qualify for the benefits under the whistleblowing regulation if the whistleblower has already made the disclosure to one of the regulatory bodies mentioned above.[62] The whistleblower would also be required, in both instances, to provide written notification to the entity of the intent to make a public or emergency disclosure.[63] In order to qualify as a *public interest disclosure*, the whistleblower would furthermore need to hold a reasonable belief that making the disclosure would be in the public interest, as well as not having reasonable grounds

---

[57] *Corporations Act 2001* (Cth), s 1317AA(1).

[58] *Corporations Act 2001* (Cth), s 1317AA(2).

[59] *Corporations Act 2001* (Cth), s 1317AAC(2).

[60] *Corporations Act 2001* (Cth), s 1317AA(3).

[61] *Corporations Act 2001* (Cth), s 1317AAD.

[62] E.g. ASIC or APRA.

[63] *Corporations Act 2001* (Cth), s 1317AAD(1)(e) and s 1317AAD(2)(c).

to believe that action is being taken to address the matter.[64] In the case of an *emergency disclosure*, the whistleblower must have reasonable grounds to believe that the information pertains to a substantial and imminent danger to the health and safety of a person/s or the environment.[65]

Explicit inclusion of disclosure to journalists under the regulatory protective umbrella is an interesting development. Arguments against extending protection to whistleblowers that disclose to the media have been offered regularly, and are often based on the perception that these whistleblowers are motivated by revenge or other improper motives, or that their allegations are typically worthless.[66] However, studies indicate that whistleblowers disclose to the media for other reasons—they typically lack power within the corporation; are concerned about a high risk of retaliation; previously reported internally without success; or they seek anonymity.[67] There is also a view that allegations about wrongdoing will only result in action being taken once they have been exposed to the media.[68] These apparent motivations seem to have been taken into consideration, when looking at the way in which permitted disclosure to the media is framed under the Australian *Corporations Act 2001* (Cth).

Whistleblowing protection under the *Sarbanes-Oxley Act* is not framed so liberally, and disclosures must be made to a federal regulatory or law enforcement agency, or to a member or committee of Congress, or to a person with supervisory authority of the employee,[69] in order to qualify for protection under the Act. Disclosures to the media will not provide the whistleblower access to the protection remedies.[70] It has been noted, however, that external reporting of wrongdoing to members or committees of Congress may also result in this information being disclosed to the media, which could have a detrimental impact on the company, particularly unwarranted where the allegations might prove not to be true.[71] The *Dodd-Frank Act* requires disclosure to the SEC in order for the whistleblower to enjoy protection under the anti-retaliation provision.[72]

The *Ontario Securities Act* provides protection against retaliation where the whistleblower discloses information, or indicates the intention to disclose information, to a person, or company, or the OSC, a recognised self-regulatory organization,

[64] *Corporations Act 2001* (Cth), s 1317AAD(1).

[65] *Corporations Act 2001* (Cth), s 1317AAD(2)(b).

[66] Dworkin and Brown (2012–2013, p. 682).

[67] Ibid.

[68] De Maria (2006, p. 651). The recent Senate Inquiry into ASIC in Australia seems to offer support for this view.

[69] *Sarbanes-Oxley Act*, s 806(a)(1).

[70] 18 U.S.C. § 1514A (Supp. II 2002), as referred to by Dworkin (2007, p. 1761).

[71] Rubinstein (2007, p. 649).

[72] *Dodd-Frank Act*, s 922. See Sect. 1.3.1 for a more detailed discussion in this regard.

or a law enforcement agency.[73] However, in order to potentially qualify for a whistleblowing financial reward, the whistleblower is required to disclose the information to the OSC.[74]

In line with previous suggestions, it is important to not be unnecessarily restrictive in relation to the requirements around whistleblowing—including whom the information can be disclosed to—in order to ensure maximum protection for whistleblowers and thus encourage whistleblowing. However, at the same it is important to recognise that the information will only be useful if it is received by an entity or body that is in a position to, for example, pursue further investigation. As such, it is understandable why disclosure to the media in the first instances is often not regarded as the most desirable approach. Another important question that frequently crops up in the context of the recipient of the disclosure is the extent to which internal disclosure should be mandated.

1.3.4.2 Emphasising Value of Internal Disclosure

The value of internal whistleblowing is recognised by many, and it has been said, for example, that '[w]histleblowing has the greatest potential for good where wrongdoing is first reported within the organization because it gives the employer the opportunity to correct the problem or at least mitigate the damages',[75] and that 'the most effective method of correcting corporate misconduct is by reporting violations internally to supervisors or senior managers who may be unaware of problems within a company'.[76] There is much to be said for a framework that encourages disclosures to be made internally first. Insiders could play a valuable role in exposing wrongdoing in a corporation much earlier and much easier, compared to having to rely on an external party to discover wrongful conduct, thus providing the entity with an opportunity to address the wrong before it escalates.[77] The 'enlightened self-interest' approach to whistleblowing[78] recognises that 'whistleblowers [benefit] their employers by offering solutions to work problems' and that 'whistleblowing can be treated as part of a strategy to maintain and improve quality'.[79]

However, in order for whistleblowing to be able to fulfil this function, corporate entities should ensure that they have comprehensive, well-publicised internal reporting policies and mechanisms in place—ideally assigning the function of receiving

---

[73] *Ontario Securities Act*, s 121.5(1)(a).

[74] OSC Policy 15-601, *Whistleblower Program*, 14(1).

[75] Rubinstein (2007, p. 650).

[76] Ibid., pp. 638–639. Also see Dworkin (2007, p. 1760), Labriola (2017, pp. 2859–2861) and Hassink et al. (2007, p. 30).

[77] It has to be conceded, however, that not all are in favour of an 'internal first' approach. See e.g. De Maria (2006, p. 651), who argues that 'the whistleblower following [mandated] internal pathways…is at the behest of complex bureaucratic processes over which he or she has little knowledge, no say and no influence'.

[78] A term used by Lewis and Uys (2007, p. 76).

[79] Ibid.

whistleblower reports and protecting whistleblowers to designated persons within the corporation.[80] This could help to alleviate concerns of whistleblowers who possess information that points to wrongdoing on the part of the directors, or concerns that the corporation will not address the issues raised by the disclosure of information. It is also desirable that these internal reporting channels are open to receive information about wrongdoing in a broad sense, and not be restricted in terms of regulatory ambit.

It is furthermore critical that the external regulatory whistleblowing framework recognises the importance of these internal whistleblowing channels. Regulations in all three jurisdictions emphasise the importance of internal frameworks in various ways, with the Australian private sector whistleblowing regulation providing the only example of mandatory internal whistleblowing policies with broad coverage.[81] Elements that must be included in such a policy include aspects such as information about protections available to whistleblowers, information about whom to and how disclosures should be made to qualify for protection, about how the company will support and protect the whistleblower, about how it will investigate disclosures, how it will ensure fair treatment of employees who blow the whistle, as well as information about how the policy is made available to those inside the organisation.[82]

An emphasis on the value of internal reporting also exists in the USA and Canada. The *Sarbanes-Oxley Act* requires the Board of Directors' Audit Committee in public companies to have procedures in place that would enable employees to confidentially and anonymously disclose concerns in relation to 'questionable accounting or auditing matters'.[83] The requirement does not extend to concerns in relation to other questionable matters. The extent to which the introduction of a whistleblowing financial reward system in the USA initially raised concerns that the existence of such a scheme may act to deter whistleblowers from using internal reporting channels due to fear of missing out on the award where they reported internally first, further demonstrate the value that is attached to internal reporting channels.[84] A decision was ultimately made against an approach that would mandate internal reporting first. However, to maintain the emphasis on the value of internal reporting channels, and in an attempt to ensure that the existence of the bounty program would not subvert these measures, certain rules were adopted. For example, the extent to which a whistleblower voluntarily participated in internal reporting systems could be a factor taken into consideration to increase the amount of the reward;[85] secondly, should an entity self-report on the basis of information that was provided by a whistleblower

[80] Australian Standard (2003) suggests the appointment of a designated Whistleblower Protection Officer [at 2.3.1], as well as the appointment of a designated Whistleblower Investigations Officer [at 2.3.2].

[81] *Corporations Act 2001* (Cth), s 1317AI(1).

[82] *Corporations Act 2001* (Cth), s 1317AI(3).

[83] *Sarbanes-Oxley Act*, s 301.

[84] See e.g. Ebersole (2011, p. 137) and Vega (2012–2013, p. 486).

[85] Securities Exchange Commission, 'Implementation of the Whistleblower Provisions of Section 21F of the Securities Exchange Act 1934', Release No 34-64545, available at https://www.sec.gov/rules/final/2011/34-64545.pdf, Rule 21F-6: Criteria for determining amount of award.

through internal reporting systems, leading to a successful action by the SEC, all the information will be attributed to the whistleblower;[86] lastly, a whistleblower reporting internally first will still be eligible to receive a whistleblowing bounty, provided that they report to the SEC within 120 days thereafter.[87]

In Ontario, employee whistleblowers are encouraged, but not required, to report potential contraventions by way of internal reporting mechanisms.[88] Similar concerns on the part of whistleblowers that internal reporting may deprive them of an opportunity to become eligible for a financial reward were recognised. If a whistleblower reports internally first and the information becomes subsequently known to the Commission through self-reporting, the whistleblower will remain entitled to an award, provided he reports the same information within 120 days of the initial internal report.[89] This is supposed to maintain the relevance and importance of internal reporting mechanisms.

1.4 Measures to Encourage Whistleblowing

1.4.1 Protecting the Whistleblower

1.4.1.1 Protection Thresholds

Corporate whistleblowers are often required to comply with various criteria in order to qualify for protection under the whistleblowing provisions. One of these—the good faith requirement—featured prominently in Australian whistleblowing regulations until recently. In terms of whistleblowing protection provisions that were in place prior to the enactment of the *Treasury Laws Amendment (Enhancing Whistleblower Protections) Act 2019* (Cth), only disclosures that were made in 'good faith' would qualify for protection.[90] The good faith requirement has been criticised by numerous commentators and for various reasons.[91] It is seen as imposing an unnecessary burden on the whistleblower to qualify for protection, and has been described as 'an

[86]Securities Exchange Commission, 'Implementation of the Whistleblower Provisions of Section 21F of the Securities Exchange Act 1934', Release No 34-64545, available at https://www.sec.gov/rules/final/2011/34-64545.pdf, Rule 21F-4(c)(3): Additional incentives to encourage reporting through internal compliance programs.

[87]Securities Exchange Commission, 'Implementation of the Whistleblower Provisions of Section 21F of the Securities Exchange Act 1934', Release No 34-64545, available at https://www.sec.gov/rules/final/2011/34-64545.pdf, Rule 21F-4(b)(7): Original source: Lookback. See Vega (2012–2013, pp. 502–505) for further discussion on these measures.

[88]OSC Policy 15-601, s 16(1).

[89]OSC Policy 15-601, s 16(2).

[90]*Corporations Act 2001* (Cth), s 1317AA(1)(e).

[91]See e.g. Lombard and Brand (2014, p. 357) and Brown (2013, p. 4).

additional ethical high jump imposed on whistleblowers'.[92] This could consequently have a detrimental impact on whistleblowing activity.

It can be surmised that this requirement was included in an attempt to avoid vexatious behaviour and to ensure that, for example, disgruntled employees would not blow the whistle on alleged 'wrongful conduct' just to cause difficulty for employers. However, the emphasis that it places on the motive of the whistleblower appears unnecessary—the quality of the information and disclosure of wrongdoing should carry more weight than the motive of the whistleblower. This has been recognised in both the Canadian and USA jurisdictions for a while now. For example, in order to enjoy protection against retaliation under s 21F(h)(1) of the *Securities Exchange Act*,[93] the Rules that were subsequently adopted to implement the program describe a whistleblower as someone who has a '*reasonable belief* that the information [they] are providing relates to a possible securities law violation…that has occurred, is ongoing, or is about to occur'.[94] The protection applies whether or not requirements, procedures and conditions to qualify for an award are satisfied.[95] The *Sarbanes-Oxley Act* similarly protects employees who *reasonably* believe that certain provisions or rules were violated.[96]

In order to assess whether a whistleblower held a 'reasonable belief' in relation to the alleged wrongdoing, it is suggested that factors such as their experience, background, and access to information could be taken into consideration.[97]

In light of the emphasis on the benefits of disclosure of wrongdoing, it would seem obvious that rules around the *eligibility* of a whistleblower to qualify for the benefits under whistleblowing regulation should be formulated as generously as possible. It is suggested that the 'reasonable belief' criterion, described by some as a 'low standard',[98] strikes the appropriate balance between providing broad access to whistleblower remedies while aiming to curtail vexatious proceedings.

1.4.1.2 Anti-retaliation Remedies

Anti-retaliation remedies feature prominently in all three jurisdictions. The Australian corporate whistleblowing regulations provide whistleblowers with protection against 'detriment' that could include, for example, dismissal, injury in the course of employment, alteration of the employee's position or duties, discrimination, harassment or intimidation, harm or injury to a person, damage to a person's property, reputation, business or financial position, or any other damage.[99] Remedies against

[92] De Maria (2006, p. 649).

[93] 15 USC 78u-6(h)(1).

[94] 17 CFR § 240.21F-(b)(1)(i) (emphasis added).

[95] 17 CFR § 240.21F-(b)(1)(ii).

[96] *Sarbanes-Oxley Act*, s 1514A(a)(1).

[97] Rubinstein (2007, p. 647).

[98] See e.g. Ebersole (2011, p. 126).

[99] *Corporations Act 2001* (Cth), s 1317ADA.

retaliation action could include compensation, injunctive relief, an apology, reinstatement, exemplary damages, or any other order the court thinks appropriate.[100]

The USA *Securities Exchange Act* provides for the protection of employee whistleblowers in prohibiting employers from discharging, demoting, suspending, threatening, harassing, or discriminating against whistleblowers.[101] An employee whistleblower who brings an action on the basis of retaliation could be entitled to a range of remedies, including reinstatement with the same seniority status as previously, two times the amount of backpay otherwise owed plus interest, and compensation for litigation costs, expert witness fees and reasonable attorney's fees.[102]

The *Sarbanes-Oxley Act* provides that companies to which the provision applies, or 'any officer, employee, contractor, subcontractor, or agent of such company [cannot] discharge, demote, suspend, threaten, harass, or in any other manner discriminate against an employee in the terms and conditions of employment' on the basis of their whistleblowing under the Act.[103] Relief available to employees under these provisions includes compensatory damages, reinstatement, back pay with interest, compensation for any special damages resulting from the reprisal, including litigation costs, expert witness fees, and reasonable attorney fees.[104] At first glance, this may appear like an extensive set of remedies. However, the restriction to compensatory damages is seen as a limitation, and inclusion of punitive and emotional injury damages is suggested, as these measures are more likely to encourage whistleblowing.[105]

Canadian employee whistleblowers enjoy similar protection against reprisals,[106] with reprisal being defined as 'any measure taken against an employee that adversely affects his or her employment', including, for example, the termination of employment, a threat to terminate employment, demotion, disciplinary action or suspension, or the threat to do so, intimidation of the employee, and so on.[107] Various civil remedies are available under such circumstances—for example, reinstatement, payment of two times the amount of remuneration the employee would have been paid if the contravention had not taken place, plus interest.[108]

1.4.1.3 Protecting the Identity of the Whistleblower

Australian private sector whistleblowing regulation attempts to protect the identity of the whistleblower through imposing criminal liability on the person or entity to whom the disclosure is made, where they cause the identity of the whistleblower to become

---

[100] *Corporations Act 2001* (Cth), s 1317AE.

[101] S 21F(h)(1)(A).

[102] S 21F(h)(1)(C).

[103] *Sarbanes-Oxley Act*, s 806(a).

[104] *Sarbanes-Oxley Act*, s 806(c).

[105] Dworkin (2007, p. 1763).

[106] *Ontario Securities Act*, R.S.O. 1990, Ch S.5, s 121.5(1).

[107] *Ontario Securities Act*, R.S.O. 1990, Ch S.5, s 121.5(2).

[108] *Ontario Securities Act*, R.S.O. 1990, Ch S.5, s 121.5(6).

known.[109] There are exceptions to the general principle, where the information is disclosed to the Australian Securities and Investments Commission (ASIC), to the Australian Prudential Regulation Authority (APRA), to a member of the Australian Federal Police, to a legal practitioner for the purpose of obtaining legal advice, or made with the consent of the whistleblower.[110]

The USA *Securities Exchange Act 1934* similarly provides for protecting the identity of the whistleblower through a prohibition on the Securities Exchange Commission to disclose any information that could reasonably be expected to reveal the identity of the whistleblower.[111] Exceptions exist, for example where it becomes necessary to disclose the identity of the whistleblower to a defendant or respondent in an action,[112] or where the Securities Exchange Commission exercises its discretion for the purposes of investor protection to provide information to appropriate regulatory authorities, the Attorney-General, and so on.[113] The *Sarbanes-Oxley Act* furthermore requires audit committees to establish whistleblowing mechanisms that would provide employees with an opportunity to raise issues anonymously.[114]

Similar regulatory measures exist in Ontario in terms of the OSC Policy 15-601, according to which the Commission will 'make all reasonable efforts to keep the identity of the whistleblower and information that could be reasonably expected to reveal the whistleblowers' identity' confidential.[115] This general protection is once again subject to certain exceptions, namely, where the Commission is required by law to disclose certain information,[116] or disclosure to an appropriate regulatory body with the permission of the whistleblower.[117] Whistleblower identity is also protected in terms of allowing for anonymous reporting.[118]

It is of critical importance that these regulatory protections are given practical application. There is a real risk of inadvertently revealing the identify of a whistleblower where a technical and digital literacy gap exists—an inventory undertaken by Martin-Bariteau and Newman shows instances of 'requesting identifying information, hosting electronic forms on unsecured web pages, or allowing submissions by email' by numerous governmental and para-public agencies.[119] It can be assumed that corporate regulatory bodies will hopefully deal with identifying information much more carefully.

---

[109] *Corporations Act 2001* (Cth), s 1317AAE.

[110] *Corporations Act 2001* (Cth), s 1317AAE(2).

[111] *Securities Exchange Act of 1934,* s 21F(h)(2)(A).

[112] *Securities Exchange Act of 1934,* s 21F(h)(2)(A).

[113] *Securities Exchange Act of 1934*, s 21F(h)(2)(D).

[114] *Sarbanes-Oxley Act,* s 301.

[115] OSC Policy 15-601, s 11(1).

[116] OSC Policy 15-601, s 11(1)(a).

[117] OSC Policy 15-601, s 11(1)(b), read with s 11(2).

[118] See, e.g. OSC Policy 15-601 [14], as well as *Sarbanes-Oxley Act*, s 301, in respect of anonymous submission of information in relation to questionable accounting or auditing matters.

[119] Marin-Bariteau and Newman (2018, p. 5).

However, there is a potential risk that internal whistleblowing mechanisms might not always be equally sophisticated in protecting the identity of the whistleblower. Even though protection of the identity of the whistleblower might not be a regulatory requirement in respect of internal reporting, similar to regulation in regard to reporting to a regulator, the underlying principle is the same—protection of the identity of the whistleblower is important to encouraging whistleblowing. Whistleblowers would likely be discouraged to come forward with information about wrongdoing by way of internal reporting mechanisms where they have concerns about their identity being adequately protected.

Whistleblower concern in relation to protection of identity is understandable, and in order to encourage whistleblowing, whistleblowers should be made confident that their identity will be protected, or should be permitted to make anonymous disclosures. However, it is clear that anonymity may not always be desirable, particularly where follow-up is required. In such instances, it is important to balance the desire to remain anonymous with the regulatory goal of being able to act on the information. It is also in cases such as that, that the availability of other protective measures is even more critical.

1.4.1.4 Culpable Whistleblowers and Protection Against Legal Action

Whistleblowers may well be deterred from disclosing information about wrongdoing where they were involved in the culpable conduct themselves, or may feel hamstrung to report wrongdoing due to confidentiality agreements. There appears to be general acceptance of the policy in all the jurisdictions referred to in this chapter that whistleblowing regulations clearly indicate that confidentiality agreements should not hinder whistleblower reporting—an approach that also appears to be generally supported by academic commentators.[120] Australian corporate whistleblowing regulations provide protection from civil or criminal liability that could arise out of the disclosure (for example on the basis of defamation), as well as placing constraints upon employer rights to seek contractual remedies against the whistleblower based on the disclosure.[121] The *Ontario Securities Act* also provides protection against any potential action that could be launched against the whistleblower on the basis that the disclosure breaches a confidentiality agreement, in that section 121.5(3) provides for any confidentiality agreement to be void, to the extent that it precludes the employee from providing information, or cooperating, testifying, or otherwise assisting in an investigation. Similarly, the USA *Securities Exchange Act* provides that

> [n]o person may take any action to impede an individual from communicating directly with the Commission staff about a possible securities law violation, including enforcing, or threatening to enforce, a confidentiality agreement…with respect to such communications.[122]

---

[120] See e.g. Dixon (2018, p. 431).

[121] *Corporations Act 2001* (Cth), s 1317AB.

[122] *Securities Exchange Act 1934*, s 21F-17.

The answer to the question as to whether whistleblowing should be encouraged to such an extent as to provide immunity from prosecution, or reduced sanctions where the whistleblowers themselves are involved in the wrongdoing, is not equally clear-cut. In Australia, disclosures that qualify as protected are not admissible in evidence against the whistleblower in criminal proceedings, other than those that might be related to falsity of the information,[123] thus providing some protection against criminal prosecution.

In the USA, however, disclosure of information to the Securities Exchange Commission will not provide protection against actions that could follow on the basis of the whistleblower's own wrongful conduct, particularly in relation to contraventions of securities laws.[124] Also, a whistleblower who is found guilty of a criminal violation may not be eligible to receive a whistleblowing financial reward.[125]

On the other hand, in Canada, the Ontario Securities Commission does allow eligibility for a whistleblowing reward on the part of a whistleblower who is complicit in the particular violation that they are reporting on.[126] Involvement in the particular violation could, however, result in a reduction of the amount that the whistleblower may receive.[127] It adopts a similar approach as the USA, however, in that provision of information to the OSC will not grant the whistleblower immunity against prosecution.[128]

In an interesting divergence, the Alberta Securities Commission—the latest provincial regulator in Canada to release a policy in relation to whistleblowing protection[129]—decided against developing a whistleblowing rewards scheme and opted for an immunity from prosecution, or reduced sanction-type of incentive instead. The ASC Policy 15-602 *Whistleblower Program* indicates that whistleblowers who are involved in misconduct could be entitled to credit pursuant to ASC Policy 15-601 *Credit for Exemplary Cooperation in Enforcement Matters*. As a result, culpable whistleblowers in Alberta could potentially not be prosecuted, or receive reduced sanction due to having blown the whistle.

1.4.2 Financial Incentives

The emphasis on whistleblower protection as a mechanism to encourage increased whistleblowing activity was referred to above. It is not surprising, therefore, that whistleblowing regulation will often focus on protection against retaliation as a key measure to encourage whistleblowing. This is done in different ways and not always

[123] *Corporations Act 2001* (Cth), s 1317AB(3).

[124] CFR Commodities and Securities Exchanges § 240.21F-15.

[125] 15 U.S.C., § 78u-6(c)(2)(B).

[126] OSC Policy 15-601 *Whistleblower Program*, [17.1].

[127] OSC Policy 15-601 *Whistleblower Program*, [17.2].

[128] OSC Policy 15-601 *Whistleblower Program*, [17.5].

[129] ASC Policy 15-602 *Whistleblower Program*; released in Nov 2018.

with equal measure of success. Also, not everybody is convinced that the anti-retaliation model is successful in encouraging whistleblowing activity, and some authors refer to the general failure of the anti-retaliation approach 'to a significant degree in the United States and almost completely in Australia' without hesitation.[130] According to some, there is 'overwhelming evidence' that 'merely protecting whistleblowers from retaliation or giving them a cause of actions' is not effective in encouraging whistleblowing.[131] As such, it could be argued that other measures should be employed to encourage whistleblowing. Insiders decide to blow the whistle for various reasons, and studies in relation to whistleblower motivation have shown that factors such as 'serious wrongdoing, strong evidence, the perceived likelihood that the wrongdoing would be corrected, and organizational atmosphere of openness that encouraged voice, and clear reporting channels', are more significant in relation to encouraging whistleblowing than fear of retaliation.[132]

It is important not to lose sight of the fact, therefore, that whistleblower protection is not the only way, or perhaps even the best way, in which whistleblower activity could be encouraged. Particularly useful could be the availability of financial incentives or 'whistleblowing bounties' as a way to encourage whistleblowing, as suggested by numerous commentators.[133] The bounty model is regarded as being better able to encourage whistleblowing, as it 'dovetails' with whistleblowers' desire that the problem be resolved through its imposition of penalties, and also because it is better at compensating the whistleblower against risk, compared to anti-retaliatory measures.[134] Financial incentives, or 'bounties' appear to have been used with much success in the United States of America.[135] The SEC's 2018 Annual Report to Congress on its Whistleblower Program[136] provides clear evidence of the growth and success of the whistleblowing rewards program. 2018 has been described

---

[130]See e.g. Dworkin (2007, pp. 1769, 1779) and Dworkin and Brown (2012–2013, pp. 654–655, 690).

[131]Dworkin (2007, p. 1769).

[132]See e.g. ibid., p. 1768.

[133]See e.g. Dworkin, p. 1774, Rapp (2007, pp. 98–99). For a contrary opinion, see e.g. Ebersole (2011, p. 124), who describes this measure as 'a misguided monetary incentive' and expresses doubt as to its usefulness to society (at p. 174).

[134]Moberley (2012, p. 49).

[135]The *Dodd-Frank Wall Street Reform and Consumer Protection Act* § 1, 124 Stat 1376 (2010), s 21F, amended the *Securities and Exchange Act* 1934, directing the Securities and Exchange Commission to 'pay awards, subject to certain limitations and conditions, to whistleblowers who voluntarily provide the Commission with original information about a violation of the securities laws that leads to the successful enforcement of an action brought by the Commission that results in monetary sanctions exceeding $1,000,000 (see United States Securities and Exchange Commission), *Implementation of the Whistleblower Provisions of Section 21F of the Securities Exchange Act of 1934*, 17 CFR Parts 240 and 249 [Release No. 34-64545; File No. S7-33-10] RIN 3235-AK78; Effective date: 12 August 2011, available at <http://www.sec.gov/rules/final/2011/34-64545.pdf> (SEC (US), Implementation of the Whistleblower Provisions of s 21F). Also see Dyck et al. (2010, p. 2251), who indicate that 'the use of monetary rewards provides positive incentives for whistleblowing' and that 'the role of monetary incentives should be expanded'.

[136]United States Securities and Exchange Commission (2018, p. 1).

as a ‘record-breaking’ year, with the SEC awarding its largest whistleblower awards to date—total whistleblowing rewards in 2018 exceeded awards paid out in all prior years combined, reaching the staggering pay-out amount of more than $168 million. So far, information provided by whistleblowers enabled the SEC to successfully pursue enforcement actions against wrongdoers resulting in monetary sanctions of over $1.7 billion being imposed.

The approach has been criticized by some as an ‘incorrect and dangerous inducement on which to expect people of goodwill to come forward’, preferring instead that they ‘come forward on the old fashioned basis of just being ethically disturbed with what they see’.[137] In spite of pronouncements such as these, other jurisdictions have now started to follow the USA bounty model.

Canada has become one of the first countries to follow the USA whistleblowing bounty model as a means to encourage whistleblowing. The whistleblowing rewards program has been established by the Ontario Securities Commission in 2016, in terms of the OSC Policy 15-601 *Whistleblower Program*. In terms of the Ontario whistleblowing rewards scheme, a whistleblower who voluntarily discloses original, high-quality information in relation to a serious contravention of securities laws to the Commission, is eligible for an award[138] where the information leads to a decision of the Commission that results in a monetary sanction or voluntary payment of at least $1 million. In the first month and a half since its inception, the OSC Office of the Whistleblower received more than 30 tips reporting potential violations of securities laws.[139] The OSC has furthermore recently made its first major payment of $7.5 million under the scheme.[140]

There has been a long-held bias in Australia against the notion of whistleblowing financial incentives.[141] However, it has been suggested that the bias against the use of bounties in Australia appears to be ‘softening’ and that ‘the [Australian] political environment is increasingly fertile for a shift towards the take-up of such provisions in respect to either the public or private sectors’.[142] This conclusion appears to have been borne out by the fact that the outcome of the recent whistleblowing reforms inquiry, presented in the Parliamentary Joint Committee on Corporations and Financial Services Report on Whistleblower Protections, recommended the adoption of a whistleblowing bounty system within certain parameters,[143] on the following basis:

---

[137] Senate Select Committee on Public Interest Whistleblowing, In the Public Interest: Report of the Senate Select Committee on Public Interest Whistleblowing (1994), at 11.15, as referred to by Dworkin and Brown (2012–2013, p. 702). Also see Lee (2011–2012, pp. 320–327) for further criticism against the whistleblowing bounty scheme under the *Dodd-Frank Act*.

[138] OSC Policy 15-601, s 14(1).

[139] Ritchie and Malik (2016).

[140] Langton (2019).

[141] See Parliamentary Joint Committee on Corporations and Financial Services *Whistleblower Protections* (September 2017), at [11.53] for examples of where this idea has been rejected in the past.

[142] Dworkin and Brown (2012–2013, p. 703).

[143] Parliamentary Joint Committee on Corporations and Financial Services *Whistleblower Protections* (September 2017), Recommendations 11.1 and 11.2, at [11.58]–[11.59].

> [A] reward system would motivate whistleblowers to come forward with high quality information. This information would otherwise be difficult to obtain. The committee considers that a reward system will motivate companies to improve internal whistleblower reporting systems and to deal more proactively with illegal behavior.[144]

Contrary to these recommendations and viewpoints, and in spite of the evident success of both the USA and Ontario bounty models, the Australian legislature has decided against a financial incentive model in its latest set of whistleblowing reforms. Instead, reforms focus on improved access to compensation for aggrieved whistleblowers.[145]

Concerns were raised that a whistleblowing bounty system that is based on paying a financial reward as a percentage of the fine or penalty levied on the wrongdoer might not be equally successful in the Australian context, due to penalties in Australia generally being much lower than those in the USA and Canada.[146] However, these concerns are partly addressed with the enactment of the *Treasury Laws Amendment (Strengthening Corporate and Financial Sector Penalties) Act 2019* (Cth) that provides for increases in fines and penalties. Even though it may still not be on par with what is available in the USA, for example, it remains a significant step forward.

The holistic whistleblowing reforms that took place therefore presented an ideal opportunity for development of a system of whistleblowing rewards that, unfortunately, has been missed. This is particularly disappointing in light of suggestions that 'cases...suggest that, at best, the civil compensation provisions offer little practical benefit to aggrieved whistleblowers'.[147]

1.4.3 Response to Disclosures

Whistleblowers are motivated by a range of different reasons when deciding to disclose information about perceived wrongdoing in the corporation.[148] One of these is the fact that they wish the right thing to be done, and thus protect the interests of the organisation, co-workers, and society more broadly.[149] Miceli and Near, with reference to expectancy theory—described as 'the most popular and most widely accepted theory of motivation'[150]—also note that whistleblowers may be concerned with 'the level of efficacy of their actions and with the level of expected retaliation'.[151] In

---

[144]Parliamentary Joint Committee on Corporations and Financial Services *Whistleblower Protections* (September 2017), at [11.55].

[145]*Corporations Act 2001* (Cth), s 1317AE.

[146]Parliamentary Joint Committee on Corporations and Financial Services *Whistleblower Protections* (September 2017), at [11.52].

[147]Dworkin and Brown (2012–2013, p. 686).

[148]Heyes and Kapur (2012, pp. 164–173) and Rapp (2012, pp. 109–113).

[149]Rapp (2012, pp. 110–111).

[150]Citing Zedeck (1977, p. 526).

[151]Miceli and Near (1985, p. 526).

other words, whistleblowers will weigh up the risk of retaliation against the extent to which their whistleblowing action will lead to correction of the wrongdoing, and will be motivated to act where there is a good likelihood of influencing a positive outcome, even where they are aware of and concerned about the risk of retaliation. In fact, according to Transparency International, 'the belief that nothing will be done, that it will not make any difference', is one of the main reasons why whistleblowers decide not to disclose information about wrongdoing.[152]

This is an important factor, and has to be contemplated when considering the action to be taken by the recipient of the information upon its reception.[153] Unfortunately, it is not always clear that the recipient of the information takes positive action on having received it, which may cause whistleblowers to question the value of disclosing information in the first place. Perceived reluctance or neglect on the part of the recipient to investigate the matter complained of may potentially serve as a deterrent to whistleblowing.[154] Whistleblowing could be encouraged, therefore, by imposition of some type of duty on the relevant regulatory authority to investigate the disclosure, or even to communicate with the whistleblower about a decision not to investigate the matter.

It is submitted, therefore, that a corporate whistleblowing regulatory framework should ideally provide that the recipient of the information must investigate the matter complained of, or refer it to an appropriate regulatory body where necessary, or at least provide reasons where it decides not to pursue the matter, in a timely fashion. It is suggested that regulatory bodies administering whistleblowing disclosures should 'update whistleblowers with the status of their case and should *communicate with whistleblowers more* to encourage reporting additional information'.[155]

This principle seems absent to a large extent in the corporate whistleblowing regulatory frameworks in respect of jurisdictions discussed in this chapter. In the Australian context, for example, it was recommended that where a whistleblower makes a protected disclosure to a law enforcement agency, the agency be required to provide regular updates to the whistleblower 'as to whether or not it is pursuing the matter', as well as whether the matter will be transferred to another agency, in which case the obligation to keep the whistleblower informed will rest on the new agency.[156] However, this recommendation appears not to have made its way into the new corporate whistleblowing legislation.

---

[152]Transparency International (2018, p. 6).

[153]Heyes and Kapur (2012, p. 177) note that '[i]t seems obvious and implicit in the design of actual policy regimes, that optimal policy toward whistle-blowing be sensitive to the motivation attributed to whistle-blowers'.

[154]De Maria (2006, p. 650) notes that research has shown that 'a major source of whistleblower grievance is the failure of authorities to conduct competent, and timely, investigations into their claims'.

[155]Ebersole (2011, p. 150).

[156]Parliamentary Joint Committee on Corporations and Financial Services, *Whistleblower Protections* (September 2017), Recommendation 8.20, at 93.

In Ontario, OSC Policy 15-601 indicates that the Commission will generally not communicate with a whistleblower about the status of a matter,[157] unless it is to inform the whistleblower that no further action will be taken, that an investigation will be undertaken, or to request additional information where necessary, should it become apparent that the whistleblower may qualify for a financial reward and information is required to confirm eligibility.[158]

The USA Securities Exchange Commission appears to follow a similar approach, as evidenced by the following comment on the website of its Office of the Whistleblower:

> The SEC conducts its investigations on a confidential basis as a matter of policy. The purpose of this policy is to protect the integrity of any investigation from premature disclosure and to protect the privacy of persons involved in our investigations. The SEC generally does not comment on whether it has opened an investigation in a particular matter or the status of its investigations.[159]

1.5 Ability to Access Whistleblowing Remedies

As was mentioned, an important part of ensuring whistleblowing protection is by way of broad application of the legislation permitting 'protected disclosures'[160] and a wide range of measures to encourage whistleblowing.[161] However, having appropriate regulatory components in place is just the first step towards enhanced whistleblowing activity. Equally important is the relative ease, from a practical perspective, with which a whistleblower could access the protection and remedies provided for in terms of the whistleblowing regulation. Whistleblower protective regulations that may appear useful on their face, could become largely ineffective in practice.[162] In addition to adequate protections and remedies, careful attention should therefore be given to having in place adequate administrative structures to ensure appropriate management of whistleblower disclosures.[163] Particularly telling in this regard is a study concerning the success of the *Sarbanes-Oxley Act* anti-retaliation measures showing dismal failure[164]—out of 286 cases that proceeded to be heard by an administrative law judge, only 2 resulted in a decision that was favourable to the employee.[165] The

---

157 OSC Policy 15-601, s 10(1).

158 OSC Policy 15-601, s 10(2).

159 See comment in relation to FAQ 12, available at https://www.sec.gov/whistleblower/frequently-asked-questions#faq-12.

160 See discussion in Sect. 1.3.

161 See discussion in Sect. 1.4.

162 See e.g. Dworkin (2007, p. 1764), Reid and David (2012, p. 909), as well as Rapp (2012, p. 82).

163 Ebersole (2011, pp. 128–130, 148–150).

164 Miceli et al. (2009, p. 391) note that 'whistleblowing legal cases related to SOX have produced few victories for the whistle-blowers'.

165 Dworkin and Brown (2012–2013, p. 661), with reference to Earle and Madek (2004, pp. 20–21).

reasons for failure can, in many instances, be attributed to surrounding structural and administrative issues, such as 'procedural complexity, misinterpretations of the statute's burden of proof, interpretations that were as strict as possible against the whistleblower, very short statute of limitations' and so on.[166] It is submitted, therefore, that it is absolutely vital to have adequate, well-resourced structures in place to support whistleblowing regulation, thus ensuring that the regulation is able to deliver optimum benefits.

1.5.1 Whistleblowing Authority or Tribunal

The *Sarbanes-Oxley Act* provides for an administrative process for complaints handling through the Occupational Safety and Health Administration (OSHA).[167] This procedure requires an employee to file a complaint with the Secretary of Labour within ninety days of the alleged discrimination, upon which the Secretary will conduct an investigation, provided the employee had shown a prima facie case that the alleged whistleblowing activity was a contributory factor to the retaliatory action.[168] The defendant employer subsequently carries the burden of proof to provide 'clear and convincing evidence' that the outcome in respect of the employee would have been the same, irrespective of the employee's involvement in the whistleblowing activity.[169] Should the employer not succeed in discharging the onus of proof, the secretary may issue a preliminary order to provide appropriate relief, if he/she finds that there is reasonable cause to believe that the retaliatory act occurred.[170]

Although sometimes described as a 'unique procedural innovation' for combining 'the efficiency of an administrative investigation with the safeguards of a federal court trial',[171] the process has also been criticised for a variety of reasons. The ninety-day period has been criticized as being too short, as 'most potential claimants don't realize what their rights are and how to pursue them in such a short period'.[172] This situation has subsequently been addressed in terms of the *Dodd-Frank Act*, that changed the period to 180 days and provided greater clarity around calculation of this period.[173] Channeling SOX whistleblower complaints to OSHA has also been criticised on the basis of OSHA's lack of experience and expertise in dealing with the

---

[166] Dworkin and Brown (2012–2013, p. 662).

[167] *Sarbanes-Oxley Act*, s 806, as summarised by Rubinstein (2007, p. 648).

[168] Rubinstein (2007, p. 648).

[169] Secretary's Order 5-2002, 67 Fed. Reg. 65,008 (Dep't of Labor Oct. 22, 2002); 68 Fed. Reg. 31,860 n.1 (May 28, 2003); see 29 C.F.R. § 1980.103(c) (2004). Also see Rubinstein (2007, p. 648) and Steinberg and Kaufman (2005, p. 449).

[170] Rubinstein (2007, p. 648).

[171] Moberley (2012, p. 9).

[172] Dworkin (2007, p. 1763). Also see Moberley (2012, p. 16).

[173] *Dodd-Frank Act*, s 922(c). Also see Moberley (2012, p. 16) for further discussion in this regard.

types of matters that SOX whistleblowers grapple with.[174] The absence of a remedy that allows for punitive damages furthermore serves as a deterrent for lawyers to take on whistleblower cases on a contingency basis, thus impeding the development of a specialised bar around whistleblower claims.[175]

One is therefore inclined to agree with Moberley that 'we ought to spend as much effort determining *who* is involved in whistleblower protection as we do deciding *what* those protections should formally entail'.[176] The model adopted by the USA in respect of its *Whistleblowing Protection Act 1989*,[177] whereby provision is made for a separate agency—the Merit Systems Protection Board—to litigate whistleblowing claims,[178] seems attractive. Such a system would circumvent the courts and address concerns around the cost of litigation to access whistleblower remedies, as well as create a specialized body with the necessary expertise and experience to deal with whistleblower claims in a particular context. However, care should be taken that regulatory disconnect does not prevent whistleblowing from performing its ultimate function, namely, enforcement actions against wrongdoers. A case in point is the way in which whistleblowing complaints under the *Sarbanes-Oxley Act* are administered by OSHA—apparently none of the complaints to OSHA have prompted an investigation by the SEC.[179] A dedicated body dealing with whistleblower claims should therefore act in close cooperation with the sector regulator, in order to ensure realization of the ultimate regulatory goals and objectives.

The issue of circumventing litigation through the court process appears less burning in regard to the way in which whistleblowing financial rewards are administered. In both the USA and Ontario, where this system has been implemented with much success, clear procedural guidelines and direct access to the process via the regulator are provided. The availability of adequate processes and systems is imperative, and the significant success of the SEC whistleblowing bounty system is likely in part due to the fact that the SEC, after enactment of the *Dodd-Frank Act*, created a central Office of the Whistleblower to manage and investigate tips.[180] It also created an Office of Market Intelligence, particularly tasked to develop technologies and systems to process tips and complaints.[181]

Concerns about an appropriate body to manage whistleblowing tips and complaints were also raised in Australia, where overwhelming support was expressed for the establishment of some form of central 'Whistleblower Protection Authority'.[182] This support resulted in a recommendation that a Whistleblower Protection Authority

---

174 See discussion and references Sect. 1.2.

175 Dworkin and Brown (2012–2013, p. 664).

176 Moberley (2012, p. 54).

177 Pub. L. No. 101-12, § 1221, 103 Stat. 1 (1989).

178 Pub. L. No. 101-12, § 1221, 103 Stat. 1 (1989), s 1221(a).

179 Rapp (2012–2013, p. 395).

180 Ibid., p. 400.

181 Ibid.

182 Parliamentary Joint Committee on Corporations and Financial Services *Whistleblower Protections* (September 2017), Ch 12.

with a broad range of powers to assist whistleblower be established.[183] The legislature decided against this recommendation, and the latest corporate whistleblowing protection legislative reforms in Australia failed to provide for the establishment of such a body.

1.5.2 Cost

Delays inherent in the process could serve as a huge disincentive to blowing the whistle, due to the costs associated with being involved in protracted legal battles to access a remedy.[184]

A delay in process is not the only potential cause of significant expense having to be incurred by the whistleblower. Adverse cost orders in jurisdictions where the shifting of cost to the unsuccessful party is the norm, such as in Australia, is another aspect that may detract from the usefulness of available remedies and protections, especially where these can only be accessed by way of litigation. Whistleblowers may be deterred from attempting to access the remedies available to them due to concerns about adverse cost orders, should they be unsuccessful with their claim. Australian private sector whistleblowing regulation includes some measures to alleviate this concern, in that the court may not order the whistleblower claimant to pay the costs incurred by the other party,[185] unless the court is satisfied that the whistleblower acted vexatiously, or without reasonable cause, or that the whistleblower's unreasonable conduct caused the other party to incur the costs.[186]

This concern will take a different guise in the USA and Canada, where cost-shifting is not used in principle. The concern in these jurisdictions is the opposite, in that the whistleblower might still have to carry a significant legal cost burden, even where the outcome of litigation is favourable to them. A contingency fee arrangement could go some way in addressing this concern. It is also possible for whistleblowers to receive a 'compensatory' cost remedy.[187] The potential success of a mechanism such as that would, however, depend on the ready availability of reasonable compensatory measures in case of a successful outcome—a criticism that was already noted in respect of the *Sarbanes-Oxley Act*. Interestingly, the US public sector legislative instrument—the *Whistleblowing Protection Act 1989*[188] provides for the possibility of cost orders in some cases.[189]

---

[183] Parliamentary Joint Committee on Corporations and Financial Services *Whistleblower Protections* (September 2017), Recommendation 12.1, at 158.

[184] Rapp (2012, pp. 115–116).

[185] *Corporations Act 2001* (Cth), s 1317AH(2).

[186] *Corporations Act 2001* (Cth), s 1317AH(3).

[187] See discussion in Sect. 1.4.1.2.

[188] Pub. L. No. 101-12, § 1221, 103 Stat. 1 (1989).

[189] Pub. L. No. 101-12, § 1221, 103 Stat. 1 (1989), s 1221(g)(1).

Ultimately, establishment of a whistleblowing tribunal may be a useful mechanism to ensure effective and efficient handling of whistleblower complaints, while being more cost-effective.

1.5.3 Burden of Proof

Another way in which the whistleblower could be provided with regulatory assistance with a view to enhance access to whistleblower remedies is through a reversed onus of proof. Under the Australian private sector whistleblowing regulation, the whistleblower claimant bears the onus of showing evidence indicating a *reasonable possibility* that the other person has engaged in conduct that would be detrimental to the whistleblower.[190] Where the whistleblower claimant is able to discharge that burden, the other party carries the onus to prove that the claim is in fact not made out.[191] This reversal of the onus of proof could significantly increase access to whistleblower remedies.

The *Sarbanes-Oxley Act* in the USA assumes the detrimental employment action, but places the burden on the employee to prove that the whistleblowing activity was a 'contributing factor' for any adverse employment action. This is regarded as a more 'employee-friendly' burden of proof than, for example, the 'but for' causation standard, or 'motivating factor' in cases where there is a mixed motive.[192] Where an employee is able to discharge this onus of proof, the burden shifts to the employer to demonstrate by 'clear and convincing evidence' that the same action would have been undertaken irrespective of the employee's engagement in whistleblowing activity—a more difficult than usual burden.[193]

A reversed onus of proof also exists in terms of section 121.5(5) in the *Ontario Securities Act*, which provides that the burden to prove that no reprisal action was taken against an employee rests on the person or company who allegedly committed the reprisal action.

1.6 Conclusion

It is well known that whistleblowers are exposed to an array of detrimental consequences that could flow from having blown the whistle. It is therefore not surprising that a key objective of whistleblowing regulation is often the protection of the whistleblower, and rightly so. However, whistleblower protection is just one piece of the puzzle—in order to encourage increased whistleblowing activity, attention should

[190] *Corporations Act 2001* (Cth), s 1317AD(2B)(a) (emphasis added).

[191] *Corporations Act 2001* (Cth), s 1317AD(2B)(b).

[192] Moberley (2012, p. 8).

[193] Ibid.

also be given to other factors that would motivate whistleblowers to come forward, for example, financial incentives, and the desire to see their actions in coming forward translating into a correction of the wrongdoing.

However, these 'regulatory incentives' to blow the whistle would only be able to achieve their function of encouraging whistleblowing if supported by an effective regulatory framework. It is therefore suggested that the regulatory goal of optimum whistleblowing activity is only achievable if careful consideration is given to the broader regulatory framework within which specific legislation or policy is operating, to assess the effect thereof on whistleblower conduct. In that respect, the scope of the relevant legislation or policies is important. The above discussion indicated that significant progress has been made in Australia, Canada and the USA to broaden the scope of application of whistleblower regulation—definitely a step in the right direction. It should be recognised, however, that where these steps are scattered over a patchwork of regulatory instruments, their impact may not be as palpable as desired, due to the confusion that it could create for potential whistleblowers. On that basis, dedicated or stand-alone whistleblowing regulation is often regarded as the more desirable option.

Another important factor to consider is the ease with which whistleblowers can access remedies under whistleblowing regulations. To this effect, a focus on aspects such as the reverse onus of proof, addressing the prohibitive cost of litigation, and the establishment of dedicated whistleblowing agencies, could be very useful. It is recognised that some of these measures may be costly to implement, but the expense may very well be worth the benefit. As Bucy noted:

> If the regulatory world wants information from insiders about complex, concealed wrongdoing motivated by economic gain, it must realize that information of this caliber from this type of whistleblower is expensive. If the regulatory world is not willing to pay for such information, it will not get it.[194]

Ultimately, an effective whistleblowing regulatory framework should operate so as to enhance accountability on the part of the corporation, and the focus at the end of the day should be on whether the whistleblowing regulatory framework as a whole is operating effectively in order to realize a wider set of policy objectives.

References

Brand V, Lombard S, Fitzpatrick J (2013) Bounty-Hunters, Whistleblowers and a New Regulatory Paradigm. *Aust Bus L Rev* 41:292

Brown AJ (2013) *Submission to the 2013 Senate References Committee Inquiry Into the Performance of ASIC*. Centre for Governance and Public Policy, Griffith University

Bucy PH (2002–2003) Information as a Commodity in the Regulatory World. *Hous L Rev* 39:905

Commonwealth of Australia (2009) *Treasury Options Paper: Improving Protections for Corporate Whistleblowers*

[194] Bucy (2002–2003, p. 948).

De Maria W (2006) Common Law—Common Mistakes: Protecting Whistleblowers in Australia, New Zealand, South Africa and the United Kingdom. *IJPSM* 19:643
Dixon O (2018) "Retaliatory" Enforcement Action for Chilling Whistleblowing Through Corporate Agreements: Lessons from North America. *Fed Law Rev* 46:427
Dworkin TM (2007) SOX and Whistleblowing. *Mich L Rev* 105:1757
Dworkin TM, Brown AJ (2012–2013) The Money or the Media? Lessons from Contrasting Developments in US and Australian Whistleblowing Laws. *Seattle J Soc Justice* 11:653
Dyck A, Morse A, Zingales L (2010) Who Blows the Whistle on Corporate Fraud? *J Finance* 65:2213
Earle BH, Madek GA (2004) The Mirage of Whistleblower Protection Under Sarbanes-Oxley: A Proposal for Change. *Am Bus LJ* 44:1
Ebersole D (2011) Blowing the Whistle on the Dodd-Frank Whistleblower Provisions. *EBLJ* 6:123
Fanto J (2007) A Social Defense of Sarbanes-Oxley. *NYL Sch L Rev* 52:517
Hassink H, de Vries M, Bollen L (2007) A Content Analysis of Whistleblowing Policies of Leading European Companies. *J Bus Ethics* 75:25
Heyes A, Kapur S (2012) An Economic Model of Whistle-Blower Policy. *J Law Econ Organ* 25:157
Labriola L (2017) Paying Too Dearly for a Whistle: Properly Protecting Internal Whistleblowers. *Fordham L Rev* 85:2839
Langton J (2019) *Tipsters Collect $7.5 Million in First-ever Payouts Under OSC Bounty Program.* Investment Executive, Quebec. https://www.investmentexecutive.com/news/from-the-regulators/tipsters-collect-7-5-million-in-first-ever-payouts-under-osc-bounty-program/
Lee J (2011–2012) Corporate Corruption and the New Gold Mine: How the Dodd-Frank Act Overincentivizes Whistleblowing. *Brook L Rev* 77:303
Lewis D, Uys T (2007) Protecting Whistleblowers at Work: A Comparison of the Impact of British and South African Legislation. *Manag Law* 49:76
Lombard S and Brand V (2014) Corporate Whistleblowing: Public Lessons for Private Disclosure. *Aust Bus L Rev* 42:351
Marin-Bariteau F, Newman V (2018) *Whistleblowing in Canada: A Knowledge Synthesis Report*
McEvoy JP (2016) The Legal Response to Whistleblowing in Canada: Managing Disclosures by the 'Up the Ladder' Prinicple. In: Thüsing G, Forst G (eds) *Whistleblowing—A Comparative Study.* Springer International Publishing, Cham
Miceli MP, Near JP (1985) Characteristics of Organizational Climate and Perceived Wrongdoing Associated with Whistle-Blowing Decisions. *Pers Psychol* 38:525
Miceli MP, Near JP, Dworkin TM (2009) A Word to the Wise: How Managers and Policy-Makers can Encourage Employees to Report Wrongdoing. *J Bus Ethics* 86:379
Moberley R (2012) Sarbanes-Oxley's Whistleblower Provisions: Ten Years Later. *SCL Rev* 64:1
Rapp GC (2007) Beyond Protection: Invigorating Incentives for Sarbanes-Oxley Corporate and Securities Fraud Whistleblowers. *BUL Rev* 87:91
Rapp GC (2012) Mutiny by the Bounties? The Attempt to Reform Wall Street by the New Whistleblower Provisions of the Dodd-Frank Act. *BYUL Rev* 73
Rapp GC (2012–2013) Four Signal Moments in Whistleblower Law: 1983–2013. *Hofstra Lab & Emp LJ* 30:389
Reid SL, David SB (2012) The Evolution of the SEC Whistleblower: From Sarbanes-Oxley to Dodd-Frank. *Banking LJ* 129:907
Ritchie LE, Malik W (2016) *Newly Introduced OSC Whistleblower Program Receives over 30 Tips Since Coming into Effect.* OSLER, Toronto. https://www.osler.com/en/blogs/risk/october-2016/newly-introduced-osc-whistleblower-program-receive
Rubinstein K (2007) Internal Whistleblowing and Sarbanes-Oxley Section 806: Balancing the Interests of Employee and Employer. *NYL Sch L Rev* 52:637
Solomon D (2004) For Financial Whistle-Blowers, New Shield is an Imperfect One. *Wall Street J,* New York
Standards Australia (2003) *AS 8004—2003 Whistleblower Protection Programs for Entities*
Steinberg MI, Kaufman SA (2005) Minimizing Corporate Liability Exposure When the Whistle Blows in the Post Sarbanes-Oxley Era. *J Corp Law* 445

Transparency International (2018) *A Best Practice Guide for Whistleblowing Legislation*

United States Securities and Exchange Commission (2018) *2018 Annual Report to Congress: Whistleblower Program*. https://www.sec.gov/sec-2018-annual-report-whistleblower-program.pdf

Vega MA (2012–2013) Beyond Incentives: Making Corporate Whistleblowing Moral in the New Era of Dodd-Frank Act "Bounty Hunting". *Conn L Rev* 45:483

Zedeck S (1977) An Information Processing Model and Approach to the Study of Motivation. *Organ Behav Hum Perform* 18:44

Sulette Lombard is a corporate and insolvency law academic at Flinders University, Australia. She has taught, researched, presented and published internationally in an array of corporate and insolvency law areas. Her research interests include corporate governance and regulatory theory, and the role and position of corporate whistleblowing in that context. Sulette is an active member of the Australian Law Council's Corporations Committee, as well as the Insolvency and Restructuring Committee, and has been invited to appear before Australian parliamentary inquiries in relation to whistleblowing on multiple occasions.

Chapter 2
The Ethics of Corporate Whistleblowing Rewards

Vivienne Brand

Abstract Corporate whistleblowing regulation has experienced rapid evolution in a number of significant jurisdictions in recent years, most notably in the United States. One of the most controversial aspects of contemporary reform in corporate whistleblowing regimes is the debate over whether or not to introduce whistleblowing rewards or 'bounties'. This chapter considers the ethical analysis that can be brought to bear in relation to the offering of corporate whistleblowing rewards, and how that might assist in ensuring that rewards have a place in an effective corporate whistleblowing regulatory environment.

Keywords Ethics of whistleblowing · Ethics of whistleblowing rewards · Expressive function of law theory · Moral development theory · Whistleblower bounty

2.1 Introduction

Whistleblowing remains an activity that exposes people to significant risk of a range of harms—including reprisal, black-listing, significant emotional stress, and loss of employment, status, income, reputation, and frequently relationships. In short, the consequences of blowing the whistle are often disastrous.[1] The harms done to whistleblowers stand in stark contrast to the social utility of increased whistleblowing activity. Whistleblowing is an important regulatory device, particularly in complex corporate environments, given its proven capacity to uncover wrongdoing that

[1] See for instance De George (2010, p. 303), Rapp (2007, pp. 95–6, 118) and Gobert and Punch (2000, pp. 34–6).

An earlier version of some of the ideas discussed in this Chapter, focussing on Australian whistleblowing reforms, appears in Brand (2018).

V. Brand (✉)
College of Business, Government and Law, Flinders University, Bedford Park, Australia
e-mail: vivienne.brand@flinders.edu.au

S. Lombard et al. (eds.), *Corporate Whistleblowing Regulation*,
https://doi.org/10.1007/978-981-15-0259-0_2

might otherwise be obscured from view.[2] In response to the clear regulatory advantages of whistleblowing, a range of interventions have been observable in various jurisdictions in recent years, including the introduction of bounties, or rewards, for whistleblowers. The most high-profile of these reforms is undoubtedly the United States' Dodd-Frank Whistleblowing bounties legislation, introduced in 2011.[3] The Dodd-Frank legislation created a rewards system for whistleblowers who bring evidence of wrongdoing to the SEC, and dramatically changed awareness of rewards as a whistleblowing regulatory device. The payment of a number of very high value rewards under the scheme has ensured on-going publicity.[4] Influenced by the US reforms, the Ontario Securities Commission introduced its own rewards system in 2016.[5]

However, despite the apparent success of the US rewards system, and the attention given to possible rewards structures as a regulatory device, whistleblowing rewards schemes have been rejected in a number of jurisdictions and remain a controversial aspect of whistleblowing regulation. Historical ambivalence about the appropriateness of paying rewards to whistleblowers is reflected in US legislation that prohibited anti-retaliation protection to whistleblowers if they stood to benefit by reporting the wrongdoing.[6] That resistance can be seen as having its roots, at least in part, in a pervasive sense that whistleblowing rewards are in some way contrary to the spirit of whistleblowing, and essentially 'unethical'. Concerns include both issues inherent in the act of whistleblowing itself (such as the perceived loyalty dilemma faced by an employee who makes a disclosure) and issues related to rewards specifically (such as the potential to create perverse incentives to delay disclosure in order to increase the size of a potential reward). It has been said that:

> [i]n spite of the alleged economic efficiencies of bounty programs, some believe they create perverse incentives and should be repealed on ethical and policy grounds. The reasoning is simple—the financial incentives of reporting are oftentimes fueled by greed or revenge. This situation may result in snitching against fellow associates, employers, relatives and even family members. Senator Reid of Nevada best captured this philosophy during a 1998 congressional debate when he labeled the Internal Revenue Service ("IRS") whistleblower program a "[r]eward for rats".[7]

In the United Kingdom, a 2013 report of the Parliamentary Commission on Banking Standards called for an investigation of the impact of financial incentives in the United States. The subsequent research note concluded incentives would not be effective, and took the view that 'financial incentives could create a number of moral and

---

[2]See for instance recent empirical work on the direct relationship between whistleblowers and increased speed and efficacy of enforcement: Call et al. (2018).

[3]Dodd-Frank Act § 922(a); FCPA § 78dd-1.

[4]The highest reward paid by the SEC to a whistleblower as of 2018 stood at almost $US50M: US Securities and Exchange Commission (2018, p. 9).

[5]Ontario Securities Commission, OSC Policy 15-601, *Whistleblower Program,* July 2016.

[6]Callahan and Dworkin (1992, p. 279), and the legislation cited there.

[7]Blount and Markel (2012, p. 1028) and the sources cited there (footnotes omitted from quotation).

other hazards.'[8] In Australia, whistleblowing rewards were endorsed by a parliamentary inquiry in 2017, but were not adopted in the resultant reforms passed by Federal Parliament.[9] In this context it is significant that the Inquiry noted that 'many submitters and witnesses focused on the ethical implications of a bounty system'.[10]

It appears that despite the clear regulatory advantages of increased rates of whistleblowing, and the potential for rewards to further enhance the effectiveness of whistleblowing, ethical concerns have been central to criticisms of whistleblowing rewards, and are likely to have delayed or prevented more widespread use of rewards systems. In light of this, this Chapter considers the extent to which an analysis of the ethics of whistleblowing rewards supports the perception of unethicality, and hence to what extent ethics ought to be seen as a barrier to the adoption of whistleblowing rewards as a regulatory tool. In doing so, it considers two theoretical perspectives that have potential to assist in understanding the regulation of whistleblowing rewards in an ethical context. The ethics of whistleblowing rewards arguably remains under-theorised, and warrants further discussion. The first theoretical perspective—the expressive function of law theory—suggests that the presence of legal norms can assist in the creation of beneficial social norms. This idea has particular salience for the historically pejorative concept of whistleblowing, since well-designed whistleblowing rewards structures could influence social perceptions of whistleblowing and rewards, and assist in establishing normative delineations between more and less ethically justifiable forms of disclosure. The second theoretical perspective—Kohlberg's theory of moral development—directs its attention to stages of moral development and makes some predictions about the moral judgments of adults that offer further support for the potential positive impact of whistleblowing rewards regulation from an ethical point of view. Taken together, these theoretical perspectives offer insight into the possible impact of legislated whistleblowing rewards systems, and indicate a way forward in addressing the perception of whistleblowing rewards as unethical.

Section 2.2 of this chapter provides a review of the ethical concerns that arise in the context of whistleblowing and the additional ethical factors applicable to whistleblowing rewards. Section 2.3 then reviews both the expressive function of law theory and Kohlberg's moral development theory in light of their potential to assist an understanding of the ethical impact of whistleblowing rewards. Section 2.4 considers how the design of a whistleblowing rewards system might address the ethical concerns identified in Sect. 2.2, with consequential implications for a reconceptualization of the ethics of whistleblowing rewards. Section 2.5 concludes the chapter.

---

[8] Bank of England Prudential Regulation Authority and Financial Conduct Authority (2014, p. 3).

[9] Parliamentary Joint Committee on Corporations and Financial Services, Parliament of Australia, *Whistleblower Protections* (September 2017); Treasury Laws Amendment (Enhancing Whistleblower Protections) Act, 2018 (Cth).

[10] Parliamentary Joint Committee on Corporations and Financial Services, Parliament of Australia, *Whistleblower Protections* (September 2017), 130.

2.2 Ethics and Whistleblowing

Ethical concerns might arise in relation to the payment of a whistleblowing reward for at least two reasons. Firstly, the payment might relate to whistleblowing activity that was not justified from an ethical point of view. Secondly, it may be that the whistleblowing was justified, but the payment of the reward is unethical. These two possibilities are considered separately in the discussion that follows.

2.2.1 Is Whistleblowing Ethical?

De George's ethical analysis of justified whistleblowing activity has been widely accepted.[11] A prominent normative business ethics academic, De George has argued against any "one-size fits all" ethical understanding of the complex actions involved in whistleblowing activity.[12] Rather, De George argues that many factors can be present in a whistleblowing event, and that each of those factors can have an effect on the ethics of any disclosure engaged in by a whistleblower. Relevant factors identified by De George are whether the disclosure is made internally or externally, the seriousness of any harm likely to result from the malfeasance being disclosed and whether that harm would be financial or physical, and the legality of any actions being disclosed.[13]

De George also distinguishes between wrongdoing that would be sufficiently serious to oblige a whistleblower to make a disclosure, and wrongdoing that would ground a justified disclosure, without being sufficiently serious to morally obligate it.[14] The following three conditions precedent to morally permissible whistleblowing have been identified by De George[15]:

1. The firm will do serious and considerable harm to employees or the public if the disclosure is not made;
2. A report has been made by an employee to an immediate superior (this being a crucial step in making whistleblowing justifiable); and
3. If the immediate superior has done nothing effective, the employee has exhausted internal procedures and possibilities within the firm—including going up the ladder to the board if necessary.

Further, two additional elements are necessary, in De George's view, to ensure an act of whistleblowing is ethically required, as opposed to merely permissible:

---

[11] Hoffman and Schwartz (2015, p. 771).

[12] De George (2015, p. 801).

[13] Ibid.

[14] Ibid.

[15] See generally, De George (2010, Chap. 14).

4. The whistleblower has documented evidence that would convince a reasonable, impartial observer of their view of the situation, and that the company's product or practice poses a serious and likely danger to the public or product users; and
5. The employee has good reasons to believe that by going public the necessary changes will be brought about. That is, '[t]he chance of being successful must be worth the risk one takes and the danger to which one is exposed'.[16]

The following section fleshes out De George's framework, and reviews a number of additional factors from the literature that can be perceived as relevant to an ethical analysis of whistleblowing, as well as positing a range of possible counter-arguments. The discussion traverses the so-called loyalty dilemma, the significance of internal versus external disclosure, issues related to procedural fairness, evidentiary standards, and the distinction between morally permissible whistleblowing and morally obligated whistleblowing.

2.2.1.1 The Loyalty Dilemma

The failure to keep corporate material within the corporation is often described in ethical terms as a breach of the employee's inherent duty of loyalty to the corporation.[17] This underlying ethical concern appears to be central to De George's analysis, with its emphasis on completely exhausting internal reporting options before reporting externally. De George specifies that a would-be whistleblower would need to have reported concerns up the ladder to the board if necessary, before it would be morally permissible to report externally. This sets a difficult standard, and raises the question whether De George's five-part set of criteria creates too high a bar for a whistleblower. Is it justifiable to require a whistleblower to put to so much of their own reputation and financial and mental health capital at risk in the pursuit of the company's and wider stakeholders' best interests when it is the organisation itself that has arguably forfeited its right to expect a duty of loyalty? That is, where a corporation has created or allowed to subsist a culture within which initial reports of wrongdoing are ignored or not sufficiently responded to, it may be appropriate to abrogate the loyalty duty proportionately.

Other commentators have offered variations of this crucial loyalty analysis. Hoffman and Schwartz appear to recognize that insisting that an attempt be made to disclose via the board before disclosing externally may be too onerous a standard to impose upon a whistleblower. They allow for external disclosure where disclosure to a supervisor or the board has not been possible, but disclosure has at least been made 'through the designated reporting channel (e.g. legal counsel, human resources manager, internal auditor…)'.[18] Velasquez suggests it will be morally justifiable to whistleblow externally where this is 'the only way to prevent the harm' to which the

[16]De George (2010, p. 311).

[17]De George (2010, p. 304).

[18]Hoffman and Schwartz (2015, p. 774).

disclosure relates.[19] Additional context is provided by empirical data that indicates it is very rare for employees to disclose externally without attempting to deal with an issue by reporting internally first,[20] and that internal whistleblowing remains a far more common form of whistleblowing.[21] This suggests that existing norms favour internal whistleblowing over external disclosure, consistent with the loyalty owed to one's employer company.

Perhaps an aggregation of evidence of the detriment borne by whistleblowers can ground a critique of De George's formulation, and allow a reframing of the loyalty dilemma which accommodates the potential for an employer to have forfeited their right to expect loyal silence from an employee. This alternative analysis would seem to be supported by the development of legislative models that acknowledge the need for whistleblowers to be able to approach external regulators—and even the media—where no adequate internal response has been forthcoming. In Australia, recent federal whistleblower protection legislation protects disclosures well short of the demanding De George test, allowing for 'emergency disclosures' to a parliamentarian or journalist in certain circumstances (that is, disclosure need not be to a regulator).[22] Another reframing of the loyalty dilemma has focussed on identifying the corporation as intrinsically linked to its surrounding context and its stakeholders.[23] This analysis allows for a 'less stark'[24] internal/external distinction, suggesting that 'external' whistleblowing may in fact be internal to the corporation's wider network of complex relationships.[25] On this formulation, the actions of a whistleblower in making external disclosure can be perceived as consistent with the duty of loyalty to the corporation, since the ultimate best interests of the corporation (widely defined) have been served.

Given the divisions between internal and external whistleblowing in terms of the loyalty duty, different categories of whistleblowing might qualify as 'ethical', depending on whether a disclosure is made internally or externally. It may be that less moral justification is required to blow the whistle internally, with a consequential increase in the number of matters that could, morally, be raised.[26] The inherent significant conflict between a duty to disclose and a loyalty duty to the firm is removed, but is replaced by a lesser conflict between a duty to disclose and a loyalty duty 'to one's immediate supervisor or one's peers'.[27] Thus, certain minor wrongdoing may only be sufficiently serious to justify internal disclosure (a lower bar, since there is no

[19] Velasquez (2018, p. 362).

[20] Hoffman and Schwartz (2015, p. 774).

[21] Ibid., p. 777.

[22] *Treasury Laws Amendment (Enhancing Whistleblower Protections) Act, 2018* (Cth), inserting s 1317AAD: 'Public interest disclosure and emergency disclosure' into the *Corporations Act, 2001* (Cth).

[23] Andrade (2015).

[24] Ibid., p. 334.

[25] Ibid., p. 332.

[26] Hoffman and Schwartz (2015, p. 777).

[27] Ibid.

loyalty obligation to the corporation in play), to be compared with more significant wrongdoing of a kind sufficient to justify external disclosure (and hence a breach of the loyalty duty). For instance, Hoffman and Schwartz offer the examples of minor theft from the stationery cupboard or the receipt of small gifts by a purchasing manager from a supplier as insufficient to justify the breaching of the duty of loyalty,[28] but different standards might apply if the disclosure was only internal.

2.2.1.2 Procedural Fairness—Warning the Wrongdoer

Normative justifications for whistleblowing can also require the whistleblower to notify the wrongdoer that their actions will be reported if they are not discontinued. Hoffman and Schwartz suggest that ensuring the whistleblower accords this level of procedural fairness to the perpetrator 'supports the moral praiseworthiness' of the whistleblower's ultimate disclosure (whether internal or external).[29] However, arguably this places a very heavy burden on the would-be whistleblower, who may risk their identity becoming known, with associated risk of reprisals. Further, the potential arises for the wrongdoer to desist—thus presumably preventing the whistleblower from disclosing—while leaving the whistleblower at risk of victimisation from the wrongdoer, without the benefit of the relevant misconduct having been disclosed. By contrast, pre-warning of the potential disclosure to the wrongdoer does not appear to be a feature of contemporary whistleblowing regulatory systems, whether they incorporate rewards or not.[30] This is not surprising for a range of reasons, including that retaliation and victimisation risks are high, encouragement of whistleblowers usually relies on assurances of anonymity, and successful prosecution of wrongdoers may necessitate the collection of evidence by authorities before a wrongdoer has a reason to suspect they are being investigated.

2.2.1.3 Evidentiary Standards

Normative discussions of the ethics of whistleblowing also suggest that the whistleblower will have to meet some sort of evidentiary standard before their disclosures will be morally obligated (or, presumably, justified).[31] Here, as in other elements of the normative analysis of whistleblowing, a range of views exist in relation to the detail of the requirement imposed upon the whistleblower—does the whistleblower need to convince others of the merits of their analysis, to gather as much evidence

---

[28] Ibid., p. 774.

[29] Ibid., p. 775.

[30] A requirement of this kind does not, for instance, form part of the existing whistleblowing systems created by the *Corporations Act, 2001* (Cth), the Ontario Securities Commission, OSC Policy 15-601, *Whistleblower Program*, or the United States Securities Exchange Commission, Office of the Whistleblower, Final Rules, § 240.21F-6 Criteria for determining amount of award.

[31] De George (2010, Chap. 14), Hoffman and Schwartz (2015, p. 775), and the commentators discussed there.

as possible, or rely upon a 'reasonable belief' standard?[32] In De George's analysis, evidentiary support for whistleblowing is relevant to a distinction between morally permissible whistleblowing and morally obligated activity.[33] This is discussed further below.

2.2.1.4 The Distinction Between Morally Permissible and Morally Obligated

A further normative factor to be taken into account in some analyses of the ethics of whistleblowing is the difference between those factors that would ensure external disclosure was morally permissible, and those that would impose a moral obligation to whistleblow externally. For De George, where evidentiary standards are met, and where the whistleblower has good reasons to believe that blowing the whistle will result in effective changes, a moral imperative arises to make disclosure by blowing the whistle.[34] Once again, this approach can be perceived as somewhat demanding of the whistleblower, given the difficulties a whistleblower may experience in determining, in a complex and multi-dimensional organisation, the likelihood of effective change being instituted. Others have argued that where insufficient legal protections exist to assist a whistleblower, there can be no moral obligation requiring the whistleblower to disclose.[35] Given the difficulty many whistleblowers experience in accessing effective protections, this analysis could be extended to justify a whistleblower not coming forward where the substance, if not the form, of an adequate system of protection is lacking.

2.2.2 *The Ethics of Whistleblowing Rewards*

In addition to the range of ethical concerns that can be identified in relation to whistleblowing activity, additional factors need to be considered when the ethics of rewards for whistleblowing are analysed. The significance of these additional factors is reflected in the pervasive sense, described earlier, of whistleblowing rewards being in some sense inherently unethical. Callahan and Dworkin have suggested that hostility to whistleblowing rewards reflects a perspective 'that disclosures motivated by gain … are not "true" whistleblowing'.[36] Yet despite this perception, clear arguments can be advanced for rewarding whistleblowing in an ethical society. It

---

[32] See Hoffman and Schwartz (2015, p. 775), and the commentators discussed there.

[33] For whistleblowing to be morally required, De George argues the whistleblower must (amongst other things) be able to produce 'documented evidence that would convince a reasonable, impartial observer that one's view of the situation is correct': De George (2010, pp. 310–311).

[34] De George (2010, p. 310).

[35] Hoffman and Schwartz (2015, p. 776).

[36] Callahan and Dworkin (1992, p. 319).

appears axiomatic that an ethical society would seek to promote transparency; the links between whistleblowing and increased transparency are clear, and hence support for whistleblowing ought to support the aims of a transparent society. Thus, it might be argued that—to the extent they increase whistleblowing activity—rewards promote an ethical society. Are rewards therefore ethically justifiable?

The following section reviews a range of arguments that can be advanced to challenge the ethicality of rewards. These concerns incorporate both normative and descriptive perspectives; that is, they encompass concerns in relation to what people *ought* to do in relation to whistleblowing rewards, as well as issues arising from *descriptions* of what people actually do in that context. Relevant factors discussed here are the risks of unethical incentives and perverse outcomes, incentives for inappropriate whistleblowing, issues arising from the randomness of rewards, problems associated with incentives to delay disclosure, the potential to create inappropriate third-party markets, and 'crowding out' and stigma problems.[37]

2.2.2.1 Anti-ethical Outcomes

A key concern with the use of rewards is that they might have the effect of militating against the creation of wide cultural acceptance of whistleblowing,[38] in that the availability of rewards may skew the development of appropriate ethical systems. This argument is presumably based in part on an intrinsic belief in the unethicality of whistleblowing rewards, which will then act as a contagion that will affect the wider ethical culture within structures in which rewards operate. Virtue ought, in this view, to be its own reward. Similarly, it has been argued that incentives to whistleblow externally operate to undermine 'management's efforts to internally handle fraud and foster an ethical culture' and thus have a deleterious effect on corporate culture and compliance efforts generally.[39] Related normative issues include the potential of whistleblowing rewards to establish unethical incentives to whistleblow,[40] and to work against the re-introduction of a good culture in an organisation.[41] That is, rewards might increase the likelihood of a whistleblower reporting information for the 'wrong' reasons, given the availability of a lucrative reward for doing so. The motive

[37]Many of these issues were discussed by a 2017 Australian Parliamentary Joint Inquiry on Whistleblower Protections, in which the introduction of rewards was considered, offering a rare opportunity for the ethical considerations associated with whistleblower rewards to be interrogated in a public forum: Parliamentary Joint Committee on Corporations and Financial Services, *Whistleblower Protections*, September 2017.

[38]Parliamentary Joint Committee on Corporations and Financial Services, *Whistleblower Protections*, September 2017, at [11.34], Dr Simon Longstaff, the Ethics Centre.

[39]Ebersole (2011, p. 139).

[40]Parliamentary Joint Committee on Corporations and Financial Services, *Whistleblower Protections*, September 2017, at [11.56].

[41]Parliamentary Joint Committee on Corporations and Financial Services, *Whistleblower Protections*, September 2017, at [11.32], the Institute of Internal Auditors.

of the whistleblower is central to these criticisms. Similarly, paying individuals to fulfil a pre-existing public duty could be seen as inappropriate.[42]

Rewards could also be capable of creating incentives for inappropriate whistleblowing activity—that is, for whistleblowing that is inherently unethical, regardless of the ethics (or otherwise) of the incentives mechanism. Where a reward makes an immoral or unethical instance of whistleblowing more likely, there are reasons to criticise the ethical basis of the reward. The discussion of normative ethics concerns above noted the potential for whistleblowing to be regarded as unethical where, for instance, adequate disclosure to a superior has not been attempted prior to the whistleblowing act. Other examples could include whistleblowing that occurs without prior warning to the offender, or is made externally without prior internal disclosure.[43] The risk of incentives undermining the introduction and maintenance of effective internal systems has been noted,[44] and given De George's analysis that internal whistleblowing is a morally superior mechanism in many instances (i.e. where external whistleblowing is not justifiable), this risk is undesirable from an ethical point of view. Further, rewards might exacerbate a moral hazard through encouraging malicious whistleblowing.[45]

2.2.2.2 Rewarding Whistleblowers for Chance Events: The Problem of Randomness

Another normative concern with regard to whistleblowers relates to the sense that whistleblowers ought not to benefit from their chance proximity to wrongdoing. That is, where an employee becomes aware of wrongdoing within an organisation and, appropriately, brings that wrongdoing to light by reporting the matter, why should they recover financially where another employee, with no 'lucky' chance proximity to the wrongdoing, would be denied the opportunity to profit from the malfeasant activity? This concern is elevated where the employee stands to receive a disproportionate wind-fall gain from the making of the disclosure that goes beyond 'restoring or maintaining the position that they held, in a financial sense, prior to a disclosure having taken place'.[46] However, it might be argued in the alternative that the employee has been, by chance alone, unfortunate in their exposure to an instance of wrongdoing within the workplace—which has now placed upon them some level of moral obligation to disclose, complete with attendant risks and potential harms. Relatedly, the concern arises that an employee not involved in making a disclosure

---

[42]Bank of England Prudential Regulation Authority and Financial Conduct Authority (2014, p. 3).

[43]On the potential for financial incentives to increase the risk of external whistleblowing without earlier internal disclosure see Hoffman and Schwartz (2015, p. 773).

[44]Bank of England Prudential Regulation Authority and Financial Conduct Authority (2014, p. 2).

[45]Parliamentary Joint Committee on Corporations and Financial Services, *Whistleblower Protections*, September 2017, at [11.14].

[46]Parliamentary Joint Committee on Corporations and Financial Services, *Whistleblower Protections* (2017) [11.35], Mr. Matthew Chesher.

and who also has access to the relevant information, might be suspected to be the whistleblower and be vicitimised as a result, yet have no access to the rewards that stand as a form of compensation for the real whistleblower.[47]

2.2.2.3 Incentives to Delay Disclosure and Obtain Information Illegitimately

The perceived ethics of rewards for whistleblowing has also been influenced by the potential for reward size to increase proportionately with the scale of the wrongdoing. Where, for instance, a reward is linked to the size of a penalty imposed upon a wrongdoer, it may be that an incentive exists for a potential whistleblower to delay disclosure, in order to increase the impact of the wrongdoing and the size of any ultimate penalty.[48] Related concerns exist in the potential for a would-be whistleblower to engage in entrapment activity in the hope of gaining information to ground a lucrative whistleblowing disclosure.[49]

2.2.2.4 Rewards and Third Parties

In addition to the ethical concerns that might be raised in relation to the impact of rewards on individual whistleblower behaviour, concerns can be identified in relation to the impact of rewards structures on third parties. Where the existence of rewards leads to the creation of a third-party market for legal or related services (as was anticipated in the United States following introduction of the Dodd-Frank reforms),[50] then one criticism of those rewards may be their potential to encourage 'ambulance chasing' by those third-party providers.[51] That is, if a market for legal advisers to would-be whistleblowers is created by a rewards system, will there be increased advertising of whistleblowing reward services, and attendant growth in wrongful (as well as legitimate) acts of whistleblowing? Will, in other words, the incentives for inappropriate or unethical whistleblowing (referred to above) be reinforced by third-party providers?

---

[47] Parliamentary Joint Committee on Corporations and Financial Services, *Whistleblower Protections* (2017) [11.30], [11.31].

[48] Parliamentary Joint Committee on Corporations and Financial Services, *Whistleblower Protections*, September 2017, at [11.39], Vivienne Brand and Sulette Lombard, Flinders University; and at [11.40], Lucas Ryan. Senior Policy Advisor, Australian Institute of Company Directors.

[49] Bank of England Prudential Regulation Authority and Financial Conduct Authority (2014, p. 3); noted by the Parliamentary Joint Committee on Corporations and Financial Services, *Whistleblower Protections*, September 2017, at [11.14].

[50] Ebersole (2011, pp. 146–7).

[51] See, for instance, the evidence of the Institute of Internal Auditors to the 2017 Australian Federal Inquiry: Parliamentary Joint Committee on Corporations and Financial Services, *Whistleblower Protections*, September 2017, at [11.45].

One response here might be that rewards operate as self-executing compensation, which more adequately protects a whistleblower than compensation that needs to be applied for and pursued. Since we know whistleblowers are likely to suffer as a result of blowing the whistle, we should protect them in meaningful (and not merely theoretical) ways. If it is necessary to harness the market to facilitate the delivery of that self-executing compensation, then perhaps that is appropriate, given the difficulties commonly placed in the path of whistleblowers. That is, while the presence of rewards may sponsor a market in third-party providers who assist in accessing that compensation, this in itself may not be a bad thing.

2.2.2.5 Descriptive Ethics Literature on Rewards: The 'Crowding Out' of Pro-social Behaviour and Stigma Issues

The majority of the ethics concerns that are raised in relation to whistleblowing rewards are normative in nature, given that very little empirical evidence is available in respect of the effect of legislative rewards on whistleblowing activity. The SEC bounties program is relatively new, with only some (admittedly highly persuasive) data available in relation to its success.[52] United States predecessors of the Dodd-Frank bounties programs have been subject to more assessment, and offer potential for longitudinal data.[53] However, it is clear that an overall shortage of data remains. Further, this shortage of descriptive evidence is not confined to whistleblowing rewards. The entire field of ethical decision-making within descriptive ethics has been described as under-developed: Schwartz has pointed out that '[w]hile much has been discovered regarding the ethical decision-making (EDM) process within business organizations, a great deal remains unknown'.[54]

Despite this general lack of evidence, some descriptive studies are available to suggest the effect of rewards on whistleblowing behaviour. There are significant bodies of organisational behaviour research in the area of rewards and a body of social-psychological research that has focused on whistleblowing.[55] This work can offer some insights into the potential for rewards to create worthwhile incentives for whistleblowing. The literature on reward structure and administration, for instance, has been summarised more than 25 years ago as indicating that paying rewards for whistleblowing activity ought to be an effective way of encouraging whistleblowing.[56] Overall, there clearly is support in the social-psychological literature for a

---

[52]The US SEC notes in its 2018 Annual Report that it received over 5200 whistleblower tips in the 2018 financial year, representing a nearly 75% increase on the same period 6 years earlier: US Securities and Exchange Commission (2018, p. 2).

[53]Call et al. (2018).

[54]Schwartz (2016, p. 755).

[55]Callahan and Dworkin (1992, p. 283).

[56]Ibid., p. 301.

well-administered rewards system as part of an effective scheme of whistleblowing regulation.[57]

Using this wider literature, it is also possible to identify a key argument to suggest that, from an empirical perspective, the use of rewards can be said to raise ethical concerns. Research has demonstrated the potential for rewards to—perhaps counter-intuitively—reduce levels of whistleblowing activity. Feldman and Orly have reported a large-scale United States study that suggested that offering monetary rewards to whistleblowers could in some cases tend to lead to *reduced* levels of reporting.[58] Feldman and Orly use so-called 'crowding out' theory to argue that introducing extrinsic motivations (for example, financial incentives) acts to reduce the space within which intrinsic motivation can operate. There are echoes here of the normative arguments raised above in relation to the negative impact of rewards on any attempt to create a culture of disclosure.[59] This effect has potentially deleterious consequences for a range of pro-social activities—including whistleblowing.[60] Essentially, Feldman and Orly argue that by externalising the motivation to report, financial incentives might—completely inadvertently—reduce inherent motivations to behave pro-socially.[61] It appears that the extent of operation of this phenomenon may vary dependent on various factors, including the size of the incentive offered. Curiously, it seems that low rewards can be the most counter-productive.[62] Perhaps relatedly, the stigma attached to blowing the whistle for a reward may further demotivate individuals from reporting wrongdoing; there is some empirical evidence that rewards carry a significant level of social stigma.[63]

Several things can be said about these crowding-out and stigma concerns. As with all empirical research, particularly in the area of ethics, care has to be taken with results generated by participants based on statements about what they would do if faced with a particular situation. It is not possible to double-blind control test the decision-making of individuals encountering serious whistleblowing choices. It is difficult to be confident that responses to complex intense ethical issues with real-life serious consequences are susceptible to duplication in experiments that use random members of the public who volunteer for surveys in return for earning online credits (as was the case in the Feldman and Orly research).[64] A second factor is the possible need to distinguish between the potential for rewards to crowd out pro-social behaviours such as painless blood donation, when compared with the potential to discourage people to do something that is both pro-social and very risky from a personal point of view. Where the desired action has seemingly inevitable negative

---

[57] Ibid., p. 302.

[58] Feldman and Lobel (2010).

[59] Parliamentary Joint Committee on Corporations and Financial Services, *Whistleblower Protections*, September 2017, at [11.34], Dr. Simon Longstaff, the Ethics Centre.

[60] Feldman and Lobel (2010, p. 1179).

[61] Ibid.

[62] Ibid., p. 1202.

[63] Ibid., p. 1205.

[64] Ibid., p. 1189.

consequences, the effect of instituting some form of self-executing compensation might well be very different. Whistleblowing may well be a quite specific kind of pro-social behaviour.

Overall, it is clear from the arguments canvassed in this section that complex ethical concerns are raised by whistleblowing activity itself, and that these are further compounded by the additional issues that can arise in the use of rewards for whistleblowing. These concerns encompass both normative and descriptive arguments, and are susceptible to alternative analyses. In light of the breadth and complexity of those issues, this Chapter suggests there is a need for further theoretical analysis to be undertaken in relation to the ethics of rewards. The next section aims to contribute to that discussion.

2.3 Theoretical Perspectives: 'Expressive Function of Law' Theory and Kohlberg's Moral Development Theory

Two theoretical perspectives are addressed in this section that have the potential to influence an ethical analysis of whistleblowing rewards. One, a perspective drawn from legal theory, has implications for the role legislative endorsement of rewards might play in legitimising whistleblowing rewards (and whistleblowing conduct generally). The other, a theory of moral development that identifies the desire of most adults to conform to shared norms and societal expectations, reinforces an analysis of whistleblowing rewards regulation as a positive step towards the creation of pro-social whistleblowing norms.

2.3.1 The Expressive Function of Law

The contribution that can be made by expressive-law theorists to the concerns of this Chapter centres on their argument that law can have a so-called 'signalling' effect on the behaviour of individuals, suggesting that certain actions may be more legitimate or deserving of dutiful compliance.[65] Thus, Sunstein has argued that 'an appropriately framed law may influence social norms and push them in the right direction'.[66] On this analysis, where a lack of pro-social norms exists in a particular regulated space, it may be possible to create positive norms by the use of the signalling power of law. Here it can be argued that 'law will have moral weight and thus convince people that existing norms are bad and deserve to be replaced by new ones'.[67] Thus, regulatory interventions can have their own impact on the creation of agreed social norms and

[65]Ibid., pp. 1183–4; Sunstein (1996).

[66]Sunstein (1996, p. 2026).

[67]Ibid., p. 2031.

on shared perceptions of appropriate behaviour, since laws 'may convey a social meaning' within a community.[68]

This theoretical framework therefore argues that what people *will do* (descriptive) will link directly to what they understand they *ought to* do (normative), and that in turn the legal frameworks within which communities operate will be relied upon by individuals as key indicators of what ought to be done. As Feldman and Lobel have argued:

> theoretical and empirical expressive-law studies indicate that when the law presents either prohibitions or obligations, the very act of expressing this norm within the legal regime provides a reason for people to act. Even in the absence of sanctions or protections, the mere existence of the law helps to shape and define our world views.[69]

This theoretical approach has significant implications for perceptions of the ethics of whistleblowing rewards. It suggests that the more whistleblowing rewards programs we have, the more socially acceptable whistleblowing, and rewards, will become. If a law can influence norms through conveying a 'social meaning that reinforces or changes the norms of a community, beyond its role in establishing and enforcing rules',[70] then increased examples of pro-whistleblowing rewards legislation may increase the normative value both of the act of whistleblowing and of doing so for reward. Where existing norms operate as obstacles to pro-social behaviour, well-designed laws may offer a corrective.[71] Thus, a rewards system may 'authorise' individuals to whistleblow who would otherwise see the behaviour as non-acceptable. On this view, whistleblowing rewards ethics concerns might be addressed at least in part by well-drafted legislation that enables clear signals to be sent, and hence norms to be created, about the acceptability of rewards. A shift in norms of this kind offers a potentially low-cost method of facilitating pro-social whistleblowing behaviour. Inherent tendencies within the population to conform to new norms enable individuals to retain choice in relation to their behaviour while shifting the reputational outcomes of certain choices.[72] Thus, a shift in whistleblowing norms could ensure an individual employee retains the ability to choose whether to blow the whistle or not, but the reputational impact of *not* doing so might become more significant than the reputational impact of disclosing information.

There is, however, presumably a limit to the extent to which laws can shift entrenched normative perspectives. The greater the alignment between a law's values and the values commonly held within the community that it seeks to govern, the more likely the law will have persuasive power and influence attitudes. This argument suggests that for whistleblowing rewards legislation to be effective in changing societal attitudes, it will need to take into account existing community concerns in

---

[68]McGinn (2015, p. 1).

[69]Feldman and Lobel (2010, p. 1184).

[70]McGinn (2015, p. 1).

[71]Sunstein (1996, p. 2053).

[72]Ibid., p. 2051. For a comparison between different design elements in whistleblowing bounty systems and their capacity to influence behavior, see Blount and Markel (2012, pp. 1029–36).

relation to the ethics of such rewards. Therefore, the more precisely a whistleblowing rewards regulatory system addresses key ethical issues in its design, the more easily it ought to be able to harness the law's expressive power. Conversely, without careful attention to the pervasive ethics concerns associated with the offering of whistleblowing rewards, it is less likely that any meaningful shift in norms would be achieved. Thus, it will be important to ensure careful design of the criteria necessary to qualify for whistleblower protection and any consequent reward: 'ethical whistleblowing rewards' would be whistleblowing rewards that are sensitive to the potential ethical concerns that can arise in rewarding whistleblowing disclosures, both from a normative and a descriptive perspective.

It is also worth noting that the regulatory design elements necessary to address ethics concerns will be to some extent situationally-specific. Just as De George has argued against a 'one-size fits all'[73] model of ethical whistleblowing, given the multi-factorial nature of any ethical analysis of whistleblowing, so the design of any ethically-sensitive whistleblowing rewards system would need to account for a plethora of factors, including local cultural settings. In some cultures, stronger pro-whistleblowing signals may be necessary in order to re-set negative societal attitudes to whistleblowing arising from historical contexts. It has been suggested that in Germany, for instance, the former encouragement by the German Stasi of a culture of 'informing' has hampered whistleblowing activity,[74] creating a stronger-than-usual perception of whistleblowing as an inherently morally compromised act. The more closely any whistleblowing rewards regulatory system accounts for prevalent ethical concerns, the higher its propensity to positively influence perceptions of whistleblowing conduct and rewards. Therefore, consideration of the many factors raised in Sect. 2.1 is likely to be necessary in the design of any ethically defensible whistleblowing rewards regulatory system.

2.3.2 *Kohlberg's Theory of Moral Development*

The foregoing analysis of the expressive function of law in the context of whistleblowing rewards legislation is largely consistent with elements of Lawrence Kohlberg's influential theory of moral development.[75] Kohlberg postulated that people move through distinct and identifiable stages of moral development as they age. While Kohlberg suggested children largely exhibit 'pre-conventional' moral thinking, with an emphasis on ego-centric behaviour, most adults are postulated to operate within either 'conventional' or (much more rarely) 'post-conventional' frameworks. Conventional moral development is characterised by Kohlberg as containing two major stages. The first includes a focus on interpersonal concordance and an attempt to demonstrate behaviours that will please others; the approval of friends and family are

[73]De George (2015, p. 801).

[74]Pittroff (2016, p. 715).

[75]Kohlberg (1981, 1984).

important in this stage. The second stage of conventional moral development incorporates an awareness of the role of shared norms in maintaining the social order, and compliance with law and order takes precedence in the individual's moral reasoning. The orientation at this stage is 'toward authority, fixed rules, and the maintenance of the social order' and 'doing one's duty, showing respect for authority'.[76] Beyond this, at the less commonly occurring post-conventional level, Kohlberg predicted that two stages could be identified, at the first of which (Stage 5) individuals are assumed to move to an awareness of others' rights and of universal principles of fairness and justice. Kohlberg's predicted Stage 6 allows for concern for the dignity of human beings and the equality of individuals to guide an individual's moral choices.[77] While critiqued on gender[78] and cultural bases[79] amongst other grounds, Kohlberg's work has nonetheless been widely influential in the field of moral development, has been described as 'the most popular and tested theory of moral reasoning',[80] and continues to be cited 'in virtually every major developmental psychology textbook on the current market'.[81]

Kohlberg's Stages 3 and 4, at which most adults are predicted to operate,[82] appear consistent with the expressive function of law's theorised operation. Within Kohlberg's model, a potential whistleblower is likely to either have regard to others' expectations and to attempt to comply with them (Stage 3), or to have regard to the importance of shared norms and compliance with law and order (Stage 4). Here, the significance of legislated whistleblowing rewards is evident. Where society has endorsed the act of whistleblowing and attached a monetary value to it, a clear signal has been sent that whistleblowing is approved pro-social behaviour and that associated rewards are socially acceptable. The desire to ensure compliance with law, order and the expectations of others ought to influence individuals towards whistleblowing behaviour. This analysis has resonances with the argument made within the expressive theory of law perspective, that legal endorsement of certain actions can signal that those behaviours are more legitimate or deserving of dutiful compliance.[83]

Thus, an application of Kohlberg's work reinforces an argument that the wider introduction of corporate whistleblowing rewards could positively influence perceptions of both the ethicality of whistleblowing activity and of the rewards themselves, removing a level of stigma, and encouraging whistleblowing activity. Under this analysis, rewards might have the effect not of under-cutting ethical behaviour in the form of unsolicited and unrewarded whistleblowing activity, but rather of positively

---

[76] Kohlberg (1973, p. 631).

[77] Kohlberg (1981, 1984).

[78] Gilligan (1982).

[79] Chang-Ho (1997) and Ma and Cheung (1996).

[80] Trevino (1992, p. 445).

[81] Gibbs (2015).

[82] Empirical evidence suggests that the higher moral reasoning levels 5 and 6 occur with low frequency, although Kohlberg argued this did not mean the stages do not exist: Kohlberg (1984, p. 328).

[83] Feldman and Lobel (2010, pp. 1183–4), see also Sunstein (1996) and Anderson and Pildes (2000).

reinforcing it. It may be that attaching monetary value to whistleblowing is a particularly effective way of expressing its ethical value. This analysis has the capacity to address a seemingly central concern of those who oppose whistleblowing rewards on ethical grounds—that the payment of rewards will be inimical to the development of ethical cultures in which whistleblowing is encouraged and viewed positively. Rather, it may be possible to argue that whistleblowing rewards, by signalling societal acceptance of whistleblowing, will reinforce the likelihood of whistleblowing conduct being perceived as a social good, and will consequently increase rates of whistleblowing activity, whether rewarded or not. If this is so, rewards may do more than give whistleblowers financial recompense—they may give both whistleblowers and society more generally a signal that assists to legitimise the action of whistleblowing as a whole.

In light of these two theoretical frameworks, it would seem clear that well-designed whistleblowing rewards regulatory structures have the potential to increase perceptions of the ethicality of whistleblowing rewards and whistleblowing generally. If it is true that '[a] large function of law may be to shift social norms and social meaning',[84] then the potential value of high-profile whistleblowing laws in norm creation can be seen. Kohlberg's work directs us to consider the likelihood that many employees will assess ethical issues in light of society's expectations and/or the importance of shared norms. Both perspectives demonstrate the potential of the expressive function of law to increase the perceived ethicality of whistleblowing as an activity. On this analysis, by expressing the validity of whistleblowing as an endorsed social good, the legislature has the capacity to influence individual perceptions of the ethics of whistleblowing—and hence of rewards for whistleblowing—in a self-fulfilling (virtuous) circle.

In addition, if those systems are carefully designed to give sufficient attention to the key ethical issues of concern, the resultant norms ought to be ethically desirable. It appears intuitively likely that without careful attention to these ethical concerns in the design of any whistleblowing rewards structure, the effectiveness of the expressive function of the scheme would be impeded (since the capacity of law to shift social norms must be a function, at least in part, of the relevant regulation allowing for or taking into account legitimate and widely-held social concerns). By contrast, identifying ethically salient issues in any rewards regulatory system ought to enhance the capacity of that system to reinforce pro-social norms that favour whistleblowing activity, including for reward.

[84]Sunstein (1996, p. 2043).

2.4 Addressing the Ethics of Rewards in the Design of Regulatory Systems

In this section, the ethical concerns discussed in Sect. 2.2 are used to identify design factors that could underpin a rewards structure that is ethically defensible, and therefore more likely to shift social norms in relation to whistleblowing rewards to a more pro-social basis. This exercise is undertaken both in respect of the factors that ought to enhance the ethical credibility of *whistleblowing activities generally* (since rewards for unethical whistleblowing will be subject to criticism) and those factors that ought to enhance the ethical credibility of *whistleblowing rewards* themselves. This section also draws on extant examples of whistleblowing rewards regulatory systems to illustrate the ways in which a number of identified ethical concerns have in fact been addressed within existing systems.

2.4.1 Designing for Factors to Enhance the Ethicality of Whistleblowing Activity

De George argues that whistleblowing will not be morally defensible unless three requirements are met: that failure to disclose will cause serious harm, that a report to an immediate supervisor has been made, and that where an initial report has not been responded to, the matter has been escalated by the whistleblower internally.

Turning to the first of these factors, one design solution might be a link between the reward and any penalty imposed for the disclosed wrongdoing. Where the rate of any reward is linked to the severity of the penalty imposed or the harm done by the malfeasance to which the disclosure relates, the incentive to blow the whistle on minor matters will be commensurately slight. The second and third criteria both relate to aspects of the loyalty duty, discussed below.

2.4.1.1 The Loyalty Dilemma

The capacity for a whistleblowing employee to be seen as acting in breach of their duty of loyalty to their employer company is, as noted above, a key ethical concern with whistleblowing.[85] Using the insights of the expressive function of law, however, it is possible to conceive of a regulation placing positive obligations on companies to prepare and disseminate whistleblowing policies,[86] with consequent shifts in social norms in relation to what amounts to a breach of loyalty. That is, mandating of whistleblower policies could be expected to increase the promulgation

[85] De George (2010, p. 304).

[86] As occurs under the Australian whistleblowing reforms of 2019: *Treasury Laws Amendment (Enhancing Whistleblower Protections) Act, 2018* (Cth), inserting s1317AI into the Corporations Act, 2001 (Cth).

of corporate policies encouraging whistleblowing. This in turn would have the likely consequence that the division between loyalty to the company on the one hand, and blowing the whistle as required by the company's own policy on the other, may in part dissolve. It has been said that 'unless an employer requests their employees to blow the whistle… we have no sufficient reason to think that employees can remain loyal to their employer and blow the whistle'.[87] However, where the employer does request that whistleblowing action, by virtue of an internal whistleblowing policy, the case is clearly otherwise.

While such policies could be expected to favour internal whistleblowing as the sole means of disclosure, legislative requirements could ensure external whistleblowing is allowed for where necessary. Relevant here is the distinction between those situations that will justify internal whistleblowing, and the more demanding preconditions postulated by De George for external disclosure. Here, the design of any whistleblowing rewards system would clearly need to take into account the risk of creating undue incentive to disclose externally before internal channels were attempted. The United States' SEC model appears to have attempted to address this concern by providing that failure to report an issue internally can decrease the size of any reward payable under the scheme.[88] Other mechanisms could include a requirement to comply with an internal whistleblowing policy before making external disclosure unless extenuating circumstances existed, or regulatory encouragement of internal incentives to be offered by corporations for internal disclosure. Further, in terms of Kohlberg's theory, a potential whistleblower is likely to have regard to others' expectations and to attempt to comply (Stage 3), or to have regard to the importance of shared norms in maintaining the social order (Stage 4). Increased requirements for internal whistleblowing policies could therefore have a significant effect in setting a level of cultural or societal understanding that whistleblowing is appropriate behaviour, and not disloyal.

Further, as noted previously, recognition of the range of complex relationships to which a corporation is a party may assist in a reconceptualisation of the loyalty dilemma that enables a less stark division between internal and external disclosure.[89] It may be possible, for instance, to conceive of whistleblowing undertaken in order to protect the corporation from further wrongdoing as in the best interests of the corporation, widely understood. At the same time, in terms of the expressive theory of law, legislative recognition of the wider stakeholder interests present in a modern corporation[90] may have the effect of re-casting social norms as to whom exactly a corporate employee owes loyalty. These normative shifts could be reinforced by whistleblowing legislation that referenced such wider conceptions of the corporation, thus directly addressing ethical concerns in relation to the loyalty duty.

---

[87]Varelius (2009, p. 272).

[88]United States Securities Exchange Commission, Office of the Whistleblower, Final Rules, § 240.21F-6 Criteria for Determining Amount of Award. See also the United States Securities and Exchange Commission (2017, p. 14).

[89]Andrade (2015, p. 334).

[90]In terms of, for example, s 172 of the *Companies Act, 2006* UK.

2.4.1.2 Procedural Fairness and Appropriate Evidentiary Standards

Further concerns arise in relation to the ethical arguments in favour of the wrongdoer being notified before a disclosure is made (procedural fairness), and the need for a reasonable level of evidence of wrongdoing. It may be that in many cases procedural fairness will be addressed by ensuring the availability of due process for the party the subject of the disclosure once it has been made. Where the disclosed conduct leads to a legal process, natural justice ought to be assured; where the disclosure is dealt with internally, some other form of protection might be required. In relation to evidentiary tests it is possible to conceive of mechanisms to address these concerns, and that could do so with some sensitivity to potential alternative ethical analyses. The level of evidence required to access a reward is, for instance, built into the US SEC's program, since a reward's availability is linked to the provision of 'original information to the Commission that [has] led to the successful enforcement' of an action.[91] This will only be possible where sufficient evidence is adduced to satisfy the Commission that the whistleblower's disclosure was instrumental in achieving a conviction. Further guidelines published by the SEC clarify that relevant concepts used in assessing eligibility for an award will include whether relevant information 'significantly contributed to the success of [an] action' or was 'sufficiently specific, credible' information.[92]

2.4.1.3 Morally Required as Opposed to Morally Permissible Whistleblowing

De George suggests that to be morally obligatory (as opposed to allowable), whistleblowing will require reasonably convincing documentary evidence of likely harm, and a reasonable belief that external disclosure will result in necessary change. If an ethical distinction between morally permissible and morally obligated whistleblowing is valid, the availability of rewards ought to be linked in some way to that difference. Perhaps the reward paid for morally obligated whistleblowing ought to be less, since the need for an incentive could be expected to be less and the existing moral obligation is more significant. This argument has resonances in concerns expressed to an Australian Parliamentary Joint Inquiry in relation to individuals being rewarded at all for disclosures they were obliged to make by reason of, for instance, their professional role.[93] If a distinction were made between compelled and voluntary whistleblowing, thought could be given to the design of the relevant reward being

---

[91] *Securities Exchange Act 1934* (US) s 21F(b)(1).

[92] Securities Exchange Commission, Final Rules Implementing the Whistleblowing Program, § 240.21F-4 Other definitions.

[93] See, for instance, the comments of the Queensland Ombudsman cited in the Parliamentary Joint Committee on Corporations and Financial Services, *Whistleblower Protections*, September 2017, [11.37].

linked to the factors identified by De George as ethically salient, such as the presence of convincing documentary evidence of harm.

Alternatively, disagreement with this aspect of De George's framework was noted earlier, and the construction of a particular regulatory system might favour those alternative policy arguments. Is it the case that ethically a whistleblower is obligated to make disclosure where they have reasonable evidence of serious danger and believe change is likely to result from disclosure, even where no adequate protections exist?[94] Or conversely, is it fair to require a whistleblower to make disclosure where the likely resultant risk of personal harm is unacceptably high?[95] These matters would need careful attention in the drafting of a regulatory system's governing principles for the payment of rewards. This could include, for instance, the presence of those factors being signalled by the use of decision-points within the reward allocation structure, ensuring awareness of those factors is raised and maintained (and appropriate norms 'signalled' by the regulatory design).

Further, one more interesting interaction of rewards and De George's framework can be imagined. There is potential for the presence of rewards to reduce the impact of De George's fifth factor, which includes an analysis of the risks taken by the whistleblower. To the extent a system of rewards is more effective at compensating or protecting a whistleblower than the common anti-retaliation provisions, the whistleblower is in a less compromised position. Therefore, arguably the whistleblower is more morally obligated to disclose than if rewards were not available, when the analysis would be that the whistleblower may be permitted—but would not be obliged—to disclose, on the basis that to do so could put them, and their livelihood, at severe risk. That is, the presence of rewards may extend the class of whistleblowers who might be said to be morally obligated to disclose.

2.4.2 *Designing for Factors to Enhance the Ethicality of Rewards for Whistleblowing Activity*

In the context of ethical concerns linked specifically to whistleblowing rewards, Sect. 2.2.2 discusses the risks of creating anti-ethical outcomes, of fortuitous and disproportionate recovery by whistleblowers, the creation of perverse incentives to delay disclosure or to obtain information by illegitimate means, the risks of encouraging third-party markets, and the risks of 'crowding out' pro-social behaviour, as well as related cultural effects.

[94] Hoffman and Schwartz (2015, p. 776).

[95] Ibid.

2.4.2.1 Anti-ethical Outcomes

The risk of rewards undermining the creation of a wider pro-whistleblowing culture through creation of unethical incentives to whistleblow is a crucial concern to be addressed in any ethical analysis of whistleblowing rewards. Moral hazards might be created by the incentive to report maliciously, or to report for the 'wrong reasons', and generally by the operation of inappropriate motives. Here the insights offered by the expressive function of law and Kohlberg's theory might be particularly useful.

If it is indeed the case that 'an appropriately framed law may influence social norms and push them in the right direction,'[96] then, as noted, whistleblowing regulatory structures might have real potential to facilitate the development of pro-whistleblowing rewards norms. This in turn ought to reduce the risk of rewards working against the creation of pro-whistleblowing cultures. Adding Kohlberg's moral development insights to this analysis, it might be argued that, as suggested above, society's endorsement of whistleblowing sends a signal that it is approved pro-social behaviour, making it more likely that many adult employees will be influenced to comply with whistleblowing policies.

In light of these arguments, it is possible that the creation of well-designed, ethically-sensitive whistleblowing rewards structures could create pro-whistleblowing cultural shifts. By designing for ethical concerns an ethical whistle blowing culture can be reinforced, by ensuring, for instance, that prior internal disclosure does not disadvantage the whistleblower's pursuit of a reward, or that natural justice for accused wrongdoers is reinforced by mandated provisions for adequate whistleblowing internal systems. Thus, the SEC model incorporates the capacity for rewards to be reduced on a range of grounds, including delay, ensuring that inappropriate delay in making a disclosure will reduce the level of reward payable.[97]

2.4.2.2 Rewarding Whistleblowers for Chance Events

Controlling the ultimate level of reward payable may be used as a technique to address the ethical concern that whistleblowers may obtain disproportionate windfall gains by chance alone (on the basis they were fortuitously in the right place to access the information, when another similar employee was not). Capping of the reward to relatively modest levels could operate as a natural brake on the capacity for disproportionate or excessive recovery. This is the approach taken in the Ontario model, where the level of recovery cannot exceed a specified total recovery.[98] Another mechanism

[96] Sunstein (1996, p. 2026).

[97] United States Securities Exchange Commission, Office of the Whistleblower, Final Rules, § 240.21F-6 Criteria for Determining Amount of Award. Similarly, the Australian 2017 PJC Report recommended that the timeliness with which a disclosure is made ought to influence the level of reward paid: Parliamentary Joint Committee on Corporations and Financial Services, *Whistleblower Protections*, September 2017, Recommendation 11.2, [11.59].

[98] Ontario Securities Commission, OSC Policy 15-601, *Whistleblower Program*, July 2016: Part 5: 18. Amount of Whistleblower Award.

to ensure that an employee does not profit disproportionately from chance proximity to the wrongdoing could be to ensure that the level of any reward approximates, in some way, compensation for the likely or possible harm resulting from coming forward. Hence, a whistleblower with no particular risk exposure in relation to the disclosed malfeasance might receive less than a central agent with high exposure to the wrongdoing who has experienced prolonged stress and anxiety.

2.4.2.3 Incentives to Delay Disclosure or Obtain Information Illegitimately

The risk of rewards creating an incentive to delay disclosure in order to increase the harm resulting from the wrongdoing (and thus increase any rewards linked to the penalty) has been addressed in extant whistleblowing rewards systems. As noted above, the US SEC model has the capacity to reduce rewards where there has been delay in bringing information forward. The Ontario Securities Commission's modified US-style rewards structure appears to further address the risk of creating a perverse incentive to withhold information through imposition of a cap on payments. This cap ensures the ultimate reward cannot increase proportionately with the impact of the wrongdoing beyond a certain point.[99] In relation to the risk of creating an incentive to obtain information illegitimately, it ought to be possible to signal the intention of any regulatory system to discourage such behaviour by ensuring legislative provisions or supporting guidelines indicate this factor will affect the availability or size of any reward. Thus, the Ontario Securities Commission mandates that a whistleblower providing 'information obtained by any means that violates criminal law' will not be eligible for a reward, and nor will 'those who obtained or provided the information in circumstances which would bring the administration of the Program into disrepute'.[100] Additionally, in terms of the expressive function of law theoretical construct, this signalling effect could have the additional virtue of reinforcing ethically-sensitive norms in relation to whistleblowing rewards.

2.4.2.4 Creating Third-Party Markets, Crowding Out of Pro-social Behaviour, Stigma and Other Cultural Issues

Creation of third-party markets, such as an industry of lawyers focused on assisting whistleblowing rewards recovery, has been identified above as a potential evil. The counter-argument noted above is that the signal failure of whistleblowing protection and compensation systems to adequately protect whistleblowers in the past suggests some form of more easily accessed compensation may be called for. Thus, design of a rewards system that facilitates access to compensation by whistleblowers—provided

[99] Ontario Securities Commission, OSC Policy 15-601, *Whistleblower Program*, July 2016, 11.
[100] Ontario Securities Commission, OSC Policy 15-601, *Whistleblower Program*, 3, 9.

it ensures there is, for instance, no 'double-dipping' through other compensatory mechanisms—could be seen as defensible from a policy point of view.

The available research on crowding out of pro-social behaviours can also arguably be accounted for in the design of a rewards system. Since the impact of the crowding-out effect may be more apparent where a lower reward is paid,[101] a nuanced system that makes calibrated decisions about the size of a reward might be capable of addressing this concern. Further context may be significant here. As noted above, Feldman and Orly's work focused on blood donation—a non-controversial pro-social behaviour; the effect of crowding out may be different where the underlying activity retains some level of stigma, as whistleblowing appears to do.[102] In addition, levels of stigma may vary according to the nature of the disclosure. There is presumably less stigma attached to making disclosures that ensure public safety than there may be for disclosing corporate wrongdoing that is technical and difficult for the general public to understand (yet may ultimately have significant consequences for the community). In each of these cases, regulatory design will need to account for the ethical nuance inherent in different pro-social behaviour contexts.

The need to ensure that allowance is made for the relevant cultural context in which a rewards system sits has also been identified above. Since local norms may differ—for example, the Stasi informer context applicable in the former East Germany—some discrimination between the forms of rewards systems in different jurisdictions is likely to be necessary. Something of this variability is evident in the contrasting design elements of the Ontario Securities Commission's rewards system when compared with the US SEC model. While the US model has no limits on the ultimate potential payout (since it is linked to the size of the penalty imposed), the Ontario model, as noted, provides for a cap on the maximum reward payable, perhaps reflecting more significant local concerns in relation to disproportionate recovery by whistleblowers.[103]

A range of factors identified in this Chapter may impact on the perceived ethicality of a whistleblowing rewards system. In many cases these concerns would appear susceptible to being addressed by carefully designed regulatory provisions. Further, it may be that by incorporating those concerns into the design of appropriate systems, shifts in perceptions of the ethicality of whistleblowing and of rewards can be achieved. These shifts might, in turn, enable the harnessing of adult conventional moral reasoning preferences to comply with perceived shared social norms, thus reinforcing pro-whistleblowing conduct. In all of this, it is likely to be important to tailor whistleblowing reward regulatory systems as closely as possible to the ethics concerns of most salience in a regulated population, to both maximise the likelihood of new pro-social perceptions of rewards being readily created, and to ensure any resultant normative delineations between more and less acceptable whistleblowing are resilient to future ethical challenges.

---

[101] Feldman and Lobel (2010, pp. 1155, 1202).

[102] See the discussion in Brand (2018, p. 418).

[103] Securities Exchange Act 1934 (US) section 21F; Ontario Securities Commission, OSC Policy 15-601, *Whistleblower Program*, July 2016, 11.

2.5 Conclusion

Whistleblowing rewards have a clear potential to increase rates of whistleblowing activity. However, whistleblowing remains a normatively complex topic and whistleblowing rewards raise additional normative and behavioural ethical issues. Historically, ethical concerns have been central to criticisms of whistleblowing rewards, and are likely to have delayed or prevented more widespread use of rewards systems. Theoretical insights suggest that pro-whistleblowing and pro-rewards regulatory provisions could have the potential to shift social norms towards a more pro-social perspective on rewards for disclosure and whistleblowing generally by re-casting perceptions of whistleblowing and whistleblowing rewards as more socially acceptable. This Chapter argues that rewards may do more than provide money to individual whistleblowers—they may provide a signal to society as a whole about the way in which whistleblowing activity is valued. Intuitively this would seem more likely to occur where those provisions take into account, so far as possible, the multifarious ethical concerns that exist in relation to whistleblowing activity itself, and particularly rewarded whistleblowing. Given the potential of whistleblowing rewards to contribute both directly and indirectly to the development of increased rates of whistleblowing, time spent carefully designing systems to account for ethical concerns would appear to be time well spent.

References

Anderson E, Pildes R (2000) Expressive Theories of Law: A General Restatement. *U Pa L Rev* 148:1503

Andrade J (2015) Reconceptualising Whistleblowing in a Complex World. *J Bus Ethics* 128:321

Bank of England Prudential Regulation Authority and Financial Conduct Authority (2014) *Financial Incentives for Whistleblowers*, July 2014

Blount J, Markel S (2012) The End of the Internal Compliance World as We Know It, or an Enhancement of the Effectiveness of Securities Law Enforcement? Bounty Hunting Under the Dodd-Frank Act's Whistleblower Provisions. *Fordham J Corp & Fin L* XVII:1023

Brand V (2018) Ethics and Corporate Whistleblowing Rewards in Australia. *Aust J Corp L* 33:402

Call A, Martin G, Sharp N et al (2018) Whistleblowers and Outcomes of Financial Misrepresentation Enforcement Actions. *J Account Res* 56:123

Callahan E, Dworkin T (1992) Do Good and Get Rich: Financial Incentives for Whistleblowing and the False Claims Act. *Vill L Rev* 37:273

Chang-Ho C (1997) Collectivism in Moral Development. *Psychol Rep* 80:967

De George RT (2010) *Business Ethics*. Prentice Hall, Upper Saddle River

De George RT (2015) A Response to My Critics. *J Bus Ethics* 127:189

Ebersole D (2011) Blowing the Whistle on the Dodd-Frank Whistleblower Provisions. *Entrepreneurial Bus L J* 6:123

Feldman Y, Lobel O (2010) The Incentives Matrix: The Comparative Effectiveness of Rewards, Liabilities, Duties, and Protections for Reporting Illegality. *Tex L Rev* 88:1151

Gibbs J (2015) Kohlberg's Theory. In: *Moral Development and Reality: Beyond the Theories of Kohlberg, Hoffman, and Haidt*. Oxford University Press. https://doi.org/10.1093/acprof:osobl/9780199976171.003.0004

Gilligan C (1982) *In a Different Voice*. Harvard University Press, Cambridge, MA

Gobert J, Punch M (2000) Whistleblowers, the Public Interest and the Public Interest Disclosure Act 1998. *Mod L Rev* 63:25
Hoffman WM, Schwartz M (2015) The Morality of Whistleblowing: A Commentary on Richard T De George. *J Bus Ethics* 127:771
Kohlberg L (1973) The Claim to Moral Adequacy of a Highest Stage of Moral Judgment. *J Philos* 70:630
Kohlberg L (1981) *The Philosophy of Moral Development.* Harper & Row, New York
Kohlberg L (1984) *The Psychology of Moral Development.* Harper & Row, San Francisco
Ma H, Cheung C (1996) A Cross-Cultural Study of Moral Stage Structure in Hong Kong Chinese, English and Americans. *J Cross-Cult Psychol* 27:700
McGinn T (2015) The Expressive Function of the Law and the Lex Imperfecta. *Roman Legal Trad* 11:1
Parliamentary Joint Committee on Corporations and Financial Services (2017) *Whistleblower Protections*, Parliament of Australia, September 2017
Pittroff E (2016) Whistle-Blowing Regulation in Different Corporate Governance Systems: An Analysis of the Regulation Approaches from the View of Path Dependence Theory. *J Manag Gov* 20:703
Rapp GC (2007) Beyond Protection: Invigorating Incentives for Sarbanes-Oxley Corporate and Securities Fraud Whistleblowers. *BUL Rev* 87:91
Schwartz M (2016) Ethical Decision-Making Theory: An Integrated Approach. *J Bus Ethics* 139:755
Sunstein C (1996) On the Expressive Function of Law. *U Pa L Rev* 144:2021
Trevino LK (1992) Moral Reasoning and Business Ethics: Implications for Research, Education, and Management. *J Bus Ethics* 11:445
United States Securities and Exchange Commission (2017) *2017 Annual Report to Congress: Whistleblower Program*
United States Securities and Exchange Commission (2018) *2018 Annual Report to Congress: Whistleblower Program*
Varelius J (2009) Is Whistle-Blowing Compatible with Employee Loyalty? *J Bus Ethics* 85:263
Velasquez M (2018) *Business Ethics: Concepts and Cases.* Pearson

Vivienne Brand is a legal academic with an early career in private commercial legal practice. She researches in corporate law, whistleblowing and business ethics, the area in which she undertook her doctoral studies. She has published widely on these topics within Australia and also internationally and has appeared by invitation before Federal parliamentary inquiries on whistleblowing and related topics. Vivienne is an active member of the Business Law Section of the Law Council of Australia's Corporations Committee and Foreign Corrupt Practices Working Party and has participated in the Council's submissions on whistleblowing matters.

Chapter 3
To Reward or Not to Reward: A Cross-Jurisdictional Comparison of the Reasons Why Securities Regulators Have Adopted or Rejected Policies to Pay Whistleblowers

Janet Austin

Abstract The idea that securities regulators should reward persons who 'blow the whistle' on fraudulent or corrupt conduct is starting to gain some traction around the world. Spurred on by the apparent success of the whistleblower award program administered by the Securities and Exchange Commission (SEC) in the United States, other countries have considered whether or not their securities regulators should adopt similar program. This article examines the reasons behind the introduction of the SEC program as well as the approach in three other jurisdictions, being Canada, Australia and the UK, all of which have considered whether to introduce such a regime. This analysis demonstrates that whether an award program for whistleblowers was adopted, and the form of the program, depended upon a number of factors. Such factors include whether or not the regulator itself supported the introduction of the program, the political landscape generally and opposition from business. Although empirical evidence about the costs and benefits of such programs contributed to the debate, it was not determinative because such empirical evidence is currently inconclusive. As such, there is a pressing need for more empirical evidence to fully assess the costs and benefits of such programs.

Keywords Whistleblower program · Whistleblower awards · Whistleblower rewards · Dodd Frank · *Qui tam* · Whistleblower bounty

3.1 Introduction

The recent momentum to consider offering financial incentives to encourage persons to blow the whistle stems from the harm caused by the 2008 Global Financial Crisis as well as the significant losses to investors that resulted from the Bernie Madoff Ponzi scheme. In the wake of these events, the US Congress passed the Dodd Frank Wall Street Reform and Consumer Protection Act (Dodd Frank Act) which was signed

J. Austin (✉)
Faculty of Law, University of New Brunswick, Fredericton, Canada
e-mail: jaustin@unb.ca

S. Lombard et al. (eds.), *Corporate Whistleblowing Regulation*,
https://doi.org/10.1007/978-981-15-0259-0_3

into law on July 21, 2010.[1] In relation to the protection of whistleblowers, the Dodd Frank Act had three key features. First, it enhanced anti-retaliation protections for those who 'blow the whistle'. Second, whistleblowers could make a report to the SEC anonymously. Finally, it directed the SEC to adopt a whistleblower awards program. Under this program, for the voluntarily disclosure of original information which leads to a successful enforcement action resulting in the imposition of monetary sanctions of over US$1 million, the SEC must pay the whistleblower a reward of between 10 and 30% of the amount collected from those sanctions.[2] In 2016, the then chair of the SEC described this program as having had a "transformative impact on enforcement" and that whistleblowers have "become key sources of very significant cases".[3] To date, the SEC has paid approximately US$326 million in whistleblower awards to 59 individuals and has ordered wrongdoers in enforcement matters involving whistleblower information to pay US$1.7 billion in total monetary sanctions.[4]

Inspired in part by the apparent success of the SEC's whistleblower program the Ontario Securities Commission (OSC), the largest securities regulator in Canada, also introduced a whistleblower awards program in July 2016.[5] This program provides that a whistleblower may become entitled to an award of between 5 and 15% of the monetary sanctions imposed if the sanctions ordered against wrongdoers are C$1 million or more.[6]

However not all jurisdictions that have considered the introduction of whistleblower awards schemes have followed suit and introduced such a program. Two other securities regulators in Canada, the Alberta Securities Commission (ASC) and the securities regulator for Quebec, the Autorité des marchés financiers (AMF), have rejected the introduction of such schemes.[7] The United Kingdom's securities commission, the Financial Conduct Authority (FCA) has also decided against the introduction of such a program.[8] In Australia, despite recommendations from parliamentary inquiries that a whistleblower reward scheme should be introduced, thus far

---

[1] See Dodd-Frank Wall Street Reform and Consumer Protection Act, Pub. L. No. 11-203 § 922(a), 121 Stat 1894 (2010).

[2] Ibid. The Act inserted a new § 21F into the *Securities Exchange Act 1934* (Pub. L. 73–291, 48 Stat. 881, enacted June 6, 1934, codified at 15 U.S.C. § 78a et seq.). The whistleblower awards program established by the SEC became effective on August 12, 2011, see SEC Rule 17 CFR Parts 240 and 249 [Release No. 34-64545; File No. S7-33-10] Implementation of the Whistleblower Provisions of Section 21F of the Securities Exchange Act of 1934 (August 12, 2011).

[3] White (2016).

[4] Securities and Exchange Commission (2018, p. 1).

[5] Ontario Securities Commission (2016b).

[6] The maximum whistleblower award under the OSC program is set at C$1.5 million if the aggregate amount of monetary sanctions and/or voluntary payments is equal to or greater than C$10 million. However if the OSC actually collects the monetary sanctions and/or voluntary payments in an amount equal to or greater than C$10 million, than the maximum award is increased to C$5 million. See ibid. and Ontario Securities Commission (2016c, para 18).

[7] Ontario Securities Commission Policy 15-601 (2016c, Parts 3.2 and 3.3).

[8] Ontario Securities Commission Policy 15-601 (2016c, Part 4).

the Federal Government and Australian securities regulator, the Australian Securities and Investments Commission (ASIC) have resisted its adoption.[9]

The primary argument in favour of paying whistleblowers financial incentives is that it will motivate them to come forward and provide information to the authorities about serious corporate wrongdoing that would not otherwise come to light.[10] It is also claimed that such whistleblowers frequently possess special skills or insight into the particular wrongdoing in question. This can allow the authorities to bring stronger and/or more successful enforcement actions and maximize the employment of their typically limited resources. Furthermore, it is argued, this increase in the ability of the authorities to detect and take action should, in turn, deter organizations from engaging in wrongdoing and thereby prod companies to enhance systems to monitor compliance so that they are able to remedy problems before they escalate.[11] If whistleblowers award programs do in fact have these effects, then it follows that this should increase protection of investors by reducing the possibility of them incurring losses due to fraud and ultimately improve the economy generally by reducing corporate malfeasance.

However, although logic may suggest that such whistleblower awards programs ought to have these outcomes and therefore be in the public interest, the empirical evidence that these programs do indeed achieve these objectives is currently incomplete, even though such evidence is gradually mounting. Furthermore, even if these programs are beneficial, there is currently no empirical evidence that the overall benefits outweigh the costs. Direct costs of whistleblower award programs include the cost of administrating the program together with costs associated with a regulator having to sift through an expected increase in the number of tips, including an increase in the number of frivolous complaints.[12] It is also argued that whistleblower reward programs increase costs for business as they undermine companies' internal compliance programs by introducing incentives for whistleblowers to go directly to regulators in the hope of a reward, rather than raise their concerns in-house.[13]

My aim in this article is to examine the reasons and background behind the decision whether or not to introduce a whistleblower award program in four countries, namely the United States, Canada, Australia and the United Kingdom and to ascertain the

---

[9]Ontario Securities Commission Policy 15-601 (2016c, Part 5).

[10]Although the effect of such a program may provide compensation for losses persons may have suffered in retaliation for blowing the whistle, this is usually not the principle reason for their introduction.

[11]Baer (2017).

[12]For example, on 12 May 2014 the SEC issued a Final Order making an individual ineligible for whistleblower claims due to repeated, frivolous claims. https://www.sec.gov/about/offices/owb/orders/owb-multiple-final-051214.pdf. Accessed 4 July 2018. It seems the individual made 196 applications for awards, including 21 in one day according to Ensign (2014). In the SEC 2017 Annual Report to Congress it was reported that unusually large numbers of tips came from two individuals in 2016 and 2017 which were left out of the tables and statistics suggesting they might have had a similar problem in those years, see Securities and Exchange Commission (2017, p. 23, footnote 51).

[13]See for example US Chamber of Commerce (2011).

key issues that influenced these decisions. As such, Sects. 3.2–3.5 detail the debate surrounding the introduction of such a program when it was proposed in each of these jurisdictions and the arguments, parties, politics and evidence which swayed the respective outcomes. Sect. 3.6 then compares and contrasts the impact of each of these various factors. I conclude by finding that matters such as the internal support within the regulator for such a program, partisan politics and the political landscape were often critical and that both sides of the debate used empirical evidence to support their case. I also conclude that to fully understand the costs and benefits of these programs there seems to be a real need to add to the empirical evidence because when new corporate scandals are exposed, as will inevitably be the case, it is likely that there will be an increase in calls for the introduction of such financial incentive schemes.

3.2 The SEC Whistleblower Rewards Program

The notion that whistleblowers should be rewarded for information they provide has a long history in the United States. In 1863 the US Congress enacted *qui tam* provisions in the False Claims Act, sometimes called the Lincoln Law, in response to fraudulent government contracts during the Civil War.[14] This legislation allowed private individuals to sue government contractors who defrauded the United States Government in return for a proportion of the proceeds.[15] This idea goes back to the old common law doctrine of *qui tam pro domino rege quam pro se ipso* ([he] who sues in this matter sues for the king as well as for himself). Under this doctrine an individual who had information about a civil or criminal wrong affecting the Crown could bring an action on behalf of the Crown and in return be given a reward if successful.[16] Reflecting the common law, the first British statutes enacted in the fourteenth century significantly relied on informers, rather than the Crown, to enforce laws affecting public order and safety. However, problems of statutory interpretation and inappropriate *qui tam* actions led to their abolition in United Kingdom in 1951.[17]

In addition to the *qui tam* provisions in the False Claims Act, other whistleblower financial incentive schemes in the United States include a provision in the US Patent Act, originally enacted in 1842, which allows an individual to sue for the mismarking of a patent in return for a proportion of the penalty.[18] The US Customs Services has

---

[14]False Claims Act 1863 31 U.S.C. §§ 3729-3733. See also Vaughn (2012, p. 127).

[15]Ibid.

[16]Also Faunce et al. (2014, p. 382).

[17]Pitzer (1972).

[18]Patent Act of 1842, ch 263 5, 5 Stat. 543, 544 (1842). This carried a penalty of US$100, half of which went to the government and the other half to the individual. This provision remains, although the penalty has increased to US$500 for every offence. See False Marking 35 USC ss 292 (2006). To succeed the relator must show that the item was marked as patented or patent pending, that the marking was false and that the marking party intended to deceive the public. *Nichols v. Newell*, 1853 U.S. App. LEXIS 737, (C.C.D. Mass. November 01, 1853). The third requirement of intent

had a scheme for awarding compensation to informers since 1930. In its current form the legislation provides that an individual who is not an employee or officer of the United States can be awarded up to 25% of the amount recovered or forfeited up to US$250,000 per case.[19] The US Internal Revenue Service (IRS) has a bounty program which dates from 1954. This program changed significantly in 2006 in a way that has led to a large increase in tips and payouts.[20] The original law gave the IRS the discretion to determine the amount of the award and the IRS was very conservative in paying awards. The 2006 amendments made awards mandatory in certain circumstances. Whistleblowers are now entitled to between 15–30% of the proceeds from an enforcement action if the information substantially contributes to a decision to take action against tax fraud of at least US$2 million by taxpayers with incomes greater than US$200,000. Whistleblowers can also appeal a decision by the IRS to deny payment. Furthermore, whistleblowers can also receive an award in relation to amounts under these set thresholds, although this is subject to the discretion of the IRS.[21]

The SEC had an award program for whistleblowers since 1988, but it was limited to information specifically provided to the SEC about insider trading. This program was created following the stock market crash of October 1987 when the US Congress passed a number of amendments to the Securities Exchange Act to improve the detection and punishment of insider trading.[22] However, a report commissioned by the SEC in 2010 found that this award program was not widely known about, even within the SEC, and that it had made only five awards in the 20 years since its inception, the highest of those being US$55,220. Other problems identified in this report were that the amount of the award was wholly within the discretion of the SEC and could be no more than 10% of the amount recovered.[23]

Although not a financial award program, in the wake of the collapse of Enron and Worldcom, in 2002 the US Congress expanded the scope of whistleblower protections by the passage of the Sarbanes Oxley Act ('SOX') with a view to encouraging the reporting of corporate fraud.[24] SOX grants private sector employees protection from

---

and the court's tendency to limit the penalty to $500 rather than $500 per item falsely marked has limited the effectiveness of the Patent office reward scheme. See Winston (2009).

[19] 19 USCS § 1619 The Customs bounty program requires the individual to detect, seize and report the vessel, baggage etc. or to provide original information so compensation cannot be given for information if the investigation was already underway or for mere testimony. See Ferziger and Currell (1999).

[20] 26 USCS § 7623 Senate Committee Report on The Restoring American Financial Stability Act of 2010, p. 111.

[21] See West et al. (2012), Brady (2012) and Rapp (2012).

[22] See section 21A(e) of the Securities Exchange Act 1934 (Pub. L. 73–291, 48 Stat. 881, enacted June 6, 1934, codified at 15 U.S.C. § 78a et seq.) which was added by the Insider Trading and Securities Fraud Enforcement Act of 1988 (ITSEA), Pub. L. No. 100-704. See also Office of Inspector General report Assessment of the SEC's Bounty Program', Report No. 474 (March 29, 2010) p. 1.

[23] Assessment of the SEC's Bounty Program, Report No. 474 (March 29, 2010) p. 1.

[24] Sarbanes Oxley Act 2002 Pub. L. No. 107-204 § 806, 116 Stat. 745 (2002). See generally Dworkin (2007).

retaliation, the right to bring a claim in federal court and requires audit committees of listed public companies to establish procedures for receiving anonymous complaints from employees in relation to accounting and audit matters.[25] Pursuant to these changes, whistleblowers can seek reinstatement, back pay and compensation.[26] It also set a relatively low standard to acquire such protection, being only that the whistleblower had a "reasonable belief of fraud".[27] Yet in the years following SOX one study found that the number of employees blowing the whistle on corporate fraud actually fell from eighteen percent to thirteen percent.[28] Many commentators put this apparent failure down to SOX not including financial incentives for whistleblowing.[29]

In 2009 there was renewed interest in the United States for revisiting the issue of how to encourage whistleblowers to come forward to report corporate wrongdoing. This was due to the failure of the SEC to respond to numerous tips about the fraudulent operations of Bernard Madoff as well as the impact of the Global Financial Crisis on the US economy.[30] Given these debacles, it seems many within the SEC believed that it needed a broad based financial reward scheme to incentivize whistleblowers to come forward. The hope was that this would allow the SEC to detect fraudulent schemes quickly before they embarrassed the SEC and rattled investors and the capital markets.[31] Jordan Thomas, who at the time worked for the SEC in developing the whistleblower award program, has stated:

> At the time the program was considered, the financial crisis had just occurred and the Madoff scandal had surfaced. At that time, the SEC and other financial watchdogs did extensive sole searching across the organization about how they could be better, and the first kind of question was, what was the vision? What was the vision for the organization? Was it to be expansive or just be better at what they were currently doing? And the answer is they wanted to be more aggressive, had a more ambitious vision for enforcement. The second question was, were the strategies and tactics that they were using essentially the status quo effective? And the answer was, it was not. And the third question was basically, what do we have to lose? Okay. Because in a whistleblower context, you pay for success. So you are developing a program that allows for it to work. If you establish a program and people don't come or they don't come with the kind of thing you want, you don't pay. And so the cost of establishing the program, yes, there are costs for establishing the office of the whistleblower. But otherwise, essentially you're just feeding more tips into your enforcement staff and you are able to triage it. Yes they have limited resources, but the thinking was they would have the opportunity to do better cases.[32]

[25]Sarbanes Oxley Act, ibid., § 301.

[26]Sarbanes Oxley Act, ibid., § 806.

[27]Ibid and Sarbanes Oxley Act, ibid., § 1514A (b). See generally King (2011).

[28]See Dyck et al. (2010). Baer (2017, p. 2226) suggests that this is because anti-retaliation law can only go so far in that back pay and the threat of lawsuits cannot protect employees from subtle stigma and discrimination.

[29]Dworkin (2007), King (2011) and Rapp (2007).

[30]For a description of the Madoff Scandal, see Langevoort (2009).

[31]Baer (2017).

[32]Ontario Securities Commission (2015c, pp. 37–38).

This resulted in the SEC seeking legislation granting it the power to reward whistleblowers, similar to IRS whistleblower award program.[33] Then Chair of the SEC, Mary Shapiro, said that she believed that such a reward program would assist the SEC to be more aggressive in its enforcement with a view to protecting investors.[34] The award scheme developed by the SEC was contained in a proposed Investment Protection Act, which the Obama Administration took to Congress on 10 July 2009.[35] This Act would have allowed the SEC to pay whistleblowers a reward of up to 30% for information that led to monetary penalties that were over US$1 million. The rationale set out in the accompanying press release was that this would encourage insiders and others with strong evidence of securities law violations to bring that evidence to the SEC and thereby improve its ability to enforce the securities laws.[36] This proposed Investment Protection Act eventually led to the enacting of SEC whistleblower award program in the Dodd Frank Act. However, the Dodd Frank Act removed some of the discretion vested in the SEC in determining the amount of the reward. Whereas the Investment Protection Act would have given the SEC the discretion to pay up to 30%, the Dodd Frank Act provides that a whistleblower providing original information to the SEC is entitled to a minimum award of 10% and a maximum of 30% if monetary penalties over US$1 million are imposed. The Dodd Frank also allows for judicial review of a decision by the SEC not to pay an award, something that was not included in the Investor Protection Act.[37]

Following the enacting of the Dodd Frank Act, on 3 November 2010 the SEC released proposed rules for the whistleblower award program and provided the public with just over a month to comment.[38] The cost benefit analysis accompanying these proposed rules stated that:

> Overall, enhanced whistleblower incentives should likely result in more frequent reporting of misconduct, which will result in greater deterrence of securities law violations and more effective and efficient enforcement on the part of the Commission.[39]

The authority cited for this statement was a paper by Dyck, Morse and Zingales. Dyck et al. collected data in relation to 216 cases of corporate frauds and found that employees were an important source for the revelation of corporate fraud. In particular, they found that 41% of frauds in the health care industry were brought to light by employees, compared to just 14% of frauds in other industries. They reasoned that the higher disclosure of frauds by employees in the health care industry was because such employees could become entitled to a reward by bringing a *qui tam* suit under the False Claims Act. They concluded that the logical implication

---

[33] Shapiro (2009, p. 10).

[34] Ibid., p. 19.

[35] U.S. Department of the Treasury Fact Sheet (2009).

[36] Ibid.

[37] Rapp (2012, p. 89) notes that there was relatively little debate of the whistleblower provisions in Congressional hearings in relation to the Dodd Frank Act.

[38] Securities and Exchange Commission (3 November 2010).

[39] Securities and Exchange Commission (2010, p. 104).

of their findings was the expansion to other industries of monetary incentives for whistleblowers.[40]

In its proposed rules the SEC acknowledged that there would be costs associated with the award program, such as possible costs to business because of an increased incentive for employees to bypass internal compliance and go straight to the SEC, as well as the costs to the SEC in dealing with a possible increase in spurious allegations. However, the SEC confined its economic analysis to those rules over which it could exercise its discretion, rather than on the costs and benefits of whether or not whistleblowers should be rewarded at all, because the US Congress had directed it to set up the program.[41]

The SEC received over 500 comment letters in response to the rules.[42] Many commentators from business groups argued that the program would divert whistleblowers from reporting internally and that companies and other entities would experience significant costs as a result.[43] The costs identified included first, the costs of increased harm due to the delay in the fraud being reported to and dealt with by the SEC, compared with it being reported internally such that the corporation would be able to take action to stem the losses. Second, there would be increased litigation costs from non-meritorious whistleblower complaints to the SEC that could have proceeded internally and been dismissed. Third, increased harm to entities and investors when non-securities law violations go unreported to the entity and instead are reported to the SEC in the hope of a reward. The SEC responded that none of the commentators had provided projections or estimates of these costs. The SEC also cited a study by Heyes and Kapur which suggests that a sizeable percentage of whistleblowers who report internally are in fact motivated by non-monetary reasons. From this the SEC concluded that it anticipated that many whistleblowers would continue to report internally first.[44] Nevertheless, in the final rules released by the SEC, it made some modifications to the draft rules in an attempt to address these concerns. This included that a whistleblower who reports internally can be entitled to a reward and that, in deciding on the amount of the award, the SEC will consider favorably the fact that a whistleblower first reported the fraud internally.[45]

The SEC adopted the final rules on 25 May 2011 and they went into effect on 12 August 2011.[46] The rules were passed by a 3–2 voting margin, with the two Republican SEC Commissioners voting against the proposal and the three Democrat SEC

---

[40]Dyck et al. (2010).

[41]Securities and Exchange Commission (2010, p. 109).

[42]Baloria et al. (2017, p. 1306).

[43]Securities and Exchange Commission (2011, p. 229).

[44]Securities and Exchange Commission (2011) citing a study by Heyes and Kapur (2009).

[45]Securities and Exchange Commission (2011, p. 231). This is in addition to the provisions included in the proposed rules (see Securities and Exchange Commission 2010) that require that in determining the amount of the award the SEC will consider whether or not the whistleblower substantially and unreasonably delayed reporting the violations in assessing the amount of the award and will view the fact that a whistleblower intentionally interfered with his or her company's compliance system as a negative factor, see Securities and Exchange Commission (2011, p. 125).

[46]Securities and Exchange Commission (2011, p. 1).

commissioners voting in favour.[47] The primary concern of the two SEC commissioners who voted against the proposal was that the rules significantly underestimated the negative impact of the program on internal compliance systems.[48] Underlying the somewhat partisan nature of support for the program is the fact that there have been subsequent attempts by some Republican members of Congress to attack elements of the program.[49] Some commentators even went so far as to argue that the Obama Administration's support for the program may have been influenced by the fact that lawyers representing whistleblowers were strong supporters of President Obama's election campaigns.[50]

3.3 Canada

Canada currently does not have a national securities regulator so each of the Canadian Provinces and Territories has its own securities regulator responsible for enforcing the provisions in their respective Securities Act.[51] The Ontario Securities Commission (OSC) is the largest securities regulator in Canada. Ontario is home to Canadian's largest securities exchange, the Toronto Stock Exchange, and Ontario based issuers comprise over 50% of Canada's equity market value.[52]

On 14 July 2016 the OSC introduced a whistleblower awards program and established an Office of the Whistleblower.[53] Yet, around the same time, two other Canadian provincial securities regulators, being the securities regulators for Quebec and Alberta, considered but ultimately rejected the idea of rewarding whistleblowers.

---

[47] Wyatt (2011).

[48] See Casey (2011) and Paredes (2011).

[49] In May 2011, prior to the finalization of the rules by the SEC, Congressman Michael Grimm (R-NY) introduced a draft bill called the Whistleblower Improvement Act but it died in Congress. This would have required internal reporting before being eligible for a bounty and eliminating the minimum amount for a bounty, see Rapp (2012, pp. 101–102). In September 2016, House Financial Services Committee Chairman Jeb Hensarling (R-Texas) introduced a bill for the Financial Choice Act, which would, among other things, allow respondents to remove proceedings from the SEC's administrative court to federal court. H.R. Rep. No. 114-883, pt. 1, at 137. Although the bill died in Congress in 2017, it appears that Representative Hansarling may reintroduce it. In February 2017, he issued a memorandum outlining changes planned to the introduced version of the Act, one of which would prohibit "co-conspirators" from receiving an award under the SEC's whistleblower bounty program.

[50] Lipton (2012). As to the benefits to trial lawyers see Ebersole (2011, pp. 146–147).

[51] Although some of the provinces are moving towards a semi-national regulator to be called the Capital Markets Regulatory Authority. See http://ccmr-ocrmc.ca/. Accessed 14 June 2018.

[52] Ontario Securities Commission (2017, p. 1).

[53] Ontario Securities Commission (2016b, c). See also The Economist (2016).

3.3.1 Ontario

Unlike the United States, Canada does not have a lengthy history of rewarding whistleblowers.[54] However, around the same time that the OSC adopted its whistle-blower award program, Canada's Federal tax regulator, the Canada Revenue Agency adopted a whistleblower award program.[55]

The driving force behind the adoption of the OSC's whistleblower award program were employees of the OSC and particularly the OSC's enforcement division.[56] This enthusiasm for adopting such a program may have been motivated by criticism over several years that the OSC has been lax in taking enforcement action compared to the SEC.[57] It has even been suggested that this low level of enforcement has resulted in a higher cost of capital for companies seeking to raise funds in Canada, verses raising funds in the US, as investors require a higher return on their funds because there is a greater risk of fraud in Canadian companies.[58] The OSC also took note of the apparent success of the SEC's whistleblower award program as indicated by the increasing number of tips the SEC was receiving each year since its introduction and statements by the SEC that over half of the tips it had received related to complex cases involving sophisticated players which would have been difficult to uncover without the assistance of the whistleblower.[59] Furthermore, Canadians were actually contacting the SEC under its whistleblower awards program, which seemed to suggest that there was an appetite from whistleblowers in Canada for such a program.[60] The OSC also conducted its own research about what drives people to blow the whistle and found that, although most whistleblowers are not motivated by financial incentives, financial incentives may offer whistleblowers a 'security blanket' in the event that they suffered retaliation.[61]

The details of the proposal for the whistleblower award program were contained in a consultation paper released by the OSC on 3 February 2015 which also invited the

---

[54]Section 30 of the Exchequer Court Act, R.S.C. 1927, c. 34 gave the Exchequer Court jurisdiction over *qui tam* suits suggesting that Canadians had the right to bring them. However, Common Law in Canada seems to have given preference to the Crown prerogative to prosecute effectively ending *qui tam* suits by the 1880s. For more on *qui tam* in Canada see Pitzer (1972) and for Crown Prerogative see Tingle (1994).

[55]In 2014, the Canada Revenue Agency (CRA) introduced a program under which whistleblowers are entitled to between 5 and 15% of the federal tax collected where the tax collected exceeds C$100,000.

[56]Franken (2017).

[57]See for example Halpern et al. (2016), Sukdeo (2009) and Puri (2012).

[58]See Coffee (2007).

[59]Ontario Securities Committee (2015a, p. 1).

[60]Franken (2017). Canadians are consistently in the top three groups of foreign nationals contacting the SEC under its whistleblower award program. See for example Securities and Exchange Commission (2012, Appendix C), Securities and Exchange Commission (2013, Appendix D) and Securities and Exchange Commission (2014, Appendix C).

[61]Franken (2017).

public to provide comments.[62] Similar to the SEC's program, the program focused on three key features. These were first, protecting the identity of whistleblowers. Second, shielding whistleblowers from retaliation and, third, offering them financial incentives.[63] The aim was to motivate those with information to come forward and, in particular, those with information that would be otherwise difficult to obtain. In addition, the program was designed to increase the number of investigations undertaken by the OSC and, at the same time, improve the efficiency of those investigations by obtaining high quality information from knowledgeable individuals. Finally, the program aimed to motivate organizations to self-report misconduct to the OSC, before they were reported by a whistleblower, so that the organization could avail itself of the OSC's "credit for cooperation" program.[64]

In relation to the impact on internal compliance systems, in this proposal the OSC adopted a similar position to that contained in the SEC whistleblower awards program, being that whistleblowers would not be compelled to report the conduct internally before approaching the OSC. However, it would view as a positive factor in assessing the amount of the award the fact that a whistleblower first reported the matter internally.[65] In support of the fact that whistleblowing awards would not adversely affect internal reporting the OSC pointed to a US study by the National Whistleblower Centre on the impact of *qui tam* reward programs on employee reporting behaviors. It found that whistleblower reward laws have no impact on the viability of internal corporate compliance programs or the willingness of employees to report suspected violations to their employers.[66]

The OSC received 17 comment letters in response to its initial proposal, 13 of which were supportive. The four letters which were against the proposal seemed primarily concerned with the impact of the rewards on internal compliance procedures.[67] The OSC also held a public roundtable in relation to the proposal. Participants at this roundtable included Jane Norberg from the SEC's Office of the Whistleblower. Jane Norberg spoke in support of the effectiveness of the SEC's program observing that it had resulted in "incredible high quality tips" causing it to open investigations and bring enforcement actions much sooner than if it had not received such information. This allowed the SEC to stop the fraud early and had frequently resulted in the SEC being able to freeze assets before fraudsters dissipated them.[68] A third of this roundtable was devoted to discussing whether or not there should be a requirement for

[62]Ontario Securities Committee (2015a).

[63]Ontario Securities Committee (2015a, p. 1).

[64]Ontario Securities Committee (2015a, p. 5). This credit for co-operation program provides for various levels of leniency depending upon factors such as when the conduct is reported, type of conduct and the organizations response to the misconduct, see Ontario Securities Commission (2014). The reward program is structured such that, if the OSC first hears of the misconduct by a whistleblower rather than the organization, the organization would be ineligible for credit for co-operation.

[65]Ontario Securities Committee (2015a, p. 24 at footnote 27).

[66]Ontario Securities Committee (2015, p. 24). See National Whistleblowers Center (2010).

[67]Ontario Securities Commission (2015b).

[68]Ontario Securities Commission (2015b, pp. 19–21).

an employee to report misconduct internally first or whether the fact that an employee reported internally first should just be a factor taken into account in determining the size of the award.[69] On 28 October 2015, and following that roundtable, the OSC published another version of the proposal which contained only minor changes from the original and gave another 60 days for public comments. It received 22 comment letters in response, the vast majority of which were supportive.[70]

The OSC adopted its final policy in July 2016. This did not require legislative approval, although the Ontario Legislature did pass some amendments to the Ontario Securities Act to enhance protection for whistleblowers against reprisals and to prohibit restrictions in employment contracts that would forbid reporting misconduct to the OSC.[71] Like its initial proposal, the final policy does not require that a whistleblower first report the misconduct through an internal compliance reporting mechanism. However, the policy endeavours to encourage internal reporting by providing that whistleblowers who report internally will be entitled to an award in certain circumstances[72] and that this will be a positive factor in determining the amount of the award.[73]

OSC's program is less generous than the SEC whistleblowing awards program and has been the subject of some criticism in relation to rules which determine the eligibility of whistleblowers to receive an award.[74] Nevertheless, the OSC has stated that the program has so far exceeded its expectations and that it has received information that it believes it would not have otherwise obtained.[75] In February 2019, the OSC announced its first award under the program comprising C$7.5 M to three individuals.[76]

3.3.2 Quebec

In February 2016, and in contrast to the position of OSC, the securities regulator for Quebec, the Autorité des marchés financiers (AMF), announced that it intended to enhance its whistleblower program but would not offer financial rewards.[77]

The AMF stated that it had rejected a financial rewards scheme based on a study it conducted of the whistleblower programs set up by the SEC, the UK Financial

---

[69] Ibid., pp. 95–145.

[70] Ontario Securities Commission (2016a).

[71] An Act to Implement Budget Measures and to Enact or Amend Various Statutes SO 2016 c 5. This inserted a new Part XXI.2 into the Ontario Securities Act RSO 1990.

[72] Ontario Securities Commission (2016c, para 16).

[73] Ibid. para 25(2)–(3).

[74] See generally Chap. 4 and Archibald et al. (2017, para 7–30).

[75] Franken (2017).

[76] Ontario Securities Commission (2019).

[77] Autorité des marchés financiers (AMF) (2016a).

Conduct Authority and the Australian Securities and Investments Commission.[78] This study found strong support from each of these authorities for whistleblower programs.[79] In relation to the issue of financial incentives, the report noted that the SEC's enforcement division pointed out that confidentiality, anti-reprisal measures as well as financial rewards were important in attracting whistleblowers[80] and that the SEC's enforcement division said that introducing a financial reward was a "game changer" in terms of reports of wrongdoing.[81] The report goes on to state:

> Americans are proud of the 20% increase in reports received since the Dodd-Frank program was set up, while the British are seeing a jump of over 400% despite the absence of any financial award. Even if we could determine with certainty the reason for the increase in reports in the U.K. (advertising about the program, its scope, recent policy changes), the growing attractiveness of the U.K. program compares favourably to the U.S. situation.
>
> Other factors should be considered if an award is to be included in a whistleblower program, such as the availability of resources to process reports, how it would be financed and the complexity of managing such a program (granting an award, possible appeals by disgruntled whistleblowers, etc.).[82]

The report then suggests that whistleblower incentives not be included in the AMF's whistleblower program at this stage because there is a lack of conclusive data in the context of the AMF's organization and market. The report suggested that the whistleblower program only focus on confidentiality and anti-reprisal measures and recommended a number of legislative changes to strengthen protections in this regard.[83]

Based on this study, the AMF then concluded that the protection of confidentiality was what primarily motivated whistleblowers to report incidents.[84] The executive director of AMF enforcement stated at the time:

> We are convinced that this protection, combined with anti-retaliation measures, as part of a structured, well-publicized program, will have a definite impact on the quantity and quality of wrongdoing reports made to the AMF, without the need for a reward.[85]

On 20 June 2016 the AMF launched its whistleblower program with enhanced confidentiality and protection from reprisals for whistleblowers but, as indicated in the earlier announcement, the AMF program does not offer financial incentives.[86] Like the OSC, the AMF did not require legislative approval for its program, although the enhanced protection from reprisals and confidentiality provisions do require some

---

[78] Ibid.

[79] Autorité des marchés financiers (AMF) (2016b, p. 1).

[80] Ibid., p. 3.

[81] Ibid., p. 14.

[82] Ibid.

[83] Ibid., pp. 10–13.

[84] Autorité des marchés financiers (AMF) (2016a).

[85] Ibid.

[86] Autorité des marchés financiers (2016c).

amendments to be made to the Quebec Securities Act. The Quebec National Assembly has not yet passed these changes.[87]

3.3.3 Alberta

Similar to the AMF, the Alberta Securities Commission (ASC) also considered but rejected a program to reward whistleblowers. In February 2017, it announced a three year strategic plan which included that the ASC was considering the creation and implementation of a whistleblower program designed to motivate individuals to report information about serious violations of Alberta securities law.[88] At the time, in statements to the media, ASC said that it has ruled out rewards for whistleblowers and will only offer whistleblowers confidentiality and protections from reprisals.[89] It seems that the ASC largely based this decision on the same study produced by the AMF, which it did not make public.[90] The ASC said that this study shows that confidentiality and protection against reprisals were the key to encouraging people to report wrongdoing and that there was not a clear indication that financial incentives will result in a more successful whistleblower program, basically the same conclusion made by the AMF.[91] In November 2018, the ASC adopted its whistleblower program that, as expected, did not include rewards to whistleblowers.[92]

A weakened provincial economy coupled with resistance from industry to any further regulatory burdens may have also contributed to the ASC decision not to consider rewards for whistleblowers. Alberta is a resource based economy and has suffered economic decline since the fall of the oil price in mid-2014.[93] In preparing the Strategic Plan the ASC stated that it had "engaged in a rigorous consultation and met with ASC Members, ASC staff and a number of external stakeholders such as issuers, law firms and other market participants to gain a broad range of perspectives" and had "performed a broad and thorough environmental scan of how our challenged provincial economy and changing industry… are impacting the securities sector."[94]

---

[87] See s571 of Bill 141 An Act mainly to improve the regulation of the financial sector, the protection of deposits of money and the operation of financial institutions. http://www.assnat.qc.ca/en/travaux-parlementaires/projets-loi/projet-loi-141-41-1.html. Accessed 15 June 2018.

[88] Alberta Securities Commission (2017).

[89] Shecter (2017) and Southwick (2017).

[90] A request by the author to the ASC under Freedom of Information and Protection Privacy Act (Alberta) for this information was unsuccessful, the ASC relying on, inter alia, section 46 of the Securities Act (Alberta) which relates to research received from other securities regulators.

[91] Ibid.

[92] Alberta Securities Commission (2018).

[93] See for example Giovannetti and Cryderman (2016).

[94] Alberta Securities Commission (2017).

3.4 The United Kingdom

In the United Kingdom the competition regulator, the Competition and Markets Authority, offers rewards up to UK£100,000 for information about cartels.[95] This program was introduced in 2008 by its predecessor, the Office of Fair Trading.[96] The UK taxation regulator, HM Revenue and Customs (HMRC), also pays awards for information from whistleblowers, however it does not publicize reward payments amounts or provide guidelines for potential whistleblowers. Such awards must be specifically requested and the amount paid is wholly at the discretion of the HMRC.[97]

However to date the UK Securities Regulator, The Financial Conduct Authority (FCA), has resisted the introduction of awards for whistleblowers despite some suggestions that it consider them. For example, in 2013, following the actions of some UK banks in contributing to the 2008 Global Financial Crisis and their participation in the Libor rate-setting scandal, the UK Parliament commissioned the Parliamentary Commission on Banking Standards to consider and report upon professional standards and culture within the UK banking sector.[98] In the resulting report the Commission "was shocked by the evidence it heard that so many people turned a blind eye to misbehaviour and failed to report it"[99] and found that it was rare to blow the whistle even where, as was the case in relation to the manipulation of Libor, there was prolonged and blatant misconduct.[100] In its final report the Parliamentary Commission made a number of recommendations designed to strengthen protection of whistleblowers. While it did not recommend financial rewards for whistleblowers, it did call on the Financial Services Authority (FSA), the predecessor of the FCA, to "undertake research into the impact of financial incentives in the US in encouraging whistleblowing, exposing wrongdoing and promoting integrity and transparency in financial markets."[101] The FSA had made submissions to this Commission in which it said that it had serious reservations about offering financial incentives to whistleblowers because of the moral hazard of paying whistleblowers and, in particular, that rewarding an individual for what was in any case arguably just their duty to report could lead to 'public disquiet'.[102]

In response to the Parliamentary Commission's call that the FSA conduct research into the impact of financial incentives to encourage whistleblowers, the FCA, together with the UK banking regulator, the Prudential Regulation Authority (PRA), produced

---

[95] Competition and Markets Authority (2014).

[96] Faunce et al. (2014, p. 386).

[97] This has led to some criticism of the scheme because of the lack information for potential whistleblowers and the lack of oversight of the scheme. Through Freedom of Information requests it has been reported that the HMRC paid out £421, 460 in 2016/2017 and £460, 433 in 2015/2016. Hodgson (2017a, b).

[98] UK Parliamentary Commission on Banking Standards Fifth Report (2013).

[99] Ibid., para 784.

[100] Ibid., para 779.

[101] Ibid., para 803.

[102] Ibid., para 802.

a research note. The note concludes "introducing financial incentives for whistleblowers would be unlikely to increase the number or quality of the disclosures we receive from them."[103] However, the evidence put forward in this note in support of this proposition is weak at best. Most of the note consists of arguments against the introduction of financial awards for whistleblowers that are not supported by any empirical evidence.[104] The closest the note comes in referencing empirical evidence is that it states that there is no empirical evidence that incentives lead to an increase in the number or quality of disclosure received by the regulators. In coming to this conclusion the authors of the note state that they have has spoken to US agencies, including the SEC, and that they have not seen a significant increase in either the number or quality of reports from whistleblowers.[105] However, it is difficult to see how they came to that conclusion as it directly contradicts publically available data and statements from the SEC regarding the increase in the number of reports they have received from whistleblowers since it introduced its awards program, as well as public statements in relation to the value of the information it is receiving.[106] The research note also states that the regulators had discussed the idea of financial incentives to whistleblowers with the British Bankers' Association who opposed the idea. It also indicates it has spoken to a number of unspecified organizations representing whistleblowers and that they were all opposed to the idea as well.[107]

Although the FCA rejected the idea of financial rewards, the note did state that it intended to introduce other changes to encourage employees to report internally, the aim being to ensure that the culture of firms is one where people are prepared to speak up. The FCA expressed concern that it should be careful to "avoid taking any action that could discourage firms from making these changes in a whole-hearted way" and be "conscious that the introduction of rules in this area could lead to

[103]Bank of England Prudential Regulation Authority and Financial Conduct Authority (2014).

[104]Ibid. Part of the justification for this position was the paper from the Department of Business Innovation and Skills (BIS) (2014). This was a report from a survey of respondents to whistleblowing issues generally, including the issue of financial rewards. The 78 respondents ranged from individuals, business representatives, businesses, trade unions and 11 of which are unclassified. The report states that the majority were not in favour of financial rewards but the report does not detail which of the respondents were in favour and which were against and who this majority comprised. Furthermore the PRA and FCA's note cites this BIS document as showing that the Government does not believe that financial incentives should form part of the whistleblowing framework." However citing this report as evidence is somewhat circular as this BIS report itself states that "the Government did not consider the evidence base strong enough to introduce this sort of system into the UK framework" but went on to say that that it would be interested to read the evidence from the PRA and FCA's note.

[105]Ibid.

[106]See n. 138 below. William Shepherd, a corporate defence attorney with Holland and Knight who apparently helped organize the U.S. meetings with British regulators was quoted as saying that the UK not introduce bounties because "They want to create culture of internally inspired ethics instead of gotcha," and were "What they're concerned about is creating the whole industry of whistleblowers and folks running around trying to drum up these cases" (Fisher 2014).

[107]A request made by the author under the Freedom of Information Act 2000 (UK) for further information in relation to this report was denied based upon a number of legislative provisions.

additional costs for firms."[108] In October 2015 the FCA did instigate rules designed to encourage employees to report internally. These include requirements that large firms must appoint a senior manager as their 'whistleblowers champion'. In addition, such firms must adopt internal whistleblowing arrangements, inform employees about the FCA's whistleblowing services, present a report on whistleblowing to the board at least annually, incorporate text in settlement agreements explaining that workers have a legal right to 'blow the whistle' and inform the FCA if it loses an employment tribunal action against a whistleblower.[109]

There is no evidence as to whether or not these changes have improved internal whistleblowing outcomes. However, it is clear that they have not resulted in a significant increase in whistleblowers reporting misconduct to the FCA, despite FCA's expectations to the contrary.[110] In 2014 the FCA received 1040 reports from whistleblowers, rising to a high of 1340 reports in 2015. However, since that time the number of such reports has fallen, the FCA receiving only 1014 reports from whistleblowers in 2016, 900 in 2017 and 1106 in 2018.[111] It is possible, of course, that the improvements in the internal whistleblower regimes is working and reducing the incidents of malfeasance.

3.5 Australia

Like the UK, to date Australia has not introduced a financial incentive scheme for corporate whistleblowers.

Serious consideration of whether there was a need to regulate to protect corporate whistleblowers seems to have begun in 2004 following the collapse of Australia's second largest insurance company, HIH Insurance. This led to the enacting of amendments in the Corporations Act intended to encourage whistleblowing. These amendments protect whistleblowers from victimization and civil actions.[112] However, a 2009 Federal Government Treasury Options Paper produced in response to the Global Financial Crisis found that these provisions were hardly ever used and

---

[108] Ibid.

[109] Financial Conduct Authority (2015).

[110] Bank of England Prudential Regulation Authority and Financial Conduct Authority (2014) which stated, at p. 6, that the FCA said that it expected reports from whistleblowers to the FCA would continue to increase, noting that the number of whistleblowing cases rose by 55% from 2011 to 2012, by a further 42% from 2012 to 2013 and that it expected that it would increase by another 30% in 2014 to reach around 1200 reports.

[111] Financial Conduct Authority (2016, p. 3) and Financial Conduct Authority (2017, p. 36). Financial Conduct Authority (2018, p. 20). See also Fantato (2017) which states that in 2016 only 13% of reports to the FCA directly contributed to enforcement action or were of significant value to the regulator.

[112] This involved the insertion of Pt 9.4AAA into the Corporations Act 2001 (Cth). See Brand et al. (2013) and Allan (2006).

were regarded as inadequate.[113] This Options Paper sought submissions on how to enhance the protection of whistleblowers by perhaps expanding the range of people covered by these provisions and/or allowing whistleblowers to remain anonymous.[114] However despite receiving a number of submissions seeking improvements to the protection of whistleblowers in response to this Options Paper, the then Government did not take any further action in relation to this issue.[115]

In 2014, the Economics References Committee of the Australian Senate conducted a broad ranging enquiry into the performance of Australia's securities and corporate regulator, the Australian Securities and Investments Commission (ASIC). The main catalyst for this review was ASIC's failure to appropriately respond to allegations of misconduct by financial advisers at a subsidiary of one of Australia's largest banks.[116] The Committee found that ASIC did not pay sufficient attention to whistleblowers who had raised serious concerns about the behaviour of these financial advisors.[117] The Committee recommended a number of changes to protect whistleblowers and their anonymity.[118] In relation to the issue of financial incentives, the Committee recommended that the Government initiate a review of the adequacy of Australia's framework for protecting corporate whistleblowers and, as part of this review, explore options for reward based incentives, including *qui tam* arrangements.[119] The Federal Government's response was to simply to note the recommendation.[120]

However, in 2016 the Australian Federal Government came under pressure to take action in relation to the protection of corporate whistleblowers. At that time, the Liberal/National Party controlled the House of Representatives but did not control the Senate. In order to obtain support for the passage of a bill that provided increased protections for persons who blow the whistle in relation to misconduct by trade unions, the Liberal/National Party Government had to commit to Senate crossbenchers that it would roll out protections for whistleblowers in the private sector.[121] As a result, on 30 November 2016 the Senate asked the Parliamentary Joint Committee on Corporations and Financial Services to conduct an enquiry into whistleblowing protections.[122] The Government stated that it gave this Senate enquiry its support and that it was committed to ensuring appropriate protections were in place for whistleblowers to expose corruption, fraud, tax evasion or avoidance, and misconduct in the corporate sector. Around the same time, it set up its own consultation process that was intended to complement the enquiry.[123]

---

[113] Treasury Options Paper (2009, p. v).

[114] Ibid.

[115] Brand et al. (2013, p. 295).

[116] Senate Economics References Committee (2014, xvii–xix).

[117] Ibid.

[118] Ibid., xxv.

[119] Ibid., xxvi.

[120] Australian Government (2014, p. 9). See also Brand (2016).

[121] Knott (2016) and Beech (2016).

[122] Parliamentary Joint Committee of Corporations and Financial Services (2017).

[123] Australian Government (2016a). See also Australian Government (2016b, p. 11).

The Senate enquiry received 75 submissions and heard evidence from a number of witnesses. In its submission to the enquiry, ASIC stated that it did not support the introduction of a financial incentives scheme for whistleblowers. ASIC observed that, in its experience, altruism motivates most whistleblowers. It suggested that there be some form of compensation for loss or damage incurred by whistleblowers and that consideration of financial incentives be deferred until the effectiveness of such a compensation scheme could be assessed.[124] ASIC also expressed concern that the quantum of penalties prescribed for corporate misconduct was too low and, as such, doubted that a financial incentive scheme would be successful. It suggested that enacting reforms similar to those introduced in the UK could foster a culture in companies to encourage whistleblowers to speak up.[125]

In September 2017, the Parliamentary enquiry produced its final report. It noted that, though there were strong arguments put forward by both proponents and opponents of financial reward systems, a reward system should be introduced. It concluded that such a reward system would motivate whistleblowers to come forward with high quality information that would otherwise be difficult to obtain. It also recognized that a reward system would motivate companies to improve internal whistleblower reporting systems and to deal more proactively with illegal behavior.[126] It further recommended that the amount of the award be within a legislated range of percentages, the actual amount to be determined by factors such as the timeliness of the disclosure and the availability of internal whistleblowing procedures.[127]

Subsequent to this report, the Federal Government introduced legislation to enhance protections for whistleblowers in the private sector. This Act expands the class of persons who are protected from reprisals and allows anonymous disclosures.[128] However, this legislation does not contain any provisions in relation to the paying of financial incentives to whistleblowers.

3.6 What Determines Whether or not a Jurisdiction Adopts a Whistleblower Award Program?

Isolating the key determinants which drove the decision to adopt or reject a whistleblower award scheme in a particular jurisdiction is complex. Nevertheless, from the above review of the decision-making processes, it is possible to isolate a few factors that significantly affected the decision and examine the impact of each.

---

[124] Parliamentary Joint Committee of Corporations and Financial Services (2017, p. 131) and Australian Securities and Investments Commission (2017, pp. 25–16).

[125] Ibid.

[126] Parliamentary Joint Committee of Corporations and Financial Services (2017, p. 138).

[127] Ibid. Xvii–xviii.

[128] Treasury Laws Amendment (Enhancing Whistleblower Protections) Act 2019 (Cth).

3.6.1 Support by the Securities Regulator

Strong support by the securities regulator appeared to be critical to the adoption of a whistleblower reward program. By way of contrast, a lukewarm or antagonistic reception by the securities regulator to such a scheme generally proved to be fatal.

In the United States and Ontario, enthusiastic internal support from within the SEC and the OSC proved crucial in pushing through the reform. It is also relevant to note that in order to garner support for the new rules, both regulators engaged in a long, transparent consultation process to ensure that all stakeholders had an opportunity to provide their views on the proposed scheme. It is not entirely clear why those within the SEC and Ontario pushed hard for these reforms but it may be that both are large regulators who are under significant political and media pressure to improve their enforcement records.

The reception by the securities regulators in Quebec, Alberta, the UK and Australia, on the other hand, seems to have resulted in the rejection of the scheme, apparently almost from the outset. The internal report commission by the AMF before it decided upon its whistleblower program was primarily focused on how to enhance protections for whistleblowers from reprisals and to protect their confidentiality.[129] Less than one page of the report is devoted to considering financial incentives.[130] The report rejects financial incentives despite the strong conclusions of the SEC of the importance financial incentives to its program, and favours instead the FCA's report of "seeing a jump of over 400% despite the absence of any financial reward."[131] The report also expresses concerns with issues such as how such a financial incentive scheme would be financed as well as the complexity of managing such a scheme.[132] The ASC in Alberta appears to have adopted the conclusions from this report, despite the report's scant analysis of the issue of financial incentives. In relation to the UK, the FSA was antagonistic to the idea of financial incentives in its submission to the Parliamentary Commission on Banking Standards. In the research note produced by the FSA's successor, the FCA, the consultation process in arriving at its decision to reject such a scheme and the evidence relied on to come to that decision remains opaque.

It is not entirely clear why each of those regulators seem opposed to the introduction of a scheme. No doubt such whistleblower awards schemes do have a significant impact on the internal operations of regulators, and, in particular, their investigation and enforcement processes and perhaps this may explain such resistance? For example, the offering of financial incentives may make it more likely that whistleblowers will engage a lawyer, which may keep a check on access by enforcement staff to the whistleblower. Whistleblower incentive programs may also result in regulators having less discretion in setting their enforcement agenda by, for example, limiting their ability to run test cases in order to send a message that a particular behaviour by

---

[129] Autorité des marchés financiers (2016b).

[130] Ibid., p. 14.

[131] Ibid.

[132] Ibid.

market participants will not be tolerated. Instead, the enforcement strategy may have to bend to pressure from whistleblowers and their lawyers to bring enforcement proceedings in relation to cases they have brought to the regulator so that they can claim the reward.[133] In fact, one study has found that since the introduction of the whistleblower reward program, the SEC's enforcement actions seem to have shifted towards those where the knowledge of the wrongdoing is relatively widespread resulting in whistleblowers coming forward (such as the investigation of Ponzi schemes), and away from those in which the knowledge of the wrongdoing is tightly confined such that a whistleblower is unlikely (for example insider trading).[134] Some within the regulator may also believe that those who are incentivized by moral outrage rather than financial rewards may produce better quality information, although the evidence here appears to be anecdotal only.[135]

3.6.2 Empirical Evidence

Empirical evidence as to the costs and benefits of whistleblower award schemes has been influential but not decisive. This seems to be because empirical evidence is only available in relation to some aspects of the costs and benefits of such schemes. For example, the empirical evidence is increasingly demonstrating that such schemes are beneficial in terms of increasing the total number of tips to regulators. However, there is a lack of evidence proving that such schemes result in efficiency savings for regulators and also that any efficiency gains outweigh the increased costs for regulators in dealing with both the upsurge in the number of tips and the rise in frivolous tips. There is also a paucity of empirical evidence quantifying the costs and benefits of such schemes to business or whether the overall cost to business outweighs the public benefit of a reduction in losses to investors from misconduct detected by such schemes. Because of this fractured picture in the empirics, both sides of the debate use aspects of empirical evidence to support their case to adopt or reject a whistleblower award scheme.[136]

Both the SEC and the OSC used the study conducted by Dyck to support the case for the introduction of their whistleblower award program. It was this study which indicated that employees are more likely to come forward and disclose fraud if offered a financial incentive.[137] In addition, both the SEC and the OSC pointed to the increase in whistleblowing tips in comparative agencies following the introduction of

[133]Ebersole (2011, pp. 140–141).

[134]Dayton (2015). In this study Dayton found that SEC enforcement actions in which a whistleblower is present has increased since 2011. These are types of action which involve multiple people there is likely to be a whistleblower, being issuer reporting and disclosure, offering fraud and market manipulation.

[135]See Austin (2017a, p. 144).

[136]For arguments against the SEC whistleblower bounty program, see generally Ebersole (2011).

[137]Dyck et al. (2010).

such a scheme to demonstrate that whistleblowing award schemes work to the extent that they generate an increase in the number of tips to regulatory agencies.[138] The SEC and the OSC also pointed to empirical evidence to counter the argument that a whistleblower award scheme would undermine companies' internal compliance systems.[139] However, perhaps recognizing the limitation of this empirical evidence, both the SEC and OSC did not wholly dismiss this as a concern and in fact modified the rules associated with their programs to encourage whistleblowers to first report internally.

In the UK, the FCA stated that it relied on empirical evidence to reach the conclusion that there is no evidence that introducing financial incentives would increase the number or quality of information provided by whistleblowers. However, as is articulated above, this empirical evidence cited by the FCA is somewhat questionable given the substantial increase in tips received by the SEC since the introduction of its whistleblower award scheme. The study relied upon by the AMF in Quebec, and seemingly also by the ASC in Alberta, similarly reviewed the empirical evidence. Although it accepted that this showed the positive impact Dodd Frank Whistleblower Program it downplayed the importance of this evidence and the increase in tips to the SEC over an alleged increase in tips as a result of the whistleblower program in the UK.[140]

In Australia, the role played by empirical evidence in the decision to not introduce a financial incentive scheme is even less clear. The Senate Enquiry seemed to accept that there was evidence that whistleblowing reward schemes do motivate whistleblowers to come forward. ASIC however did not refer to any empirical evidence to support its submission to this enquiry that such a scheme should be rejected.

3.6.3 The Business Lobby

The purported benefit for business from whistleblower reward programs is that it should prod them to improve internal compliance systems. An internal compliance system where employees are encouraged to come forward and raise concerns without fear of retribution should allow the organization to become aware of problems at an early stage thereby enabling them to correct the problem and mitigate any losses. However, there are costs associated with instigating and maintaining such a compliance system. For small business in particular these costs may be disproportionally high.[141] In addition, as is referred to above, it is argued that whistleblower rewards

[138]The SEC pointed to the increase in tips and payouts at the IRS after it introduced its award program, see Shapiro (2009, p. 19). The OSC pointed to the increase in tips and payouts to the SEC after it introduced its award scheme, see Ontario Securities Commission (2015a, p. 4).

[139]Ontario Securities Commission (2015a, p. 24) which cited National Whistleblowers Center (2010) and Securities and Exchange Commission (2011) citing a study by Heyes and Kapur (2009).

[140]Autorité des marchés financiers (2016b, pp. 1–2, 14).

[141]Ebersole (2011, pp. 137–138).

undermine internal compliance in that if a company becomes aware of misconduct first it can take steps to rectify the problem. However, once a whistleblower reports the misconduct to the regulator companies face the possibility of penalties, reputational costs if the alleged misconduct becomes public and will forgo any possible opportunity to receive leniency for voluntarily reporting the issue to the regulator.[142] It will also face legal costs in dealing with the regulator, even if the whistleblower's report has no merit or is vexatious. There is also the cost to some businesses associated with an increased risk of being reported by a whistleblower in relation to behaviour which, though illegal, they may view as valuable to a company's bottom line and competitive position such as the paying of bribes to secure contracts.

As such, when the introduction of a whistleblower award program is proposed, it could be expected that there would be opposition by some businesses who view the cost to their particular company as outweighing the benefits. In particular, it would be expected that there may be opposition from those companies with weak internal compliance systems who may be more vulnerable to reports by whistleblowers and as a result would have to incur cost to improve their internal reporting systems.[143] In fact, an analysis by Baloria, Marquardt and Wiedman showed that in response to the SEC draft proposal rules for its whistleblower award scheme, 87% of individuals who provided comments favoured the proposals.[144] However corporate managers strongly disapproved, particularly the provision allowing whistleblowers to report potential violations directly to the regulator without first reporting the violation through internal compliance systems.[145] Baloria et al., found that firms that lobbied against the implementation of the SEC whistleblower provisions were those with significantly weaker internal whistleblower programs and as such more vulnerable to whistleblower allegations.[146] Nevertheless, the impact of this lobbying did not result in the SEC abandoning its proposal for a whistleblower award system. It also did not result in a change in the rule that whistleblowers did not have to report internally first to be eligible for a reward, although, as is referred to above, the SEC did amend the rules to encourage internal reporting. Similarly, although most respondents to the OSC's proposed rules were supportive, some were concerned about the impact on internal compliance systems. However, these concerns did not stop the OSC pursuing its proposal for a whistleblower award system.

By way of contrast, opposition from business may have had an impact on the FCA and ASCs' decision to reject whistleblower award schemes. The FCA noted that it took into account opposition from unspecified organizations and the British Bankers' Association in making its decision to reject rewards for whistleblowers. Similarly, the ASC stated that it considered the views of external stakeholders in developing its

---

[142]Ebersole (2011, pp. 137–138).

[143]Bowen, Cal and Rajopal found that companies with weak internal compliance programs are more likely to be subject to whistleblowing but that such whistleblowing was justified (Bowen et al. 2010).

[144]Baloria et al. (2017).

[145]Ibid.

[146]Ibid.

three year plan which ruled out awards for whistleblowers. In relation to the AMF and ASIC, it is not clear if business opposition had any impact upon their decision not to support a whistleblower reward scheme.

It is also not possible to fully assess the influence of the business lobby on the decision of regulators because direct lobbying by business is not the only way business can influence decisions by securities regulators. Regulatory capture, that is, processes by which a regulated industry influences policy makers in pursuit of its own self-interest, can take a number of forms.[147] In addition to direct lobbying, political campaign contributions can influence who is appointed to regulators, industry may have unparalleled access to regulators and business can sometimes shape the intellectual environment within which policy decisions are made.[148]

3.6.4 The Political Landscape

In some instances, the influence of partisan politics can be detected in the decision to adopt or reject a whistleblower award program. This is perhaps not surprising because of the choices inherent in the design of securities regulation generally. In particular, the design of securities regulation must always balance what can often be competing objectives. Two primary objectives of securities regulation are the protection of investors and the promoting of fair and efficient capital markets. Frequently, regulation which serves one of these goals can detract from the other.[149] Whistleblower rewards programs can enhance investor protection by exposing fraud at an early stage before investor funds are lost. Yet at the same time such schemes may result in costs to business and thereby detract from the efficiency of capital markets. In the interest of fostering efficient capital markets, right wing political parties are traditionally more concerned with not overburdening business with the costs associated with additional regulation. Conversely, left leaning political parties tend to view any such business costs as justified by enhanced investor protection and the public interest.

Certainly, the whistleblowing reward program proposed by the SEC obtained critical political support from the left leaning Democrat administration, and may not have been passed, at least in its current form, if Republican commissioners had been in the majority at the SEC when the rules were finalized. In Australia, the right leaning Liberal/National party government had to, somewhat reluctantly, commit to enhancing whistleblowing protection regulation in the private sector in return for laws to protect whistleblowers in trade unions. However, while it did draft legislation to enhance protections in the private sector, it did not take the extra step of introducing a whistleblower award program. In the UK, while there is no direct evidence of political influence in the rejection of a whistleblower award scheme, the FCA's rejection of a

[147] Stigler (1971).

[148] See further Armour et al. (2016, pp. 560–561).

[149] See generally Austin (2017b).

whistleblower award scheme does happen to coincide with a right wing government being in power.

Partisan politics appear to have played less of a role in relation to the adoption and rejection of whistleblower award programs in Canada. Although a left leaning government was in power when the whistleblower reward program was introduced by the OSC, left leaning governments were also in power in Quebec and Alberta when the AMF and ASC rejected whistleblower rewards. The marginal influence of partisan politics in Canada is perhaps a reflection of the fact that legislatures have vested securities regulators with very broad powers to set policy and regulations with minimal legislative interference.[150]

3.7 Conclusion

As the above analysis demonstrates, factors other than just empirical evidence influenced the decision whether or not to introduce a whistleblower award program in the United States, Canada, the United Kingdom and Australia. This seems to be primarily because the empirical evidence in relation to the costs and benefits of such programs is currently incomplete. In particular, the receptiveness of the regulator itself appeared to play a critical role in the decision.

No doubt the reasons why a whistleblower chooses to come forward are often multifaceted and perhaps are not always based on a rational analysis by them of the costs and benefits of their action. They could include the professional position of the person, an ethical motivation to 'do the right thing', a chance to tell their story, avoidance of personal liability, retaliation for been dismissed and/or working for a competitive rival of the fraudster.[151] Nevertheless, the empirical evidence continues to mount in support of the hypothesis that a financial award may change the calculus and may motivate some people to come forward who would not have done so otherwise.[152] In particular, each year the SEC is reporting a steady increase in the number of

[150] See for example Ontario Securities Act RSO 1990 c 5, s 143.

[151] For a discussion of possible motivations by whistleblowers and countervailing incentives to blow the whistle see Rapp (2012, pp. 109–118) and Feldman and Lobel (2010).

[152] See Dyck et al. (2010). Berger, Perreault and Wainberg also found that there was a higher likelihood that a fraud would be reported when there was a financial reward, although also found that there was a higher likelihood of reporting being delayed if the value of the fraud fell below the threshold for a financial incentive, see Berger et al. (2017). Feldman and Lobel found that the highest level of reporting occurs when there is both a duty and high reward and the least reporting occurs when there is a low reward. Although they did also find that were there is a low level of moral outrage about the conduct, the introduction of small bounties may actually decrease the rate it is reported, see Feldman and Lobel (2010). However, interviews conducted by Kesselheim, Suddert and Mello of 17 federal qui tam cases against the pharmaceutical manufacturers found that all said that the financial bounty had not motivated their participation in the qui tam lawsuit. Motivations were four non-mutually exclusive themes being integrity, altruism or public safety, justice and self-preservation (Kesselheim et al. 2010).

whistleblowers and a 75% increase since the introduction of the program.[153] By way of contrast reports from whistleblowers to the FCA, which does not offer rewards, has not increased year to year.[154] There is also a recent study, using data from the SEC, that found that enforcement proceedings are brought more quickly when whistleblowers are involved and that whistleblower involvement is associated with higher monetary penalties and longer prison sentences for culpable executives.[155]

In relation to the impact of whistleblowing on internal compliance systems, the evidence from data released by the SEC seems to show that whistleblowing reward programs do not significantly disrupt internal compliance systems and that most whistleblowers first report the problem internally.[156] This is consistent with empirical studies in other areas where whistleblowing rewards are available.[157] Furthermore, a study by Bowen, Call and Rajgopal found that whistleblowing complaints are usually justified in terms of disclosing previously unknown issues, are not usually motivated by those with an axe to grind or to avoid disciplinary proceedings, and can result in improved compliance.[158]

Nevertheless, there remain many unanswered questions. For regulators, while it is becoming clear that the adoption of such programs do increase the number of tips, the number of frivolous tips also increase thereby necessitating filtering systems to sort

---

[153]Tips to the SEC have increased by over 75% since the program became operational and have increased each year from the time it was introduced. The SEC received 3001 tips in 2012, see Securities and Exchange Commission (2012, p. 4). In 2013 the SEC received 3238, see Securities and Exchange Commission (2013, p. 1). In 2014 the SEC received 3620 tips, see Securities and Exchange Commission (2014, p. 3). In 2015 the SEC received 3923, see Securities and Exchange Commission (2015, p. 21). In 2016 the SEC received 4218 tips, see Securities and Exchange Commission (2016, p. 23). In 2017 the SEC received 4484 tips, see Securities and Exchange Commission (2017, p. 23). In 2018 the SEC received 5200 tips, see Securities and Exchange Commission (2018, p. 6). The SEC also has said that the program has been of tremendous value to the SEC's enforcement efforts by assisting the SEC uncover and stop fraudulent investment schemes and allowing hundreds of millions of dollars to be returned to investors, see Securities and Exchange Commission (2017, p. 1).

[154]In 2014 the FCA received 1040 reports from whistleblowers, 1340 in 2015, 1014 in 2016, 900 in 2017 and 1106 in 2018. See Bank of England Prudential Regulation Authority and Financial Conduct Authority (2014, p. 6), Financial Conduct Authority (2016, p. 3, 2017, p. 36, 2018, p. 20).

[155]See Call et al. (2018). This seems to corroborate statements made by the SEC that the quality of those tips have been high which has enabled it to bring enforcement actions much quicker and save on resources which it would have to have otherwise spend on investigations and prosecutions. The program has also resulted in information as to the whereabouts of investors' funds and that this has enabled it to obtain orders to freeze assets and thereby stop investor funds from being dissipated by the fraudsters. See comments by Jane Norberg, Head of the SEC Office of the Whistleblower, Ontario Securities Commission (2015c, p. 19).

[156]The 83% of SEC whistleblowers who were current or former employees reported that they raised their concerns internally first, see Securities and Exchange Commission (2018, p. 17).

[157]In the Kesselheim study, 18 out of the 22 insiders interviewed tried first to fix the problem internally by talking to their superiors, filing an internal complaint or both. Kesselheim et al. (2010, p. 1834).

[158]Bowen et al. (2010).

through these and identify valuable information.[159] There are currently no publically available figures about whether these costs are significant or otherwise. There are also real questions as to the costs and benefits of such programs for business, whether these costs outweigh the benefits or if approving corporate compliance can be achieved in an alternative and perhaps cheaper way. Moreover, although such programs may be in the interests of investors and the public generally in terms of reducing waste from fraud and misconduct, at this point of time it is simply not possible to calculate whether this benefit outweighs the burden to the economy as a result of an increase in business compliance costs.

Overall, the analysis in this article suggests the need for more empirical evidence so that decision makers can fully assess the costs and benefits of whistleblower reward programs. Until such time, the debate as to the merit of such programs is vulnerable to hijack by vested interests, selective use of empirical evidence, anecdotal evidence and partisan politics. Further research into the costs and benefits of such programs is also important in that it is unlikely that the call for the introduction of such programs will disappear in jurisdictions in which they have not yet been introduced. This is because history has shown, from events such as Enron, the Bernie Madoff Ponzi scheme and the Libor rate-setting scandal, that regulators and governments periodically find themselves having to respond to wrongdoings that perhaps could have been exposed by whistleblowers before they caused much more substantial damage. At the same time, the pressure on regulators to improve their enforcement results without further relying on taxpayer funds is inevitably likely to continue. Such whistleblower award programs, which pay whistleblowers from monetary penalties imposed on wrongdoers and not from the public purse, may assist them to improve their enforcement record in the face of such fiscal challenges.

References

Alberta Securities Commission (2017) *ASC Strategic Plan*. https://www.albertasecurities.com/-/media/ASC-Documents-part-2/About-the-ASC/ASC-3yr-strat-plan-summary.ashx?la=en&hash=C8ABB687AF1C021BDA0EA5C7808C84B2. Accessed 8 May 2019

Alberta Securities Commission (2018) *Alberta Securities Commission Policy 15-602 Whistleblower Program*. https://www.albertasecurities.com/-/media/ASC-Documents-part-2/Enforcement/15-602-Whistleblower_Policy.ashx?la=en&hash=A80AFAFF4F0B0E68567342BD92926192. Accessed 8 May 2019

Allan G (2006) The HIH Collapse: A Costly Catalyst for Reform. *Deakin Law Rev* 11(2):137

Archibald T, Jull K, Roach K (2017) *Regulatory and Corporate Liability from Due Diligence to Risk Management*. Thomson Reuters, Toronto

Armour J, Awrey D, Davies P et al (2016) *Principles of Financial Regulation*. Oxford University, Oxford

Austin J (2017a) *Insider Trading and Market Manipulation, Investigating and Prosecuting Across Borders*. Edward Elgar, Cheltenham

[159]See 12 SEC (12 May 2014) Final Order. https://www.sec.gov/about/offices/owb/orders/owb-multiple-final-051214.pdf. Accessed 4 July 2018, and SEC 2017 Annual Report to Congress: Whistleblower Program, p. 23.

Austin J (2017b) What Exactly Is Market Integrity? An Analysis of One of the Core Objectives of Securities Regulation. *Wm & Mary Bus L Rev* 8(2):215

Australian Government (2014) *Response to the Senate Economics References Committee Report: Performance of the Australian Securities and Investments Commission*. https://www.aph.gov.au/Parliamentary_Business/Committees/Senate/Economics/ASIC/Additional_Documents. Accessed 13 June 2018

Australian Government (2016a) *Review of Tax and Corporate Whistleblower Protections in Australia*. https://static.treasury.gov.au/uploads/sites/1/2017/06/C2016-059_CP-whistleblowing.pdf. Accessed 13 June 2018

Australian Government (2016b) *Australia's First Open Government National Action Plan 2016–18, Draft for Consultation*. https://ogpau.pmc.gov.au/sites/default/files/files/2016/10/Australias-first-Open-Government-National-Action-Plan-Draft-for-consultation-Accessible.pdf. Accessed 13 June 2018

Australian Securities and Investments Commission (2017) *Review of Tax and Corporate Whistleblower Protections in Australia Submission by the Australian Securities and Investments Commission*. https://www.aph.gov.au/Parliamentary_Business/Committees/Joint/Corporations_and_Financial_Services/WhistleblowerProtections/Submissions. Accessed 13 June 2018

Autorité des marchés financiers (2016a) *No Rewards for Whistleblowers*. https://lautorite.qc.ca/en/general-public/media-centre/news/fiche-dactualites/no-rewards-for-whistleblowers-1/. Accessed 12 Dec 2017

Autorité des marchés financiers (2016b) *Proposed Framework for a Whistleblower Program*. Whistleblower Task Force (February 20, 2016 version). On file with the author

Autorité des marchés financiers (2016c) *AMF Launches Whistleblower Program*. https://lautorite.qc.ca/en/general-public/media-centre/news/fiche-dactualites/amf-launches-whistleblower-program/. Accessed 12 Dec 2017

Baer MH (2017) Reconceptualizing the Whistleblower's Dilemma. *UCD L Rev* 50(2280):2235

Baloria V, Marquardt C, Wiedman C (2017) A Lobbying Approach to Evaluating the Whistleblower Provisions of the Dodd-Frank Reform Act of 2010. *Contemp Acc Res* 34(3):1305

Bank of England Prudential Regulation Authority and Financial Conduct Authority (2014) *Financial Incentives for Whistleblowers*. https://www.fca.org.uk/publication/financial-incentives-for-whistleblowers.pdf. Accessed 4 July 2018

Beech A (2016) Government Agrees to Whistleblower Protection Laws in Bid to Pass Industrial Relations Bills. *abc.net*. http://www.abc.net.au/news/2016-11-21/government-agrees-whisteblower-laws-industrial-relations-bills/8044402. Accessed 8 June 2018

Berger L, Perreault S, Wainberg J (2017) Hijacking the Moral Imperative: How Financial Incentives Can Discourage Whistleblower Reporting. *Audit: A J Pract Theory* 36(3):1

Bowen RM, Call AC, Rajgopal S (2010) Whistle-Blowing: Target Firm Characteristics and Economic Consequences. *Acc Rev* 85(4):1239

Brady EL (2012) Does Tax Crime Pay (Whistleblowers). *Taxes* 90:49

Brand V (2016) Still 'Insufficient or Irrelevant': Australia's Foreign Bribery Corporate Whistleblowing Regulation. *UNSW L J* 39(3):1072

Brand V, Lombard S, Fitzpatrick J (2013) Bounty Hunters, Whistleblowers and a New Regulatory Paradigm. *AB L Rev* 292

Call AC, Martin GS, Sharp NY et al (2018) Whistleblowers and Outcomes of Financial Misrepresentation Enforcement Actions. *J Acc Res* 56(1):123

Casey KL (2011) *Statement by SEC Commissioner: Adoption of Rules for Implementing the Whistleblower Provisions of Section 21F of the Securities Exchange Act of 1934*. https://www.sec.gov/news/speech/2011/spch052511klc-item2.htm. Accessed 6 July 2018

Coffee J (2007) Law and The Market: The Impact of Enforcement. *U Pa L Rev* 156:268

Competition and Markets Authority (2014) *Informant Rewards Policy*. https://www.gov.uk/government/publications/cartels-informant-rewards-policy?event-category=Outbound%20Link&event-action=Open-Rewards&event-label=Cartels_2018_Outbound_Rewards-Policy. Accessed 4 July 2018

Dayton CE (2015) An Empirical Analysis of SEC Enforcement Actions in Light of the Dodd-Frank Whistleblower Program. *NYU J L & Bus* 12(1):215

Department of Business Innovation and Skills (2014) *Whistleblowing Framework Call for Evidence, Government Response*. https://www.gov.uk/government/uploads/system/uploads/attachment_data/file/323399/bis-14-914-whistleblowing-framework-call-for-evidence-government-response.pdf. Accessed 4 July 2018

Dworkin TM (2007) Sox and Whistleblowing. *Mich L Rev* 105(8):1757

Dyck A, Morse A, Zingales L (2010) Who Blows the Whistle on Corporate Fraud? *J Fin* 65(6):2213–2253

Ebersole D (2011) Blowing the Whistle on Dodd-Frank Whistleblower Reform. *Ohio St Entrepren Bus L J* 6:123

Ensign RL (2014) SEC Bans Would-Be Whistleblower Over Annoying Filings. *Wall Street J*. https://blogs.wsj.com/riskandcompliance/2014/06/04/sec-bans-would-be-whistleblower-over-annoying-submissions/. Accessed 4 July 2018

Fantato D (2017) Whistleblowing Reports to FCA Fall for Second Year. *Finan Adviser*. https://www.ftadviser.com/regulation/2017/03/22/whistleblowing-reports-to-fca-fall-for-second-year/?page=1. Accessed 7 June 2018

Faunce T, Crow K, Nikolic et al (2014) Because They Have Evidence: Globalizing Financial Incentives for Corporate Fraud Whistleblowers. In Brown AJ, Lewis D, Moberly R et al (eds) *International Handbook of Whistleblowing Research*. Edward Elgar, Cheltenham

Feldman Y, Lobel O (2010) The Incentives Matrix: The Comparative Effectiveness of Rewards, Liabilities, Duties, and Protections for Reporting Illegality. *Tex L Rev* 88:1151

Ferziger MJ, Currell DG (1999) Snitching for Dollars: The Economics and Public Policy of Federal Civil Bounty Programs. *U Ill L Rev* 1141

Financial Conduct Authority (2015) *FCA Introduces New Rules on Whistleblowing*. https://www.fca.org.uk/news/press-releases/fca-introduces-new-rules-whistleblowing. Accessed 4 July 2018

Financial Conduct Authority (2016) *Annual Report 2015/2016*. https://assets.publishing.service.gov.uk/government/uploads/system/uploads/attachment_data/file/537002/fca_annual_report_15_16_dot_gov.pdf. Accessed 7 June 2018

Financial Conduct Authority (2017) *Annual Report 2016/2017*. https://www.gov.uk/government/publications/financial-conduct-authority-annual-report-2016-to-2017. Accessed 9 July 2018

Financial Conduct Authority (2018) *Annual Report 2017/2018*. https://www.fca.org.uk/publication/annual-reports/annual-report-2017-18.pdf. Accessed 8 May 2019

Fisher D (2014) UK Commission Takes A Pass on U.S.-Style Whistleblower Bounties. *Forbes*. https://www.forbes.com/sites/danielfisher/2014/07/31/uk-commission-takes-a-pass-on-u-s-style-whistleblower-bounties/#271ad5266aaa. Accessed 7 July 2018

Franken H (2017) *Comments by OSC Chief Office of the Whistleblower, Flinders University Whistleblowing Bounties as an Anti-Corruption Measure 2017 A Panel Discussion*. http://video.flinders.edu.au/events/Whistleblowing_Bounties_as_an_AntiCorruption_Measure_2017.cfm. Accessed 26 June 2018

Giovannetti J, Cryderman J (2016) Alberta Braces for Longest Economic Slump Since 1980s. *Globe and Mail*. https://www.theglobeandmail.com/news/alberta/alberta-ndp-confirms-provinces-recession-to-last-into-2016/article28877029/. Accessed 11 Dec 2017

Halpern P, Cakebread C, Christopher et al (2016) *Back from the Brink: Lessons from the Canadian Asset-Backed Commercial Paper Crisis*. University of Toronto Press, Toronto

Heyes A, Kapur S (2009) An Economic Model of Whistleblower Policy. *J L Econ & Org* 25:157

Hodgson C (2017a) The UK Tax Collector has Paid Informants Nearly £2 Million Since 2013. *UK Business Insider*. http://uk.businessinsider.com/hmrc-paid-informants-nearly-2-million-2017-10. Accessed 12 June 2018

Hodgson C (2017b) The Millions HMRC Pays to Informants May Not be Value for Money. *UK Business Insider*. http://uk.businessinsider.com/millions-hmrc-pays-informants-value-2017-10. Accessed 12 June 2018

Kesselheim AS, Studdert DM, Mello JD (2010) Whistle-Blowers' Experiences in Fraud Litigation Against Pharmaceutical Companies. *N Engl J Med* 362(19):1832

King ME (2011) Blowing the Whistle on Dodd-Frank Amendments: The Case Against the New Amendments to the Whistleblower Protection in Section 806 of Sarbanes-Oxley. *Am Crim L Rev* 48:1457

Knott M (2016) Revealed: Senate Deal Could See Whistleblowers Paid a Bound for Exposing Wrongdoing. *Sydney Morning Herald*. https://www.smh.com.au/politics/federal/revealed-senate-deal-could-see-whistleblowers-paid-a-bounty-for-exposing-wrongdoing-20161122-gsur7b.html. Accessed 8 June 2018

Langevoort DC (2009) The SEC and the Madoff Scandal: Three Narratives in Search of a Story. *Mich St L Rev* 899–914

Lipton E (2012) A Legal Circle Reaches Deep to Aid Obama. *NYTimes.com*. https://www.nytimes.com/2012/10/02/us/politics/whistle-blower-lawyers-donate-to-obama-campaign.html. Accessed 23 May 2018

National Whistleblowers Center (2010) *Impact of Qui Tam Laws on Internal Corporate Compliance: National Whistleblowers Center Report to the Securities and Exchange Commission*. http://www.whistleblowers.org/index.php?option=com_content&task=view&id=1169&Itemid=1167. Accessed 22 June 2018

Ontario Securities Commission (2014) *OSC Staff Notice 15-702 Revised Credit for Cooperation Program*. http://www.osc.gov.on.ca/documents/en/Securities-Category1/sn_20140311_15-702_revised-credit-coop-program.pdf. Accessed 6 July 2018

Ontario Securities Committee (2015a) *OSC Staff Consultation Paper 15-401, Proposed Framework for an OSC Whistleblower Program*. http://www.osc.gov.on.ca/documents/en/Securities-Category1/rule_20150203_15-401_whistleblower-program.pdf. Accessed 6 July 2018

Ontario Securities Commission (2015b) *Comment Letters for 15-401 Proposed Framework for an OSC Whistleblower Program*. http://www.osc.gov.on.ca/en/47231.htm. Accessed 4 June 2018

Ontario Securities Commission (2015c) *Unedited Transcript, Roundtable Discussion Re Whistleblower Roundtable*. http://www.osc.gov.on.ca/en/SecuritiesLaw_rule_20150609_15-401_whistleblower-program-roundtable-transcript.htm. Accessed 6 July 2018

Ontario Securities Commission (2016a) *Comment Letters Fir 15-401—Whistleblower Program*. http://www.osc.gov.on.ca/en/49883.htm. Accessed 9 July 2018

Ontario Securities Commission (2016b) *OSC Launchers Officer of the Whistleblower*. http://www.osc.gov.on.ca/en/NewsEvents_nr_20160714_osc-launches-whistleblower.htm. Accessed 7 Dec 2017

Ontario Securities Commission Policy 15-601 (2016c) *Whistleblower Program*. http://www.osc.gov.on.ca/documents/en/Securities-Category1/20160714_15-601_policy-whistleblower-program.pdf. Accessed 9 July 2018

Ontario Securities Commission (2017) *Annual Report*. http://www.osc.gov.on.ca/documents/en/Publications/Publications_rpt_2017_osc-annual-rpt_en.pdf. Accessed 12 Dec 2017

Ontario Securities Commission (2019) *News Release, OSC Awards $7.5 Million to Three Whistleblowers*. https://www.osc.gov.on.ca/en/NewsEvents_nr_20190227_osc-awards-to-three-whistleblowers.htm. Accessed 8 May 2019

Paredes TA (2011) *Statement at Open Meeting to Adopt Final Rules for Implementing the Whistleblower Provisions of Section 21F of the Securities Exchange Act of 1934*. https://www.sec.gov/news/speech/2011/spch052511tap-item2.htm. Accessed 6 July 2018

Parliamentary Joint Committee of Corporations and Financial Services (2017) *Whistleblower Protections*. https://www.aph.gov.au/Parliamentary_Business/Committees/Joint/Corporations_and_Financial_Services/WhistleblowerProtections/Report. Accessed 13 June 2018

Pitzer DD (1972) The Qui Tam Doctrine: A Comparative Analysis of Its Application in the United States and the British Commonwealth. *Tex Int'l L J* 7:415

Puri P (2012) Securities Litigation and Enforcement: The Canadian Perspective. *Brook J Int'l L* 37(3):967

Rapp G (2007) Beyond Protection: Invigorating Incentives for Sarbanes-Oxley Corporate and Securities Fraud Whistleblowers. *BU L Rev* 87:91

Rapp G (2012) Mutiny by the Bounties—The Attempt to Reform Wall Street by the New Whistleblower Provisions of the Dodd-Frank Act. *BYUL L Rev* 73:151

Securities and Exchange Commission (2010) *Proposed Rules for Implementing the Whistleblower Provisions of Section 21F of the Securities Exchange Act of 1934*, 17 CFR Parts 240 and 249, [Release No. 34-63237; File No. S7-33-10]. https://www.sec.gov/rules/proposed/2010/34-63237.pdf. Accessed 6 July 2018

Securities and Exchange Commission (2011) *Whistleblowers Incentive and Protections Final Rules*, [Release No. 34-64545; File No. S7-33-10]. https://www.sec.gov/rules/final/2011/34-64545.pdf. Accessed 4 July 2018, p 229

Securities and Exchange Commission (2012) *Annual Report to Congress Whistleblower Program*. https://www.sec.gov/files/annual-report-2012.pdf. Accessed 6 July 2018

Securities and Exchange Commission (2013) *Annual Report to Congress Whistleblower Program*. https://www.sec.gov/files/annual-report-2013.pdf. Accessed 6 July 2018

Securities and Exchange Commission (2014) *Annual Report to Congress Whistleblower Program*. https://www.sec.gov/about/offices/owb/annual-report-2014.pdf. Accessed 6 July 2018

Securities and Exchange Commission (2015) *Annual Report to Congress on Dodd-Frank Whistleblower Program*. https://www.sec.gov/files/owb-annual-report-2015.pdf. Accessed 9 July 2018

Securities and Exchange Commission (2016) *Annual Report to Congress on Dodd-Frank Whistleblower Program*. https://www.sec.gov/files/owb-annual-report-2016.pdf Accessed 9 July 2018

Securities and Exchange Commission (2017) *Annual Report to Congress Whistleblower Program*. https://www.sec.gov/files/sec-2017-annual-report-whistleblower-program.pdf. Accessed 15 Dec 2017

Securities and Exchange Commission (2018) *Annual Report to Congress Whistleblower Program*. https://www.sec.gov/sec-2018-annual-report-whistleblower-program.pdf. Accessed 8 May 2019

Senate Economics References Committee (2014) *Performance of the Australian Securities and Investments Commission*. https://www.aph.gov.au/Parliamentary_Business/Committees/Senate/Economics/ASIC/Final_Report/index. Accessed 12 June 2018

Shapiro M (2009) *Testimony to the Subcommittee of Financial Services and General Government Appropriations Committee (111 Congress)*. https://www.scribd.com/document/328584364/SENATE-HEARING-111TH-CONGRESS-FINANCIAL-SERVICES-AND-GENERAL-GOVERNMENT-APPROPRIATIONS-FOR-FISCAL-YEAR-2010. Accessed 23 May 2018

Shecter B (2017) Alberta Securities Watchdog Considering Whistleblower Program—But Sorry, No Financial Reward. *Financial Post*. https://business.financialpost.com/news/fp-street/alberta-securities-watchdog-considering-whistleblower-program-but-sorry-no-reward. Accessed 11 Dec 2017

Southwick R (2017) Alberta Adopting Whistleblower Program for Securities Violations Without Rewards for Tips. *Calgary Herald*. https://calgaryherald.com/business/local-business/alberta-adopting-whistleblower-program-for-securities-violations. Accessed 11 Dec 2017

Stigler G (1971) The Theory of Economic Regulation. *Bell J Econ Manag Sci* (now *RAND J Econ*) 2:3

Sukdeo V (2009) Corporate Crime: The Need to Increase Enforcement and Compliance. *CLEA 2009 Annual Meeting Paper*. https://papers.ssrn.com/sol3/papers.cfm?abstract_id=1427508. Accessed 6 July 2018

The Economist (2016) *Payouts for Whistelblowers: Whistle While You Work*. https://www.economist.com/finance-and-economics/2016/07/14/whistle-while-you-work. Accessed 9 July 2018

Tingle BC (1994) The Strange Case of the Crown Prerogative Over Public Prosecutions or Who Killed Public Interest Law Enforcement? *UBC L Rev* 28:309–365

Treasury Options Paper (2009) *Improving Protections for Corporate Whistleblowers*. http://archive.treasury.gov.au/contentitem.asp?ContentID=1620. Accessed 15 June 2018

UK Parliamentary Commission on Banking Standards Fifth Report (2013) *Changing Banking for Good*. https://publications.parliament.uk/pa/jt201314/jtselect/jtpcbs/27/27ii02.htm. Accessed 12 June 2018

US Chamber of Commerce (2011) *U.S. Chamber Warns New SEC Whistleblower Rule will Undermine Corporate Compliance Programs*. https://www.uschamber.com/press-release/us-chamber-warns-new-sec-whistleblower-rule-will-undermine-corporate-compliance. Accessed 23 May 2018

U.S. Department of the Treasury Fact Sheet (2009) *Administration's Regulatory Reform Agenda Moves Forward Legislation for Strengthening Investor Protection Delivered to Capitol Hill*. https://www.treasury.gov/press-center/press-releases/Pages/tg205.aspx. Accessed 6 July 2018

Vaughn RG (2012) *The Successes and Failures of Whistleblower Laws*. Edward Elgar, Cheltenham

West R, Skarbnik JH, Brunetti FL (2012) A Primer for Tax Whistleblowers. *Taxes* 90:27

White MJ (2016) *SEC Chair White Offers A New Model for Enforcement*. https://www.sec.gov/news/speech/chair-white-speech-new-york-university-111816.html. Accessed 11 May 2018

Winston EI (2009) The Flawed Nature of the False Marking Statute. *Tenn L Rev* 77:111

Wyatt E (2011) S.E.C. Adopts Its Revised Rules for Whistle-Blowers. *New York Times*. https://dealbook.nytimes.com/2011/05/25/s-e-c-adopts-final-rules-for-whistle-blowers/. Accessed 6 July 2018

Janet Austin is an Associate Professor in the Faculty of Law, University of New Brunswick, Canada. She previously lectured at the University of New South Wales, Sydney, Australia and spent many years as a senior prosecutor at Australia's federal prosecution service, the Commonwealth Director of Public Prosecutions, where she conducted significant prosecutions for securities fraud. During her career she also practiced as a lawyer for Australia's corporate and securities regulator, the Australian Securities and Investments Commission and for private commercial law firms. She obtained her Ph.D. from Osgoode Law School, York University, Canada and has published many journal articles and book chapters in relation to white-collar crime and its detection, investigation and prosecution.

Part II
Regulatory, Theoretical and Governance Aspects in Relation to Corporate Whistleblowing

Chapter 4
Paid Whistleblowers and Paid Compliance Programs: Opposite Sides of the Same Coin

Ken Jull

Abstract The phrase "paid whistleblower" conjures up for most people the image of a person "coming in from the cold" to the office of a governmental regulator and receiving a bounty for so doing. In this chapter, I argue that the flip side of the coin (that is, payments to a whistleblower) is the concept of paying people for compliant behaviour as part of their annual performance or compensation review. Why should we wait for really bad events to occur in order to pay people for ethical conduct? To the contrary, a compensation system should recognize and reward compliant behavior. This is not the norm in North America, but should be.

Keywords Employee compensation · Compliance culture · Compensation for compliance · Whistleblower incentive · Whistleblower award · Compliance program

4.1 Introduction

The phrase "paid whistleblower" conjures up for most people the image of a person "coming in from the cold" to the office of a governmental regulator and receiving a bounty for so doing.[1] In an academic forum on compliance, the topic of paid whistleblowing prompted some commentators to argue that it should not be necessary to pay people to do the right thing.[2] This is a nice platitude, but ignores the reality faced by most whistleblowers. Only a whistleblower can explain the feeling of being excluded from future prospects and social circles. Only a whistleblower can explain

---

[1] We have to live without sympathy, don't we? We can't do that forever. One can't stay out of doors all the time. One needs to come in from the cold" The Spy Who Came in from the Cold (1965), Quotes, https://www.imdb.com/title/tt0059749/quotes and see Archibald and Jull (2018a).

[2] Canadian Business Ethics Research Network (CBERN) CEU Educating for Integrity Conference. Thursday, November 5–Saturday, 7 November, 2015. York University, Toronto.

K. Jull (✉)
Gardiner Roberts LLP, Toronto, Canada
e-mail: kjull@grllp.com

S. Lombard et al. (eds.), *Corporate Whistleblowing Regulation*,
https://doi.org/10.1007/978-981-15-0259-0_4

the reaction of spouses and significant others to loss of income and an uncertain future.

The concept of whistleblowing is generating a lot of research and thought, as demonstrated by a two-day conference held in Toronto in 2017 devoted only to that topic.[3] A recurring theme at that conference was the retaliation experienced by many whistleblowers, in both economic, emotional and in some cases physical forms of intimidation. The conference highlighted the complexity of designing a system that protects and compensates or incentivizes whistleblowers to come forward in a manner that leads to useful evidence being obtained.

In this chapter, I argue that the flip side of the coin (that is, paying a whistleblower) is the concept of paying people for compliant behaviour as part of their annual performance or compensation review. Why should we wait for really bad events to occur in order to pay people for ethical conduct? To the contrary, a compensation system should recognize and reward compliant behavior. This is not the norm in North America, but should be.

4.2 Paid Whistleblower Regimes

A prime example of a paid whistleblower programme is that run by the United States Securities and Exchange Commission. The Commission has awarded over $326 million to 59 individuals since the beginning of the whistleblower program. In FY 2018 alone, the SEC awarded more than $168 million in whistleblower awards to 13 individuals whose information and cooperation assisted the Commission in bringing successful enforcement actions. This amount exceeds the total amount awarded in all prior years combined and reflects the significance of the information that whistleblowers are reporting to the Commission.[4]

The SEC is proud of the program's added value in the protection of the investors. Since the program's inception, the SEC has ordered wrongdoers in enforcement matters brought with information from meritorious whistleblowers to pay over $1.7 billion in total monetary sanctions, including more than $901 million in disgorgement of ill-gotten gains and interest, of which approximately $452 million has been, or is scheduled to be, returned to harmed investors.[5]

Whistleblower awards have received significant media attention in the United States. Bradley Birkenfeld, a former UBS banker, blew the whistle on how UBS wooed thousands of rich Americans and helped them evade U.S. taxes. Not only did Mr. Birkenfeld lose any prospect of future employment in the banking industry, he was also prosecuted for taking part in the UBS scheme he reported upon and was sentenced to 40 months in prison, 10 more months than the prosecutors sought.

[3]The Canadian Institute, Corporate Whistleblower Compliance, https://www.canadianinstitute.com/corporate-whistleblower-compliance. See also Chap. 2, Baer (2017) and Givati (2018).

[4]Securities and Exchange Commission (2018a, p. 1).

[5]Ibid.

Mr. Birkenfeld was paid a whistleblower bounty of $104 million. The information provided by Bradley Birkenfeld helped the Internal Revenue Service (IRS) collect more than $5 billion in unpaid taxes from banks and individuals.[6] A 2017 article uses this case to develop an economic model that assists in determining how much whistleblowers should be paid. In "Of Snitches and Riches: Optimal IRS and SEC Whistleblower Rewards",[7] Yehonatan Givati develops an economic model that takes into account complex factors beyond the mere magnitude of the rewards and gains. Givati provides the following example of other factors to consider:

> A higher personal cost to whistleblowers from blowing the whistle requires a higher whistleblowing reward. This means that different whistleblowers may receive different amounts, depending on their circumstances, even when the same type of information is provided. For example, it may be necessary to pay higher rewards to young employees at a start-up firm than to older employees who are about to retire from a car manufacturing firm, since the cost of blowing the whistle to the former group, in terms of the reduction in future employment prospects, is likely higher.[8]

The Ontario Securities Commission (OSC) announced on June 16, 2016 the appointment of a Chief of the Office of the Whistleblower. The Office of the Whistleblower opened to receive tips on July 14, 2016. The OSC's Office of the Whistleblower is the first paid whistleblower program by a securities regulator in Canada.[9]

The OSC whistleblower program is complex.[10] If there is an award eligible outcome (defined in terms of the meaningful assistance to Commission Staff in investigating the matter and other criteria) the Commission will pay an eligible whistleblower an award of between 5 and 15% of the total monetary sanctions imposed and/or voluntary payments made. The amount is capped at $1.5 million or if collections exceed $10 million, the cap is $5 million.[11]

In 2019 the Ontario Securities Commission paid $7.5 million to whistleblowers in the inaugural use of a first-of-its-kind program in Canada that pays for tips leading to findings of wrongdoing under securities law. The three recipients receiving the cash were not identified by the OSC, which pledges to take "all reasonable efforts" to protect the identity of whistleblowers. "These individuals voluntarily provided high quality, timely, specific and credible information, which helped advance enforcement actions resulting in monetary payments to the OSC," the OSC Office of the Whistleblower said in a statement. "These whistleblower awards are the first ever by a Canadian securities regulator."[12]

---

[6] Givati (2018, pp. 106–107).

[7] Givati (2018).

[8] Ibid., p. 111.

[9] Ontario Securities Commission (2016a).

[10] Ontario Securities Commission (2016b).

[11] Ibid.

[12] Schecter (2019).

The OSC scheme contains a clause disentitling a whistleblower from an award in certain circumstances. I have previously described this clause as "the Achilles heel of the programme".[13] The "no award clause" reads as follows:

> No award - circumstances
>
> 20. The Commission will generally not make a whistleblower award in the following circumstances: (a) there is a determination that an individual who submitted information to the Commission is not an eligible whistleblower; or (b) the outcome of any proceeding resulting from a whistleblower submission is not an award eligible outcome (e.g., the matter is pursued quasi-criminally, the voluntary payments made and/or monetary sanctions ordered are less than $1,000,000 or the Commission's decision to order monetary sanctions is overturned on appeal).[14]

The fundamental flaw with the above "no award clause" is that a whistleblower does not have a crystal ball to predict how a proceeding will unfold. The programme requires that a whistleblower take a leap of faith and risk her career, in the expectation that the OSC whistleblower policy will offset that career loss with compensation.

If an Ontario securities matter is pursued quasi-criminally, there is no entitlement to an award. Presumably the reason for this is that any fines received in that offence forum would go to the provincial government and not the OSC directly. The problem with this is that the whistleblower has no control over, nor any ability to predict, which enforcement route the OSC will take. The irony is that a whistleblower may feel morally that more serious conduct deserves to be reported and yet this more serious conduct which ought to be prosecuted as a quasi-criminal matter will not yield an award.

The same problems of predictability present with the threshold amount of $1 million and the issue of a sanction being overturned. Again, a whistleblower has no ability to predict such contingencies. A related problem is delay in the appeal process. A whistleblower may be forced out of a job as a result of reporting to the OSC and during that period of unemployment will be in need of immediate funds; an appeal that delays receipt of funds is worrisome.

Some regulators have chosen not to use paid whistleblower programmes. Quebec's securities regulator has launched a whistleblower program to attract tips about crimes, but says it will not pay for the information. The Autorité des marchés financiers (AMF) said on June 20, 2016 that it has launched a whistleblower program that is intended to offer protections to individuals who report wrongdoing, including offering tippers immunity from potential civil lawsuits as a result of their reporting.[15] But the Quebec regulator said it will not take the approach of the Ontario Securities Commission:

> The AMF said it has reviewed whistle-blower programs in Britain and Australia, which do not pay for tips, and said it cannot be "established with certainty" that financial incentives

[13] Archibald and Jull (2018b), 7:20:18.10—Whistleblowers: Another Reason to Compensate Compliance.

[14] Ontario Securities Commission (2016b).

[15] Autorité des marchés financiers (2016).

> lead to better information. The regulator said it believes whistle-blowers want confidentiality and protection more than cash payments.[16]

A paid whistleblower programme is useful, although it is not a panacea or replacement for corporate compliance techniques or robust law enforcement. A paid programme recognizes the reality that companies who are engaged in illegal behaviour may retaliate against whistleblowers and terminate their employment immediately. A paid programme ensures that whistleblowers have a safety net for themselves and their families that will be available during a very stressful period.

4.3 The Zone of Non-discovery by Government and Internal Whistleblowing

Scholarship in the area of whistleblowing has explored the difference between incentives created by paid whistleblower schemes and corporate incentives to come forward (such as deferred prosecution programs).[17]

In *Digital Realty*,[18] the Supreme Court of the United States held that the whistleblower provisions of the Securities Exchange Act of 1934 (Exchange Act) require that a person report a possible securities law violation to the U.S. Securities and Exchange Commission ("SEC") in order to qualify as a whistleblower protected against employment retaliation under Section 21F(h) of the Dodd-Frank Wall Street Reform and Consumer Protection Act (Dodd-Frank), thus invalidating the SEC's rule interpreting that provision's anti-retaliation protections to apply regardless of whether a report of possible securities law violations was made to the Commission, to a different government agency, or internally to an employer.[19] The ruling resolved a Circuit Court split regarding whether individuals who had reported only to their employers, rather than to the Commission, were protected under Dodd-Frank's anti-retaliation protections. This is a significant change in whistleblower protections, and potential whistleblowers should be mindful of this ruling when deciding when to report their concerns to the SEC. Following the ruling, the SEC proposed amendments to bring the Whistleblower Rules in line with the holding of the Court.[20]

In the OSC scheme, the Commission encourages whistleblowers who are employees to report potential violations of Ontario securities law in the workplace through an internal compliance and reporting mechanism in accordance with their employer's internal compliance and reporting protocols. However, the Commission does not require whistleblowers to do so, recognizing that there may be circumstances in

[16] McFarland (2016).

[17] Baer (2017).

[18] 138 S. Ct. 767 (2018).

[19] Securities and Exchange Commission (2018, p. 1).

[20] Securities and Exchange Commission (2018b).

which a whistleblower may appropriately wish not to report to an internal compliance and reporting mechanism.[21]

The "zone of non-discovery by government", is an area where government regulators have no knowledge of the issue and there is no reason for government authorities to suspect or investigate a company. The zone of non-discovery is depicted in the following diagram.

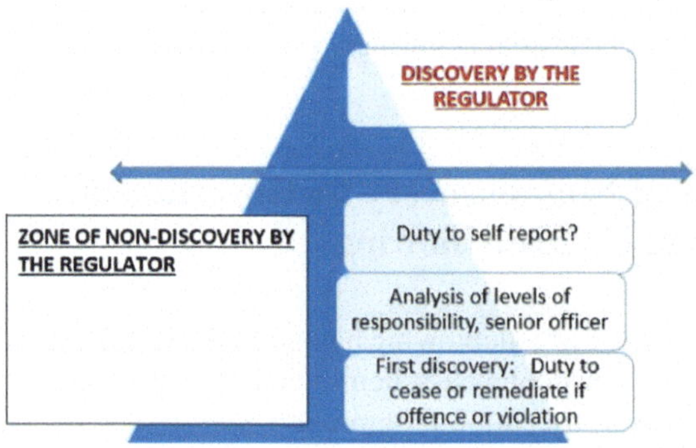

In the zone of non-discovery, whistleblowing may occur that is internal to an organization. An organization must consider the risks that if an internal investigation is not commenced, or prompt action is not taken, the whistleblower may consider going to the regulatory authorities, particularly if there is a paid whistleblowing policy.

In rare cases, a whistleblower may demand compensation, or settlement of a grievance by way of monetary payment, in return for silence or a promise to not go outside the zone of non-discovery to regulatory authorities. Under no circumstances should an organization make any payment or compensate a whistleblower to "buy silence" or prevent the report of potentially criminal conduct to the authorities. The act of "buying silence" is potentially a criminal offence known as "compounding", which is prohibited in the following section of the Canadian *Criminal Code*[22]:

> Compounding Indictable Offence
>
> 141 (1) Every one who asks for or obtains or agrees to receive or obtain any valuable consideration for himself or any other person by agreeing to compound or conceal an indictable offence is guilty of an indictable offence and liable to imprisonment for a term not exceeding two years.

Where the alleged offence is not criminal within the meaning of the Criminal Code (such as a provincial regulatory offence in Canada) or is an alleged violation subject to an administrative monetary penalty, as a matter of policy, the same considerations apply. Organizations should not buy silence or cover up violations of the law.

An incentive for an organization to do a proper investigation following an internal whistleblower submission is the existence of a deferred prosecution programme.

---

[21]Ontario Securities Commission Policy 15-601 (2016b, para 16).

[22]RSC 1985, c C-46.

Canada has recently enacted such a programme in a new part of the Criminal Code concerning "Remediation Agreements".[23] The recent political furor over whether SNC-Lavalin ought to be considered for a deferred prosecution agreement may have put a temporary chill in the air for those thinking of coming in from the cold.[24]

4.4 Proactive Compensation for Compliance

A compliance system must be implemented at the operational level. Different groups in an organization may have competing interpretations of how to best implement a compliance system. This very important point is made by Donna Kennedy-Glans and Bob Schulz in their book *Corporate Integrity: A Tool Kit for Managing beyond Compliance*.[25] Kennedy-Glans and Schulz develop an integrity grid, which is similar to matrix planning. One insight they add is that different people in an organization may have different levels of commitment to corporate integrity. They give a hypothetical example of a small, family-run business where different generations of the family may have different views toward environmental compliance.[26]

The solution to bringing corporate walk into line with corporate talk, and to implement value change throughout the organization, is linked to compensation. Simply put, most companies in North America do not compensate employees or managers for positive regulatory compliance, although most treat non-compliance as grounds for discipline. Compensation schemes must be revised to reward integrity, a point made by Kennedy-Glans and Schulz:

> In order to encourage corporate walk on integrity, employees must be rewarded for behaviours that are aligned to the corporate talk on integrity.
>
> A corporation's clarity in defining business integrity expectations and measuring outcomes of strategy influences its organizational ability to assess individual, departmental, and overall organizational business integrity performance. If there is a lot of talk about the importance of business integrity — but without corresponding recognition and rewards for positive employee and departmental alignment with corporate business integrity expectations in corporate compensation schemes — the commitments quickly become nothing more than rhetoric.[27]

Feedback mechanisms are essential to organizational learning. An excellent contribution to this literature is Pentti Sydanmaanlakka's creative book entitled *An Intelligent Organization*.[28] Sydanmaanlakka was the former director of human resources

---

[23] Archibald and Jull (2018b), INT:90:100:10 Legislation to Enact a Canadian Deferred Programme.

[24] See Buzzetti (2019), CBC (2019), LeBlanc and Fine (2019), K. Jull's testimony as an expert witness on remediation (deferred prosecution) agreements, Standing Committee on Justice and Human Rights (2019) and Jull (2019).

[25] Kennedy-Glans and Schulz (2005).

[26] Kennedy-Glans and Schulz (2005, Chap. 9).

[27] Kennedy-Glans and Schulz (2005, p. 276).

[28] Sydanmaanlakka (2002).

at Nokia. Sydanmaanlakka considered that "a good feedback culture needs openness, trust, respect for the individual, informative communication, an acceptance of mistakes, good team spirit, support for other people and an ambition for continuous learning. The feedback system does not work without all these values".[29]

Theories of management that were popular in the 1990s developed a "balanced scorecard" that went beyond financial issues to include learning and growth.[30] If one looks at the standard performance appraisal form (and I suggest that the reader should try this test on his or her own organization), a box for "compliance culture" feedback probably does not exist. Instead, what one will see are categories such as "contribution to work of others, attitude, customer satisfaction etc."

Perhaps one reason for the absence of a box for "compliance" is the difficulty in quantifying ethical behaviour. I do not see this as an insurmountable obstacle. We should look at performance appraisals in other countries that have successful compliance records. For an example, Nokia's Performance Management form ranked values such as "respect for the individual", "knowledge sharing" and "continuous learning".[31]

Quantifying ethical behavior could be tied to factors such as low rates of regulatory complaints, good record keeping, and principled decision-making. Regulatory compliance will involve trade-offs that may result in lower profits in some cases. It may require that a firm turn away business that appears to skate too close to the regulatory line. If the individual is not compensated for ethical behaviour, there is incentive to fly below the radar and hope that one does not get caught with regulatory non-compliance. Enron teaches this important lesson, if nothing else.

There should be a box in the performance appraisal form for compliance. It should be taken seriously. It is a fact of human nature that in a competitive environment where there are many tasks, due diligence will be shunted to the bottom of the pile unless it is rewarded along with the other tasks.

The relationship between performance appraisal and ethical conduct can be seen to some degree in the microcosm of a law school class. Students are taught ethics as part of legal options, but they generally will not read the materials unless they are told that the ethics materials are examinable. It is not that law students are not interested in ethics; rather, given the competition for marks and the high volume of work, they tend to view their assignments from a competitive and practical viewpoint. If ethics are not on the exam, then they are losing valuable reading time while studying ethics when the other students are using their time to study the core courses. This dynamic is translated into the competitive business world. Employees are rarely rewarded with a monetary benefit for outstanding ethical behaviour.

Compensation as a driving force goes right to the top of the corporate ladder. In her book entitled *Value Shift*,[32] Professor Paine of the Harvard Business School makes a convincing case for new ethical standards as a method of increasing profits.

---

[29] Sydanmaanlakka (2002, p. 45).

[30] Sydanmaanlakka (2002, pp. 104–5).

[31] Sydanmaanlakka (2002, Appendix 1).

[32] Paine (2003, p. 141).

The power of compensation is illustrated by Paine in using the case study of Sears, Roebuck and Co., which revised its compensation system in the auto repair centres in the 1990s. Those responsible for inspecting cars and advising customers on needed parts and repairs were switched to a combined salary and commission system. Paine described the results:

> By the summer of 1992, things had only gotten worse. Customer complaints against Sear's auto repair business — at the time, the largest company-owned automotive service organization in the United States — were spiraling out of control, and Sears had become the target of misconduct charges by officials in 44 states. Employees and former employees were coming forward with stories about the "pressure, pressure, pressure to get the dollars" and about the practices employed to do so. Across the country, 18 class action suits were pending against the company. The charges covered a host of alleged misdeeds including misleading customers, selling unnecessary repairs, charging for unauthorized work, issuing false invoices, carrying out negligent repair work, and violating various laws and regulations governing the auto repair business.[33]

Paine concluded that while no one foresaw nor intended the ethical violations that ensued, "they were a natural and predictable outcome of the new compensation and quota systems given the context in which they were implemented."[34]

Compensation as a strong motivator is not limited to employees. In the last decade directors were increasingly compensated with stock options that they could sell within a relatively short period of time, thereby creating a short-term focus that could lead to the ignoring of longer-term productivity or regulatory issues.[35] Roger Martin, Dean of the Rotman School of Management at the University of Toronto, draws a parallel to the world of sports in arguing that stock options are analogous to inside betting. In a creative and entertaining book entitled *Fixing the Game: Bubbles, Crashes, and What Capitalism Can Learn from the NFL*,[36] Martin uses the sports world of the National Football League to demonstrate parallels for good governance.

Martin extols the focus on the customer by the NFL, and the focus on actual results as compared to the "expectation market" created by betting on results, which is forbidden to players. By contrast, Martin argues that compensation models in business based on share options and other techniques focus on the expectation market in the stock market which creates incentives that may not be consistent with maximizing shareholder value.

In summary, Martin argues that the NFL, which is the most successful sports league in America, has many lessons for business:

> In part, we can learn from the NFL just what to do. We can begin by keeping our players from betting on the games they play. We can provide the right incentives to our executives — returning the focus to the real market and away from the expectations market. Like Peter Rozelle and his successors, we can endeavor to consistently tweak the rules to keep our fans happy, focusing our executives on customer delight rather than shareholder value.[37]

---

[33] Paine (2003, p. 169).

[34] Ibid.

[35] Millstein (2002, p. 22).

[36] Martin (2011).

[37] Martin (2011, pp. 217–218).

Apart from business culture, the judiciary also has a role to play in encouraging compensation for compliance. While courts cannot force companies to financially compensate employees for due diligence, they can reward those companies who do, by recognizing this culture as constituting an integral part of due diligence. In *R. v. National Waste Services Inc.*[38] the court recognized that the defendant company compensated employees by way of a bonus for regulatory compliance, and deducted pay for infractions:

> Drivers who follow safety measures receive at the beginning of each year a monetary bonus or are deducted an amount for infractions. In the case at bar, after this offence, the driver was suspended for three days, was deducted an infraction amount, and no longer works for the defendant company.[39]

The defendant driver in this case had driven a truck loaded with asphalt and insulation which was not properly covered, in breach of a regulation under Ontario's *Environmental Protection Act*. The driver had telephoned his manager to advise of problems with the tarp and was given instructions to use an alternate tarp arrangement, which he failed to comply with. The evidence of a due diligence program at the defendant's company was significant, including safety manuals that addressed tarps, and mandatory meetings discussing tarping, which the drivers were paid to attend. The company also had an independent company perform random spot checks and had a system for circle checks of the trucks before each trip.

Given the extensive due diligence system in place, the company was acquitted, even though in this particular case the driver had not complied with company policy. The compensation system of a bonus for compliance and the payment of drivers to attend training sessions was part of the overall program of due diligence.

In summary, on the issue of compensation, I encourage companies to pro-actively compensate for compliance, rather than waiting for bad things to prompt whistle-blowers.

4.5 Matrix Analysis and Compensation for Compliance

The use of matrix analysis is a core concept of risk management. A standard matrix in risk management balances two competing axes: "precautions taken to avoid the event" are weighed against "systems to measure potential gravity of impact". This matrix then gives an organization a plan of action based on priorities that should be accomplished first, second and so on.[40] The concept of compensation for compliance could be baked into a matrix analysis to compensate both accurate predictions made within the model and concrete actions taken in accordance with the priorities set by the model.

---

[38] 2004 ONCJ 53.

[39] Ibid. at para 7.

[40] Archibald and Jull (2018b), INT:10:40 Risk Matrix: Basic Principles.

I want to suggest that we can take this compensation model to the next level, in a further attempt to proactively encourage compliance (and by implication reduce the need for people to become paid whistleblowers). This next level is the positive matrix.

On one axis one could plot time, which is a standard graphical measurement. On the other axis one could plot reward/risk. In other words, risk can lead to rewards as well as negative outcomes. The following is an example[41]:

Profit			
Significant	Emotional wellness	Provides hope	Transcendence
Moderate	Quality	Fun/Entertainment	Affiliation/belonging
Minor	Simplifies	Integrates	Reduced anxiety
	Low	*Medium*	*High*
			Likelihood of achieving profit

The positive matrix can be used as an effective mechanism to change behaviour by providing rewards and incentives which will lead to corporate and organizational growth and prosperity. Instead of levels of harm, the positive axis plots level of profit. Instead of probability of harm occurring, the other axis plots the probability of reaching that profit through the mechanism of superior risk management and compliance.

Positive values such as hope, affiliation/belonging and fun/entertainment are actively promoted in the positive matrix to enhance profit and the likelihood of making that profit.

Step back and think about the positive matrix for a moment. When was the last time that you thought of your own workplace as fun or entertaining? Forward-looking companies explicitly provide for an atmosphere that enhances fun, creativity, and entertainment. Amid the fun, the paid whistleblower may become a relic of the past.

4.6 Conclusion

In his seminal book *Motivation and Personality* Abraham Maslow studied healthy self-actualized people in order to identify the traits of a healthy personality.[42] Maslow identified a hierarchy of human needs as follows:

1. the Physiological Needs

---

[41] Archibald and Jull (2018b), INT:10:160 Positive Risk Matrix—Basic Principles.

[42] A. H. Maslow's classic model was developed in his work, Maslow (1970).

2. the Safety Needs
3. the Belongingness or Love Needs
4. the Esteem Needs
5. the Need for Self-Actualization.

Maslow's hierarchy provides some signposts for an analysis of whistleblowing.

1. The Physiological Needs and 2. The Safety Needs

A whistleblower will likely have a mortgage to pay, and a family to support. Most people are dependent on a regular bi-weekly or monthly income. If a whistleblower feels that she may be sacrificing her regular income in order to come forward, this will significantly reduce the potential for her to do the right thing. Alternatively, she may fear that long term employment in a sector or industry may be threatened.

Basic human needs underline the importance of compensation for compliance, and creating a culture where compliance is rewarded. Industry compensation for assisting an organization to improve its compliance will reduce the need for regulators to compensate later for whistleblowing.

3. Belongingness or Love Needs

It is not all about money, however. Employees who feel that they are part of a welcoming business community are happier, and according to Maslow, will be healthier.

It is essential that an organization encourage feedback, perhaps anonymously, that improves compliance. In some cases compliance lapses may involve criticism of other employees, who will in turn isolate and retaliate against those who are seeking change.

In order to align with belongingness needs, there must be a safe harbor where people are encouraged, for the better good of the organization as a whole, to come in from the cold. Only in this way will belongingness be encouraged, as part of the holistic organization.

4. The Esteem Needs and 5. The Need for Self-Actualization

This chapter has attempted to argue that compliance requires a paradigm shift in culture. A person should feel that contribution towards compliance is not only rewarded, but increases their own self-esteem. A self-image of being a moral person who contributes to a larger goal of a just and fair workplace will contribute to both self-esteem and self-actualization.

These goals are easy to state, but much harder to put into practice. Imagine a corporate retreat where the agenda included discussion of topics such as occupational health and safety, gender and racial equity, environmental awareness, anti-corruption compliance, and the integrity of financial documents.

I ask the reader: Would the organization that you presently work with support a corporate retreat where these type of compliance topics were on the agenda? I bet that the answer is "No", as compliance is viewed as a back burner necessity that can be handled by a designated compliance group.

Until the paradigm shifts to encourage a compliance culture as part of an organization's future path to prosperity, I suspect that there will be more paid whistleblower rewards.

References

Archibald T, Jull K (2018a) *Coming in from the Cold: Deferred Prosecution (Remediation) Agreements in Canada*. Toronto Lawyer's Association. https://www.lexology.com/library/detail.aspx?g=7e176f28-6bbe-478e-8040-4b1bf808db67. Accessed 26 Apr 2019

Archibald T, Jull K (2018b [2019]) *Profiting from Risk Management and Compliance*. Thomson Reuters, Toronto

Autorité des marchés financiers (2016) *AMF Launches Whistleblower Program*. https://lautorite.qc.ca/en/general-public/media-centre/news/fiche-dactualites/amf-launches-whistleblower-program/. Accessed 26 Apr 2019

Baer MH (2017) Reconceptualizing the Whistleblower's Dilemma. *UCD L Rev* 50(2280):2235

Buzzetti H (2019) La ligne rouge a-t-elle été franchie? *Le Devoir*. https://www.ledevoir.com/politique/canada/548843/la-ligne-rouge-a-t-elle-ete-franchie. Accessed 26 Apr 2019

CBC Power and Politics (2019) *Bombshell Testimony Rocks the Government*. CBC Television

Givati Y (2018) Of Snitches and Riches: Optimal IRS and SEC Whistleblower Rewards. *Harv J Legis* 55:105

Jull K (2019) *The Case for–and Problem with–Remediation Deals Like the One SNC-Lavalin Wants*. Maclean's. https://www.macleans.ca/politics/the-case-for-and-problem-with-remediation-deals-like-the-one-snc-lavalin-wants/. Accessed 26 Apr 2019

Kennedy-Glans D, Schulz B (2005) *Corporate Integrity: A Tool Kit for Managing Beyond Compliance*. Wiley, Mississauga

LeBlanc D, Fine S (2019) SNC-Lavalin was Trudeau's Priority for New Minister of Justice, Wilson-Raybould Says. *The Globe and Mail*. https://www.theglobeandmail.com/canada/article-snc-lavalin-was-trudeaus-priority-for-new-minister-of-justice-wilson/. Accessed 26 Apr 2019

Martin R (2011) *Fixing the Game: Bubbles, Crashes and What Capitalism Can Learn from the NFL*. Harvard Business Review Press, Brighton

Maslow A (1970) *Motivation and Personality*, 2nd edn. Harper & Row, New York

McFarland J (2016) Quebec Securities Regulator Establishes Whistle-Blower Program, But Will Not Pay for Tips. *The Globe and Mail*. https://www.theglobeandmail.com/report-on-business/quebec-securities-regulator-establishes-whistle-blower-program/article30528133/ Accessed 26 Apr 2019

Millstein I (2002) *Greed, Governance and Self-Correction*. Professional Administrator (Institute of Chartered Secretaries and Administrators in Canada) 26:22

Ontario Securities Commission (2016a) *OSC Launchers Officer of the Whistleblower*. http://www.osc.gov.on.ca/en/NewsEvents_nr_20160714_osc-launches-whistleblower.htm. Accessed 26 Apr 2019

Ontario Securities Commission Policy 15-601 (2016b) *Whistleblower Program*. http://www.osc.gov.on.ca/documents/en/Securities-Category1/20160714_15-601_policy-whistleblower-program.pdf. Accessed 26 Apr 2019

Paine L (2003) *Value Shift: Why Companies Must Merge Social and Financial Imperatives to Achieve Superior Performances*. McGraw-Hill, Toronto

Schecter B (2019) Ontario Market Watchdog Pays $7.5 Million to Three Whistleblowers in Canada's First Reward for Tips. *Financial Post*. https://business.financialpost.com/news/fp-street/ontarios-market-watchdog-to-pay-7-5-million-to-three-whistleblowers Accessed 26 Apr 2019

Securities and Exchange Commission (2018a) *Annual Report to Congress Whistleblower Program.* https://www.sec.gov/files/sec-2018-annual-report-whistleblower-program.pdf. Accessed 5 Apr 2019
Securities and Exchange Commission (2018b) *SEC Proposes Whistleblower Rule Amendments.* https://www.sec.gov/news/press-release/2018-120. Accessed 26 Apr 2019
Standing Committee on Justice and Human Rights (2019) *House of Commons, Canada Evidence.* https://www.ourcommons.ca/DocumentViewer/en/42-1/JUST/meeting-133/evidence. Accessed 26 Apr 2019
Sydanmaanlakka P (2002) *An Intelligent Organization: Integrating Performance, Competence and Knowledge Management.* Capstone Publishing, Oxford

Kenneth Jull is a co-author of "Profiting from Risk Management and Compliance", an adjunct Professor at University of Toronto Faculty of Law and Osgoode Hall Law School and counsel at Gardiner Roberts LLP in the area of corporate compliance which includes internal investigations and trials where compliance is an issue.

Chapter 5
External Regulation and Internal Whistleblowing Frameworks: An Australian Perspective

Sulette Lombard and Vivienne Brand

Abstract Internal corporate whistleblowing systems, or 'institutionalised' whistleblowing, could offer valuable corporate governance benefits, particularly around notions of compliance and risk management. There are sound regulatory theories to explain the value of such systems as part of a corporate governance framework. The Australian legislature clearly recognises the benefits of such systems, as is illustrated by recent legislative reform that includes mandatory development of such systems for some companies. This chapter provides an overview of recent legislative reforms in relation to corporate whistleblowing, particularly around provisions aimed at ensuring development of internal whistleblowing frameworks. In addition, it analyses the approach adopted by the Australian legislature with reference to theories in relation to corporate governance and regulatory approaches to ensure development of such internal whistleblowing systems. The chapter lastly provides some comparison between the pre-reform practices of some of Australia's largest companies and the requirements of the new regime.

Keywords Whistleblowing · Corporate whistleblowing · Internal whistleblowing · Corporate regulation · Whistleblowing policies

5.1 Introduction

The 'doctrine of disclosure' has been entrenched in the corporate regulatory framework since its earliest iterations.[1] The focus in respect of the obligations imposed on

[1]Davies (2008) at 711 indicates that 'the founding fathers' of company law thought that providing information about the company to the public and members, would serve as 'a sure shield' and describes disclosure as 'the fundamental principle' underlying corporate regulation.

S. Lombard · V. Brand (✉)
Flinders University, Adelaide, Australia
e-mail: vivienne.brand@flinders.edu.au

S. Lombard
e-mail: sulette.lombard@flinders.edu.au

S. Lombard et al. (eds.), *Corporate Whistleblowing Regulation*,
https://doi.org/10.1007/978-981-15-0259-0_5

companies to report information has typically been on their value as a protective measure for those who have dealings with a corporate entity, for example shareholders, creditors, and potential investors.

Voluntary disclosure of information by insiders, in particular information about wrongdoing inside the organisation (whistleblowing), is also widely recognised as being very valuable,[2] as it presents an opportunity for early-intervention to address the wrongdoing that may not otherwise have been detected, or detected much later, thus potentially preventing or reducing harm to the corporate entity and/or its stakeholders.

In addition to the obvious benefit above, insider disclosures also offer regulatory benefits, as it reduces the monitoring or oversight burden on the regulator. It is accepted that 'public regulators will not be intimately familiar with the ongoing or inchoate wrongdoing committed by private individuals and business' and that '[i]nformation from insiders about such activity is needed before regulators can address it'.[3] Information provided by whistleblowers would not only be valuable in relation to detection of wrongdoing, but would also be valuable during a subsequent investigation of the alleged wrongdoing.[4]

This chapter aims to provide an overview of recent corporate whistleblowing legislative reform in Australia,[5] particularly with reference to the extent to which the new legislative provisions attempt to ensure development of internal whistleblowing frameworks. It also explores how the regulatory approach adopted by the Australian legislature aligns with certain governance and regulatory theories in relation to internal whistleblowing frameworks, and lastly aims to offer some practical insights into the practices of large, listed Australian corporations prior to the introduction of a more prescriptive legislative regime.

5.2 Legislative Reform and Internal Corporate Whistleblowing Frameworks

In line with the amount of regulatory interest generated by whistleblowing reforms in other jurisdictions in recent years,[6] the Australian legislature embarked on a project to review the effectiveness of private sector whistleblowing provisions. The process that initiated the legislative reforms commenced on 30 November 2016 with Senate referring an inquiry into *Whistleblower Protections in the Corporate, Public and Not-for-Profit Sectors* to the Parliamentary Joint Committee on Corporations and Financial Services, for report by 30 June 2017. The Australian government followed with the release of a discussion paper: Review of tax and corporate whistleblower

[2]See e.g. Devine et al. (2011), at 165; Pascoe and Welsh (2011), at 144; 146; Rapp (2013), at 389; Brand et al. (2013); Dixon (2016), at 169; and Mathiopoulos et al. (2017), at 262.

[3]Bucy (2002), at 940.

[4]Ibid., at 943.

[5]The *Treasury Laws Amendment (Enhancing Whistleblower Protections) Act 2019* (Cth) received Royal Assent on 12 March 2019.

[6]See Chap. 1 for a more detailed discussion in this regard.

protections in Australia (20 December 2016), and received numerous submissions up to the submission deadline of 10 February 2017. The reporting date was subsequently extended to 14 September 2017. The Report of the Parliamentary Joint Committee on Corporations and Financial Services *Whistleblower Protections*[7] was eventually released in September 2017, with the Inquiry culminating in the *Treasury Laws Amendment (Enhancing Whistleblower Protections) Act 2019* (Cth) receiving Royal Assent on 12 March 2019.

The Committee Report on Whistleblower Protections highlighted a number of issues in relation to existing whistleblowing regulations,[8] including focussing its attention on internal disclosures. The Committee indicates general support for protection for internal disclosures.[9] However, the Committee seems to regard internal reporting as an instance of 'first reporting', with a whistleblowing regulatory framework that also provides for *regulatory* reporting (reporting to a regulator) as a requirement to contribute to more effective disclosure of information. It is seen that a 'tiered approach' such as that would 'act as an additional incentive for organisations in the private and not-for-profit sectors to ensure that their internal reporting procedures and practices met best-practice criteria'.[10] The Committee Report on Whistleblower Protections, therefore, does not appear to contain a direct recommendation in relation to mandating internal reporting channels, but does recognise the benefits of internal disclosure, and the importance of ensuring that whistleblower protections are available where a whistleblower elects to disclose information about wrongdoing through an internal reporting channel.

However, the legislation went one step further and has chosen the path of providing for mandatory whistleblower policies for public companies,[11] large proprietary companies[12] and proprietary companies that are trustees of registrable superannuation entities.[13] Non-compliance with the statutory obligation to have such a policy

---

[7] Hereinafter 'Committee Report on Whistleblower Protections'.

[8] A number of these falls outside the scope of discussion for the purposes of this chapter, but include, for example, issues around a fragmented approach, thresholds for protection, anonymity of whistleblowers, remedies and sanctions for reprisals, whether a rewards system is desirable, etc. A copy of the complete report is available at https://www.aph.gov.au/Parliamentary_Business/Committees/Joint/Corporations_and_Financial_Services/WhistleblowerProtections/Report.

[9] Committee Report on Whistleblower Protections, Recommendation 8.1, at [8.10].

[10] Committee Report on Whistleblower Protections, at [8.15].

[11] *Treasury Laws Amendment (Whistleblowers) Act 2019* (Cth), ss 1317AI(1).

[12] *Treasury Laws Amendment (Whistleblowers) Act 2019* (Cth), ss 1317AI(2). In terms of the *Corporations Act 2001* (Cth), s 45A(3), a proprietary company is defined as a large proprietary company for a financial year if it satisfies at least 2 of the following paragraphs:

(a) the consolidated revenue for the financial year of the company and the entities it controls (if any) is $50 million or more
(b) the value of the consolidated gross assets at the end of the financial year of the company and the entities it controls (if any) is $25 million or more;
(c) the company and the entities it controls (if any) have 100 or more employees at the end of the financial year.

[13] *Treasury Laws Amendment (Whistleblowers) Act 2019* (Cth), ss 1317AI(3).

in place, is an offence of strict liability that would carry a fine.[14] The compulsory development of internal policies is justified on the basis that '[t]ransparent internal whistleblower policies are essential to good corporate culture and governance'[15] and are seen to be able to deter wrongdoing.[16]

The legislation also contains specific requirements in relation to the matters that must be set out in such a policy—these include information about the protections available to whistleblowers, to whom disclosures should be made and how they should be made, how the company will support whistleblowers and protect them from detriment, how the company will investigate disclosures, how the company will ensure fair treatment of employees, how the policy is to be made available to officers and employees of the company, as well as any matters prescribed by the regulations.[17] The rationale for leaving room to prescribed matters by regulation, is to ensure that there is sufficient flexibility to allow whistleblower policies to adapt to future changes and developments in relation to whistleblower protections and remedies.[18]

5.3 Regulatory Theories, Elements and Instruments

5.3.1 Regulatory Theories

5.3.1.1 New Governance Ideals

One could potentially argue that companies should be free to choose to develop internal whistleblowing systems, or not, as the benefits would speak for themselves, and the consequences of the decision not to do so (not reaping the subsequent governance benefits) will be carried by the companies who decide not develop such systems. On that basis, it could be argued that there is no need for regulation to 'demand' that companies develop such systems.

However, as indicated previously, internal whistleblowing systems are not exclusively to the benefit of the particular company. It is beneficial to the regulatory system as a whole, as it serves to alleviate the regulatory burden; it provides increased regulatory efficiency; and it aids in protecting the interests of corporate stakeholders who will benefit from a timely discovery and handling of wrongdoing within the company.

---

[14] *Treasury Laws Amendment (Whistleblowers) Act 2019* (Cth), s 1317AI(4).

[15] Explanatory Memorandum to the *Treasury Laws Amendment (Enhancing Whistleblower Protections) Bill 2017*, at [2.119].

[16] Explanatory Memorandum to the *Treasury Laws Amendment (Enhancing Whistleblower Protections) Bill 2017*, at [2.122].

[17] *Treasury Laws Amendment (Whistleblowers) Act 2019* (Cth), ss 1317AI(5).

[18] Explanatory Memorandum to the *Treasury Laws Amendment (Enhancing Whistleblower Protections) Bill 2017*, at [2.125].

In addition, internal whistleblowing systems have an important role to play as part of a company's compliance and risk management framework, as it serves as a mechanism by which the company can essentially 'police' its own behaviour.[19] The method of 'self-policing' is regarded as advantageous, due to suggestions that these 'corporate compliance programs can more cheaply and effectively regulate corporate employees than outside regulators'.[20]

On that basis we agree that development of internal whistleblowing systems should not be left as a purely voluntary step. However, neither should it be made a legal obligation, non-compliance with which will carry particular sanctions. A more preferable option would be for external regulation that would *encourage*, rather than *compel*, the development of such systems, also leaving room for some flexibility as to what such an internal whistleblowing system should look like. This raises the obvious question of the approach that regulation should take, or the type of regulatory approach that is required, to ensure that companies voluntarily 'elect' to develop internal whistleblowing systems. An approach that could be useful, is one which allows

> blurring the boundaries between the roles and functions of the public and private sectors in regulation, [whereby] policy-makers can create a new governance regulatory regime with the flexibility to adjust to problems as they arise, and with the necessary 'buy-in' from the private sector to encourage cooperation.[21]

The emphasis on new governance here is clear. New governance is sometimes referred to as 'a new approach in legal scholarship that emphasizes not legal doctrine or formal jurisprudence, but rather how change actually happens within complex real-life social systems'.[22] It could also be used as a term 'to describe a regulatory strategy or tool' or 'regulator attitude',[23] which is particularly relevant for this discussion. New governance emphasises the public-private collaboration, encourages a bottom-up approach, and views the regulator as a 'facilitator', rather than as a 'centralised rule-maker'.[24] The role of the regulated party is also transformed under new governance ideals, where they could be seen as 'partners in regulation, implicitly and explicitly enlisted to fill out the substance of legal norms and develop the means for implementing those broader principles locally'.[25]

Also useful in this context is Feaver and Sheehy's suggestion that legal concepts such as rules and legislation should be characterised as 'devices that influence actor behaviour, and hence, social practices'.[26] We suggest that these notions may offer

---

[19] See Austin and Lombard (2019).

[20] Baer (2008), at 526.

[21] Solomon (2010), at 624.

[22] Ford (2008), at 27.

[23] Solomon (2010), at 593.

[24] Simmons (2013), at 1153.

[25] Bamberger (2006), at 392.

[26] Feaver and Sheehy (2015), at 964.

some insights into how adoption and development of internal whistleblowing frameworks could occur, in line with the idea that the purpose of regulation should be to 'influence actor behaviour and…social practices'.[27]

Scholz's discussion in relation to the 'opposing' strategies of regulatory enforcement, namely deterrence and cooperation, as means to regulate business, adds an interesting perspective here. The deterrence or rule-making strategy, described as seeking to 'coerce compliance through the maximal detection and sanctioning of violations of legal rules' and often associated with distrust, is seen as the appropriate approach in respect of 'bad' firms.[28] The cooperative strategy adopts a different approach and 'emphasizes flexible or selective enforcement that takes into consideration the particular circumstances of an observed violation'—an approach that could be used for 'good' firms.[29] It is not suggested that the focus on 'cooperation' should be interpreted as an indicator of complete alignment with new governance ideals, even though clearly more closely aligned with new governance than the deterrence model, for the simple reason that the cooperative strategy still relies on a 'rule' that must be enforced, even though in a different, more 'cooperative' way. It does therefore not seem to allow as much scope for a 'cooperative', 'bottom-up', 'inside-out' development of the rule as new governance would suggest. What is interesting, however, is the suggestion that 'cooperative' regulation is appropriate for 'good' firms, whereas a stricter, 'top-down' enforcement should be used in the case of 'bad' firms. If this idea is extrapolated to the new governance context, the conclusion should be that new governance regulation could be appropriate for 'good' firms, whereas the deterrence model, which follows a much harsher top-down, rules-based, sanctioned approach, would be appropriate for 'bad', non-compliant firms.

5.3.1.2 Responsive Regulation and Smart Regulation

Also useful in this context is to look at whistleblowing regulation aimed at encouraging development of internal whistleblowing frameworks through the lense of well-known regulatory theoretical principles around responsive regulation and smart regulation.

Responsive regulation, described as a 'highly influential approach' in relation to regulation,[30] is a concept that was developed by Ian Ayres and John Braithwaite.[31] The idea underpinning the responsive regulation approach is that governments should be responsive to the conduct of those they seek to regulate in deciding whether a more or less interventionist response is needed. In particular, law enforcers should

[27] Ibid.

[28] Scholz (1984), at 179; 182.

[29] Scholz (1984), at 179; 182–183.

[30] Baldwin and Black (2008), at 61.

[31] Ayres and Braithwaite (1992).

be responsive to how effectively citizens or corporations are regulating themselves before deciding whether to escalate intervention.[32]

It is often expressed with reference to the well-known 'regulatory pyramid', to illustrate how enforcement action should escalate from a broad base of persuasion, to the most severe punitive measure at the apex of the pyramid, as shown below:[33]

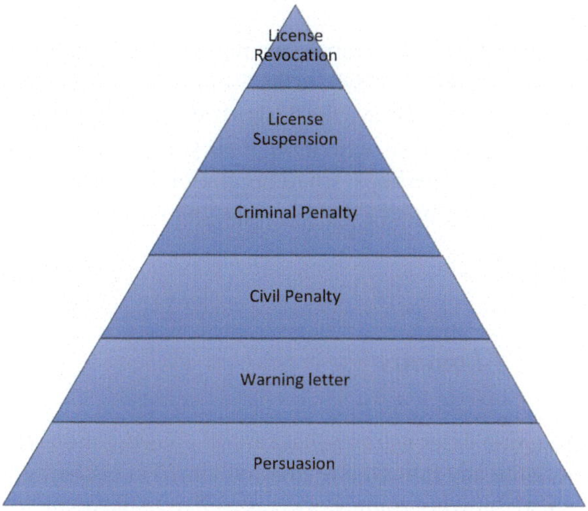

In the context of regulation aimed at ensuring development of internal whistleblowing systems, regulatory 'enforcement' should start from a base of 'persuasion' in order to achieve compliance. Only in cases where companies fail to respond to the 'softer' layers of regulation at the lower levels of the pyramid, should enforcement action become more punitive. In some ways, this corresponds with the suggestion above that 'good' firms should be exposed to less 'forceful' regulatory compliance measures than 'bad' firms.

'Smart regulation', as described by Gunningham, Grabosky and Sinclair,[34] builds on the principles underlying the approach of responsive regulation. However, in terms of smart regulation, enforcement is not only the responsibility of the role of the state, but also other parties who act as 'surrogate regulators'[35] and thus it embraces regulatory pluralism.

In both instances, the underlying principle is that enforcement action should become increasingly intrusive, only once the bottom layers of enforcement failed to succeed in achieving the desired behaviour on the part of the regulated entity. Both responsive and smart regulation also emphasise 'processes, instruments, and institutions that can be used in order to further regulatory objectives'.[36]

---

[32]Braithwaite (2002), at 29.

[33]Ayres and Braithwaite (1992), at 35.

[34]Gunningham et al. (1998).

[35]Gunningham and Sinclair (2011), at 135.

[36]Baldwin et al. (2011), at 267.

This outcome-driven focus, along with consideration of various mechanisms to achieve the desired regulatory outcome, appear to align well with new governance notions. Furthermore, responsive and smart regulation both allow room for adherence to the ideals of new governance concepts to the extent that regulated entities would be permitted to 'experiment',[37] thus potentially resulting in optimum regulatory outcomes, without the fear of immediately being 'sanctioned' for non-compliance with the 'letter of the law'.

However, it has been noted that responsive regulation ultimately relies on 'some form of "rule" that can...be enforced where the "softer" layers of regulation at the bottom parts of the pyramid fail to achieve the desired outcome'.[38] Such an interpretation would indicate that the 'responsive regulation' theory may not sit as comfortably with notions of new governance as perhaps 'smart regulation', which would instead permit 'regulatory pluralism that embraces flexible, imaginative and innovative forms...of control'.[39]

5.3.2 Regulatory Elements

The preceding discussion demonstrates that careful consideration should be given to the elements comprising any potential regulation aimed at encouraging the development of internal whistleblowing frameworks, as well as to the regulatory enforcement approach that is adopted. Regulation in terms of which corporate behaviour is to be influenced, requires two elements to have a chance of success. The first is the element that relates to the ability to cause future pain (sanctions), and the second relates to desired long-term results (what is desired?). This could be likened to the 'carrot-and-stick' type approach to achieve particular regulatory outcomes.

However, it is important to emphasise that the reference to 'the stick' element should not be interpreted as a desire for external regulation compelling development of internal whistleblowing systems (a typical top-down regulatory approach), coupled with regulatory sanction in cases of non-adherence to the rule, as a way to encourage the development of such systems. This approach is undesirable for a number of reasons.

Firstly, an external, top-down approach to force the development of internal whistleblowing systems would require regulatory policing to establish whether companies are complying with the obligation, as well as sanctions to ensure compliance, thus leading to an increased regulatory burden. In the Australian context this burden typically falls on the corporate regulator, the Australian Securities and Investment Commission, which is already perceived by some to be over-burdened and under-resourced.[40]

---

[37]Described as a 'hallmark' of new governance by Baer (2009), at 954–955.

[38]Austin and Lombard (2019).

[39]Gunningham and Sinclair (2011), at 133.

[40]See e.g. Gilligan (2013) and Maiden (2013).

Secondly, in line with the theories and concepts discussed above, an approach that facilitates and encourages internalisation of particular norms over time would be more effective to bring about a change in corporate culture and achieve the desired behaviour on the part of companies, compared to a traditional, top-down regulatory approach. It has been noted that 'the benefits of internal whistleblowing mechanisms include the fact that a well-developed internal system provides a "signal" to would-be whistleblowers that disclosures of wrongdoing are encouraged, thus creating a culture of transparency within an organisation'.[41] Once a culture of transparency is established, it could in fact be more successful in preventing wrongdoing, compared to external monitoring and sanctions.[42] Also, a free-flow of information up and down the corporate ladder, something that could be facilitated by internal whistleblowing systems, could serve to reduce wrongdoing within the corporation, 'in part because employees feel constrained to do the right thing'.[43]

Thirdly, command-and-control type regulation often leaves little room for discretion and flexibility, as it is aimed at formulating a particular 'rule' that could be applied universally. As such, its focus is traditionally 'narrow', rather than broad. This could prove to be especially problematic in the context of a rule that would apply to all companies, where their size and context could vary significantly. One is inclined to agree with Bamberger that rules that 'direct behavior towards compliance with an incomplete set of detailed provisions…may frustrate, rather than further, the broader regulatory goal in particular circumstances'.[44]

For these reasons our initial emphasis is on 'the carrot' aspect of the regulation, in line with an incentive-based regulatory approach.[45] It has been suggested that the 'carrot' in this instance could be a reduction in penalties where a company is found criminally liable,[46] or complete avoidance of sanctions where the company can demonstrate *bona fide* compliance efforts—an internal whistleblowing system being an example of such efforts.[47] In this way, the 'good' firm is rewarded for its good behaviour.

It is acknowledged, however, that these examples of 'the carrot' would only serve as a regulatory incentive where corporate criminal liability is a real threat. Where corporate criminal liability is unlikely, there is no real incentive to develop internal whistleblowing systems in order to obtain a reduction in penalty, or to avoid possible sanctions. For that reason, the 'carrot' aspect of the regulation should be framed

[41] Austin and Lombard (2019).

[42] Baer (2008), at 542.

[43] Baer (2008), at 542.

[44] Bamberger (2006), at 387.

[45] However, not all commentators are convinced of the success of such an approach. See e.g. Malloy (2003), at 512–516 for a summary of perceived flaws of this approach.

[46] There are already examples of analogous concepts in the 'adequate procedures' defence in terms of the UK *Bribery Act 2010*, s 7(2).

[47] Near and Dworkin (1998), at 1559. Examples of similar models already exist in other contexts: *Bribery Act 2010* (UK), s7; Ministry of Justice (UK) 'The *Bribery Act 2010:* Guidance' (Guidance, March 2011); US Department of Justice, *Principles of Federal Prosecution of Business Organizations* (2008) 14 [9-28.800].

broadly as an inducement ('a means of prompting behaviour using self-interest'[48]) that will serve to apply pressure to achieve the desired outcome in a broader context.[49]

Another way to 'induce' development of internal whistleblowing frameworks, is through the adoption of 'internal first' type regulation that would require whistleblowers to generally disclose internally first, where there are well-developed internal systems in place. In the absence of such systems, whistleblowers could potentially be permitted to report externally, even to the media.[50]

It is assumed that not all companies would necessarily be influenced to the same extent to develop internal whistleblowing systems by the above inducements. For those companies some form of external regulatory burden and/or sanction could still fulfil a useful purpose.

Mandatory reporting by companies in relation to the extent to which internal whistleblowing frameworks have been developed, could be useful here.[51] A mandatory reporting requirement could be integrated with existing corporate statutory reporting obligations to avoid an additional cost and regulatory burden being imposed on the company.[52] The purpose of a reporting obligation in this instance is to emphasise the importance of having such measures in place, and thus change corporate behaviour accordingly.[53]

5.3.3 Regulatory Instrument

Encouraging the development of internal whistleblowing systems through regulatory and quasi-regulatory measures is not an unknown concept. However, the question here is what would be an appropriate regulatory instrument, if the aim is to encourage the development of internal whistleblowing systems? One option is for the regulatory instrument to take statutory form. Another option is to encourage the development of internal whistleblowing systems by way of codes, rather than legislation.

In the Australian context, the significance of internal whistleblowing structures has been recognised increasingly by the ASX Corporate Governance Council, potentially indicating a preference for the 'code' option, rather than 'legislation' option. The Council introduced specific reference to whistleblowing into the Corporate Governance Principles in the second edition, released in 2007, and this material was

[48]Feaver and Sheehy (2015), at 986.

[49]Ibid.

[50]See Lombard and Brand (2018), at 39.

[51]The benefits of mandatory disclosure in relation to internal corporate whistleblower systems are discussed in Moberly (2006), at 1169–1170; see also Vivienne Brand and Sulette Lombard, submission to the Senate Standing Committees on Economics, Economics References Committee Inquiry into the performance of the Australian Securities and Investments Commission 19 February, 2014, at 3–4.

[52]Lombard and Brand (2018), at 39.

[53]See in general Hess (2007) and Topping (2012), at 46 who suggests that '[q]ualitative disclosure drives strategic thinking'.

carried over to the 2014, third iteration of the Principles.[54] The fourth iteration of the ASX Corporate Governance Council's Principles and Recommendations was released in February 2019. In relation to the possible content of a company's code of conduct the third edition suggested that such a code might:

> [i]dentify the measures the organisation follows to encourage the reporting of unlawful or unethical behaviour. This might include a reference to how the organisation protects "whistleblowers" who report violations in good faith.[55]

These provisions, while permissive rather than 'command-and-control' in their expression, appear to have created sufficient impetus amongst ASX listed entities to ensure the vast majority made provision for some form of internal whistleblower system. The relevant data is discussed further below. The most recent, fourth, iteration of the ASX Principles has further strengthened the encouragement given to listed entities to ensure they have a whistleblowing policy, with such a policy now being recommended and a list of suggestions being made for what such a policy might include.

In its continued emphasis on a 'light touch' approach, the ASX Corporate Governance Principles appear to offer a useful example of a regulatory system that allows for a public-private collaboration where companies have the flexibility to design their own programs and structures (albeit with increased encouragement and suggested detail being offered in the fourth edition of the Principles). Further the ASX Principles as a whole rely upon an 'if not why not' regulatory model, where compliance is not mandated but non-compliance must be explained.[56] This approach, combined with a flexibly worded recommendation on whistleblowing policy content differs very clearly from a 'top-down' regulatory approach of the kind we suggest may be counter-productive.

However, we recognise that these requirements only apply to listed entities, and even though the wider influence of 'soft' regulation such as the ASX Corporate Governance Principles should not be under-estimated,[57] legislative intervention could be required in order to ensure compliance across the spectrum.

5.3.4 How Do the Australian Legislative Reforms Compare?

On the face of it, the Australian legislature appears to have opted for a more traditional 'command and control' type of regulation to achieve the desired regulatory

---

[54] ASX Corporate Governance Council's *Corporate Governance Principles and Recommendations*, (3ed) 2014.

[55] Ibid., at 20.

[56] ASX Corporate Governance Council's *Corporate Governance Principles and Recommendations*, (4ed) 2019, 2.

[57] The impact of 'soft' regulation has been noted by numerous commentators. See e.g. Kingsford-Smith (2012), at 91, who explains that these types of guidelines could 'seep into the cracks and crannies of the organisation and into the expectations of its officers'.

outcome of ensuring that companies develop internal whistleblowing frameworks. This is evident from the instrument that is used; the way in which it is formulated to mandate, rather than to encourage particular behaviour; the amount of detail in order to prescribe what the internal whistleblowing framework should look like, as well as the fact that there is little by way of encouragement or a 'carrot' to ensure achievement of the desired regulatory outcomes, but the immediate 'stick' in the form of criminal liability and a fine in cases of non-compliance is at the forefront. There is little room for public-private collaboration between regulated entity and regulator in designing tailor-made programs and rules that are flexible and that could achieve optimum regulatory benefit, and real potential for regulated entities to comply with the minimum standards as set out in the legislation, merely to achieve 'compliance'.

The 'mandatory' model adopted by the Australian legislation could arguably offer certain advantages, in that it ensures participation in the scheme through directly triggering compliance by way of a sanction, instead of relying on 'indirect' influence to ensure adoption of the regulatory goal in question.[58]

5.4 Elements Comprising an Internal Whistleblowing Framework

As noted, existing external regulatory frameworks in Australia have not, until recently,[59] required the creation of good internal corporate whistleblowing structures. In spite of this, some companies, voluntarily sought the benefits of good internal structures, having chosen to implement their own frameworks. An interesting question is whether the 'voluntary' internal whistleblowing practices adopted by certain companies prior to the enactment of the new whistleblowing legislation, gave sufficient cause for concern to explain the approach that was adopted. Were internal whistleblowing frameworks absent to such an extent, or developed so poorly, that a legislative mandate was needed?

A review of some of the pre-existing 'voluntary' systems offers useful insight into prior practices, with a view to answering the above question. It also offers the opportunity to link the theoretical models discussed in this paper to concrete examples of whistleblowing in practice. The following section draws on available evidence of existing models from Australian corporate practice in place before the recent legislative amendments, and discusses linkages between those models and theoretical perspectives discussed in this paper.

[58] See e.g. Malloy (2003), at 518.

[59] See discussion Sect. 5.2 above.

5.4.1 A Comparison with Some Evidence from Prior Practice

Two separate reports are available in relation to the whistleblowing policies of Australia's largest corporations that were in place prior to the passage of the new mandatory requirements. The first study undertook a review of Australia's 200 largest listed corporations with a focus on anti-retaliation protections for whistleblowers in codes of conduct (T200 study).[60] The second study (by the authors of this Chapter), took a broader, thematic approach, identifying key themes in the whistleblowing policies of 20 of Australia's largest companies (T20 study).[61] Some interesting comparisons can be made between the reports of those studies and the mandated contents of internal whistleblowing policies under the new legislative provisions. The discussion that follows investigates those contrasts, structured by reference to the themes identified in the T20 study. Interestingly, both studies indicated that the vast majority of the companies reviewed had an internal whistleblowing policy of some kind,[62] suggesting that the non-prescriptive encouragement offered by the ASX Corporate Governance Principles was reasonably effective in ensuring broad implementation of whistleblowing policies.

Five major themes were identified by the T20 study in particular that offer an insight into the style and format of pre-regime policies. Those were: the presence of a description of whistleblowing and its importance; an effort to integrate the place of whistleblowing within the corporation's existing reporting and governance structures; the use of 'hotlines'; an attempt to normalise whistleblowing as standard corporate governance practice, and evidence of innovation in approaches to whistleblowing.[63]

5.4.1.1 Description of Whistleblowing and Its Importance

The T20 study indicated ASX 20 companies commonly provided a description of the company's internal whistleblowing systems. This occurred either within a separate whistleblowing policy or as part of the company's code of conduct. Reassurance was frequently given in that description as to both the importance of whistleblowing and as to the protection that would be offered to whistleblowers. Several policies provided additional supporting detail in relation to the categories of conduct that would warrant disclosure, while several companies undertook to provide feedback to the whistleblower on the outcome of investigations resulting from a disclosure. This approach is broadly consistent with the new mandatory requirement that companies' internal policies provide information in relation to the protection available to whistleblowers.[64] However the existing policies' emphasis on the importance of

[60]Dixon (2016).

[61]Lombard and Brand (2018, pp. 29–47).

[62]Lombard and Brand (2018), at 42; Dixon (2016), at 184.

[63]Lombard and Brand (2018), at 44.

[64]Corporations Act, 2001 (Cth), section 1317AI(5)(a).

whistleblowing as a valuable measure not provided for in the mandated contents. We would suggest this is a good thing, as this kind of qualitative material is best left to individual entities to devise, with reference to current practice within individual corporations, rather than being prescribed by 'top-down' regulation.

5.4.1.2 Integration into Existing Reporting Structures and Chains of Responsibility

Interestingly, a number of the T20 study companies provided publicly available material that described the place of internal whistleblowing processes within the company's broader internal governance structures. This would appear sensible: given the extensive information obligations to which listed companies are subject, well-designed connections between whistleblowing policies and existing reporting structures is likely to enhance implementation of the policies. Thus T20 companies described the reporting of whistleblowing data to audit committees, risk committees, governance committees, or sustainability committees. The identification of clear chains of responsibility for disclosure would presumably allow for direct connection between disclosures and senior management within a company and assist in ensuring information is not lost in transmission through intervening layers of management. The T200 study indicated that disclosures were commonly permitted to be directed to a direct or immediate supervisor, suggesting a more diffuse set of reporting channels.[65] Thus the data suggests the potential for variation in whistleblowing reporting lines between companies. This approach appears largely consistent with the new mandatory requirement that company policies specify to whom disclosures may be made and how they may be made,[66] but does not take the further step of prescribing appropriate reporting channels by legislative fiat.

5.4.1.3 External or Internal Reporting 'Hotlines'

A third theme identified in the T20 study was the widespread use of reporting hotlines, whether anonymous or not. Approximately three-quarters of the companies reviewed provided for some form of anonymous whistleblowing hotline. By contrast approximately a third of T200 organisations provided for a hotline.[67] In the vast majority of cases both within the T20 and T200 studies it was clear that reports by way of hotlines could be made anonymously.[68] Provision is also made for the protection of the identity of the whistleblower by way of confidentiality measures under the new legislation, although anonymous disclosure is not expressly mentioned.[69]

[65] Dixon (2016), at 190.

[66] Corporations Act, 2001 (Cth), s1317AA(1)(c).

[67] Ibid.

[68] Lombard and Brand (2018), at 44; Dixon (2016), at 197.

[69] *Corporations Act 2001* (Cth), s 1317AAE.

This has the beneficial effect of enabling corporations to continue to evolve their systems as technology and other developments allow for new disclosure mechanisms. Thus while 'hotlines' were prevalent at the time of the T20 and T200 studies, emergent technology offers the possibility of reporting online to artificially intelligent entities.[70]

5.4.1.4 'Normalisation' of Whistleblowing as Standard Corporate Governance Practice

An interesting theme identified in T20 was the availability of some limited evidence to suggest companies were making attempts to ensure internal whistleblowing activity was perceived as a 'normal' component of standard corporate governance within the company. This effort might presumably have been in part a response to earlier perceptions that whistleblowing was a form of 'dobbing', with pejorative connotations.[71] Thus corporate governance statements for some companies made reference to the company's whistleblowing program as part of the risk or governance framework, or located coverage of whistleblowing provisions in the corporate governance sections of the company's websites.

These explicit connections between corporate governance practice and whistleblowing are perhaps in part reflective of the *ASX Corporate Governance Principles*' then inclusion of whistleblowing systems as a potential item within a company's code of conduct.[72] Nonetheless such references may have assisted in reinforcing internal perceptions of a connection between good corporate governance and whistleblowing. Further, some evidence was available of an evolution in nomenclature amongst T20 companies, with references to 'whistleblowing' being absent but use instead of terms that might have been perceived to be less stigmatised, such as 'speaking up', or 'raising a business conduct concern'.[73]

By contrast, the mandated whistleblowing policy requirements of the new Australian provisions require that information be provided to 'whistleblowers', and deal with the mechanics of 'whistleblowing'.[74] This consistency of nomenclature is necessary in a legislative context where penalties are imposed for non-compliance. It is likely however to exercise a restrictive effect on future use of alternative, and possibly less pejorative, terms. While presumably companies could choose to use their own descriptors for their internal whistleblowing process, most companies are perhaps likely to follow the wording dictated by the Act, to avoid any suggestion of

[70]See for instance the services advertised by Hello Ethics: https://www.helloethics.com/en/index.html (accessed 24 June 2019).

[71]Brand (2005), at 273.

[72]ASX Corporate Governance Council, *Corporate Governance Principles and Recommendations*, 2014, 3ed, at 20.

[73]Lombard and Brand (2018), at 44.

[74]Corporations Act, 2001 (Cth), s1317AI.

non-compliance. An outcome of the new provisions may thus be to discourage companies from recharacterising whistleblowing as part of a wider, positive governance structure.

5.4.1.5 Innovative Developments

The fifth theme identified in the T20 study was the presence of some innovative developments amongst surveyed companies.[75] One ASX 20 company had chosen for instance to identify whistleblowing not just as a risk or governance matter but also as a means of stakeholder engagement (e.g. with employees). This characterisation suggests a possible expanded role for future whistleblowing programs, beyond compliance and risk minimisation. Other companies had imposed a mandatory requirement on employees to whistleblow where they had become aware of suspect conduct, or had enunciated a clear expectation that a report would be made. One company was reported to have gone still further, imposing a requirement on suppliers that they have their own whistleblowing processes. Similarly, the T200 study reported a majority of ASX200 companies imposed a duty to whistleblow on employees.[76] The placing of a positive obligation on employees to report wrongdoing, rather than merely providing a mechanism for doing so, again suggests a path for potential evolution in corporate internal whistleblowing processes.

Nothing in the requirements of the new Australian legislative provisions specifically prohibits this kind of extension of whistleblowing policy. Indeed it may be that the mandating of policies for all larger companies, and of at least some of the contents of those policies, will encourage many more companies to consider whistleblowing systems and to seek to integrate them into their wider corporate governance practices. However it seems at least equally possible that innovative or expanded systems of the kind seen in earlier whistleblowing systems will be less likely in the future as compliance efforts respond to a more prescriptive regulatory environment and focus on aligning with legislative requirements.

5.4.2 Links to Theory and Evidence of the Prior Practices of Australian Corporations

There are identifiable connections between the public-private partnerships model of 'new governance' and the prior whistleblowing practices of Australian companies identified in the T20 and T200 studies. New governance sees external regulatory practices as facilitative of rule-making in a more decentralised way, rather than via a prescriptive approach. Pre-legislative development by Australia's largest companies of incremental, 'bottom-up' internal disclosure systems provides some evidence of

[75]Lombard and Brand (2018), at 44.

[76]Dixon (2016), at 186.

the way such a new governance approach might work in the context of whistleblowing.

Although whistleblowing mechanisms may in part have been implemented in an effort to ensure compliance with existing (albeit minimal) whistleblowing protections, and in particular the prohibitions on victimisation of whistleblowers,[77] the range and depth of the observed systems went well beyond legislative requirements. The systems reviewed in the T20 study demonstrated considerable variety including in relation to such central matters as the name chosen for whistleblowing; the location of the policy also varied (for instance, in a separate whistleblowing policy, or a general code of conduct, or elsewhere).[78] The T200 study similarly reported wide variation in the details of existing systems including in relation to the nature of violations to be reported; who reports were to be made to; key elements of policies and guidelines; and aspects associated with protection from retaliation.[79] In general both studies were suggestive of the pre-mandatory internal policies regulatory environment having been productive of varied, individual approaches by corporations.

This evidence of prior practice contrasts with the more controlled and specific nature of the new legislative provisions. While a number of legislatively mandated requirements reflect standard elements of prior practice (e.g. the need to specify to whom a report may be made and the need to provide information about the protection available to whistleblowers), others do not. The specification of content necessarily involves a standardisation of terms and approaches (including, as noted, of the term used to describe whistleblowing). A new governance analysis of desirable whistleblowing regulation would preference companies being able to develop systems that suit their needs and their circumstances, including as to nomenclature and structural settings. That said, the new Australian provisions are not completely prescriptive and do leave room for some flexibility; as noted, while the provisions require that internal policies specify to whom disclosures may be made, they do not for instance mandate the recipients of disclosures.

Perhaps the biggest risk of Australia's new provisions is that the presence of a 'list' of mandatory content will artificially limit the extent to which companies will reflect on their own internal governance needs, and introduce innovative approaches. By specifying the necessary contents of a policy the new legislation may disempower those within the corporation who might otherwise look to design more tailored whistleblowing solutions. We have noted the power of intrinsic motivators in the regulatory process and the beneficial effects of the freedom to choose a course of action best suited to individual circumstances.[80] Some evidence of the effect of those ideas appears to have been present in the prior practice of Australian corporations in relation to internal corporate whistleblowing policies (in the case of the largest and most scrutinised entities at least). It will be interesting to observe the operation of Australia's new whistleblowing provisions, and to see whether the level of discretion

---

[77] *Corporations Act 2001* (Cth), s1317AC.

[78] Lombard and Brand (2018, pp. 29–47).

[79] Dixon (2016, Tables 3, 4, 5 and 6).

[80] Feaver and Sheehy (2015), at 984.

that has been left to corporations is sufficient to encourage similarly self-motivated adoption of innovative and tailored policies.

5.5 Conclusion

The value of information that could be provided by those with inside knowledge is increasingly being recognised—information that is valuable not only from a regulatory perspective, or the perspective of corporate stakeholders, but also valuable from a governance perspective, as a means to allow those in control of the company to ensure compliance and accountability.

In order for 'inside information' to serve a corporate governance function, well-developed systems of institutionalised whistleblowing are necessary, as an integral part of a comprehensive, well-developed corporate governance system.

There is clear evidence that Australia's largest companies have commenced the process of developing such internal whistleblowing systems, and have started doing so even in the absence of regulatory mandates to this effect. An overview of these systems demonstrates variation and diversity, along with several common themes. This suggests that companies have both personalised elements of their approach, while recognising core elements of a functional internal whistleblowing system. The voluntary development of such nuanced systems serves to demonstrate recognition of their value, as well as the benefits in allowing organic development of such frameworks, instead of attempting to 'compel' development in terms of strict and prescriptive regulation.

Even though these listed companies, to a large extent, appear therefore to have behaved as 'good' firms, the Australian legislature opted for a regulatory approach and enforcement model that is traditionally associated with distrust and 'bad' firms.[81] Rather than viewing this as a reflection on the large corporates, we suggest, instead, that it emphasises the value that is attached to internal reporting mechanisms and the obvious benefits they offer.

There are undeniably advantages in the approach of mandating internal whistleblowing frameworks—the approach adopted by the Australian legislature—in that it ensures consistency and avoids a 'time lag' in relation to adoption of these policies, which could occur in regard to relying on voluntary adoption of internal whistleblowing systems. It has the added benefit of 'capturing' a larger number of companies, rather than just relying on listed companies to develop internal whistleblowing systems.

However, concerns remain in relation to the approach where a statutory obligation is imposed to develop internal whistleblowing frameworks. Firstly, mandating an internal whistleblowing framework could potentially carry the risk that companies adopt these frameworks as a result of a 'box-ticking approach' merely in order to

[81] See par 3.1.1 above, with reference to Scholz (1984).

comply with the legislation,[82] and thereby opting for the lowest common denominator in devising an internal framework.[83] This could furthermore also result in a culture of disclosure and transparency not becoming an integral part of the cultural fabric of the company, leading to principles associated with well-developed institutionalised whistleblowing frameworks not being internalised by the company. In addition, the possibility that regulations may be drafted to prescribe the content of internal whistleblowing policies could mean that insufficient opportunity is left for 'tailor-made' policies which further detracts from an opportunity to 'internalise' notions underpinning a culture of transparency and disclosure. It also fails to appreciate that companies may have and use their 'superior knowledge of their particular firm needs and vulnerabilities to innovate, while remaining accountable for their performance'.[84] Lastly, a statutory obligation carries the risk of increased regulatory burden and oversight.

In this respect, one is inclined to agree with Langevoort that compliance systems (such as internal whistleblowing systems) are 'good things', but that

> any direct requirement forcing the maintenance of reasonable systems, which in fact may well be low-powered monitoring system in many firms, will be extremely difficult to apply accurately, leading to excessive investment in window-dressing, and scapegoating…[and that] compliance adequacy should mainly be something that firms struggle with *ex ante* rather than something that law struggles with in hindsight.[85]

References

Austin J, Lombard S (2019) *The Impact of Whistleblowing Awards Programs on Corporate Governance*. Windsor Yearbook of Access to Justice (forthcoming)

Ayres I, Braithwaite J (1992) *Responsive Regulation*. OUP, Oxford

Baer MH (2008) Corporate Policing and Corporate Governance: What Can We Learn from Hewlett-Packard's Pretexting Scandal? *Univ Cincinnati Law Rev* 77:523

Baer MH (2009) Governing Corporate Compliance. *Boston College Law Rev* 50:949

Baldwin R, Black J (2008) Really Responsive Regulation. *Modern Law Rev* 71:59

Baldwin R, Cave M, Lodge M (2011) *Understanding Regulatory Theory, Strategy and Practice*. OUP, Oxford

Bamberger KA (2006) Regulation as Delegation: Private Firms, Decisionmaking, and Accountability in the Administrative State. *Duke Law J* 56:377

Braithwaite J (2002) *Restorative Justice and Responsive Regulation*. OUP, NY

Brand V (2005) Sanctioned "Dobbing": Whistleblowing Under the Corporations Act. *Keep Good Co* 57(5):272

Brand V, Lombard S, Fitzpatrick J (2013) Bounty Hunters, Whistleblowers and a New Regulatory Paradigm. *Australian Business Law Rev* 41:292–293

---

[82] Ford (2008), at 29.

[83] This is in line with the opinion of Ford (2008), at 19, who argues that 'prescriptive requirements emphasize the wrong things…they encourage firms to focus on detailed compliance rather than to exercise sound judgment'.

[84] Ford (2008), at 28.

[85] Langevoort (2002), at 117–118.

Bucy PH (2002) Information as a Commodity in the Regulatory World. *Houston Law Rev* 39:905–940

Davies PL (2008) *Gower and Davies' Principles of Modern Company Law*. Sweet & Maxwell, London

Devine T, Maassarani TF, Wigand J (2011) *The Corporate Whistleblower's Survival Guide: A Handbook for Committing the Truth*. Berrett-Koehler Publishers, San Francisco

Dixon O (2016) Honesty Without Fear? Whistleblower Anti-Retaliation Protections in Corporate Codes of Conduct. *Melbourne Univ Law Rev* 40:168

Feaver D, Sheehy B (2015) Designing Effective Regulation: A Positive Theory. *Univ New South Wales Law J* 38(3):961

Ford CL (2008) New Governance, Compliance and Principles-Based Securities Regulation. *Am Bus Law J* 45:1

Gilligan G (2013) *The Ethics of Whistleblowing: PRISM Evaluated*. Centre for Law, Markets & Regulation, University of New South Wales, 17 June 2013

Gunningham N, Sinclair D (2011) Smart Regulation. In: Drahos P (ed) *Regulatory Theory: Foundations and Applications*. ANU Press, Canberra, p 133

Gunningham N, Grabosky PN, Sinclair D (1998) *Smart Regulation: Designing Environmental Policy*. OUP, Oxford

Hess D (2007) Social Reporting and New Governance Regulation: The Prospects of Achieving Corporate Accountability Through Transparency. *Bus Ethics Q* 17:453

Kingsford-Smith D (2012) Governing the Company: The Role of 'Soft' Regulation. *Univ New South Wales Law J* 18:82

Langevoort DC (2002) The Behavioral Economics of Corporate Compliance with Law. *Columbia Bus Law Rev* 71:7

Lombard S, Brand V (2018) Whistleblowing and Corporate Governance: Regulating to Reap the Governance Benefits of "Institutionalised" Whistleblowing. *Company Secur Law J* 36:29–47

Maiden M (2013) ASIC has Far Too Much on Its Plate. *The Age*, 18 June 2013

Malloy TF (2003) Regulation, Compliance and the Firm. *Temple Law Rev* 76:451

Mathiopoulos JA, Hogan K, du Plessis JJ (2017) Whistleblowing Reforms: A Critical Analysis of the Current Law and the New "Bells and Whistles" Proposed. *Company Secur Law J* 35(261):262

Moberly R (2006) Sarbanes-Oxley's Structural Model to Encourage Corporate Whistleblowers. *Brigham Young Univ Law Rev* 5:1107

Near JP, Dworkin TM (1998) Responses to Legislative Changes: Corporate Whistleblowing Policies. *J Bus Ethics* 17:1551

Pascoe J, Welsh M (2011) Whistleblowing, Ethics and Corporate Culture: Theory and Practice in Australia. *Common Law World Rev* 40:144–146

Rapp GC (2013) Four Signal Movements in Whistleblower Law 1983–2013. *Hofstra Labor Employ Law J* 30:389

Scholz JT (1984) Cooperation, Deterrence, and the Ecology of Regulatory Enforcement. *Law Soc Rev* 18:179

Simmons OS (2013) The Corporate Immune System: Governance from the Inside Out. *Univ Illinois LR* 1131

Solomon JM (2010) New Governance, Preemptive Self-Regulation, and the Blurring of Boundaries in Regulatory Theory and Practice. *Wis Law Rev* 591

Topping N (2012) How Does Disclosure Drive Behavior Change? *J Appl Corp Finance* 24:45

Chapter 6
Directors' Duties and Whistleblowing

Rosemary Teele Langford

Abstract The relationship between whistleblowing and directors' duties is not straightforward. Directors' core duties (duty of care, duties to act in good faith in the interests of the company and for proper purposes, and duties to avoid unauthorised conflicts and profits) are owed to the company and not directly to whistleblowers or employees. On the other hand, a company's reputation is a key factor in its success and one that is increasingly recognised in the application of the duty to act in good faith in the interests of the company and, more recently, in the application of the duty of care. Corporate codes may also contain material concerning whistleblowing, and a question arises as to how binding these codes are and the consequences of non-compliance. This chapter explores the interaction between whistleblowing and directors' core duties, as well as the potential implications of non-compliance with whistleblowing provisions in corporate codes by companies and directors. The analysis relates primarily to Australian law, but comparison is made with other Commonwealth jurisdictions.

Keywords Directors' duties · Corporate governance · Company law · Best interests · Oppression · Duty of care

6.1 Introduction

Given the pivotal role played by directors in the oversight and direction of a corporation, the effectiveness of whistleblowing measures is very much influenced by directors' initiatives and responses. The chapter critically analyses the interaction between directors' duties and whistleblowing from an Australian perspective, as well as how this interaction may evolve. It does so within a wider context of developments in other jurisdictions, which this chapter also references. The specific focus of this chapter is on the potential liability of directors in relation to whistleblowing

R. T. Langford (✉)
Melbourne Law School, University of Melbourne, 185 Pelham Street, Carlton 3053, VIC, Australia
e-mail: rosemary.langford@unimelb.edu.au

S. Lombard et al. (eds.), *Corporate Whistleblowing Regulation*,
https://doi.org/10.1007/978-981-15-0259-0_6

and, more specifically, in relation to any failure in a company's response to whistle-blowing or in the implementation or monitoring of a whistleblowing policy. Such liability may arise from a number of sources. These include amended sections of the Corporations Act 2001 (Cth) resulting from new whistleblowing legislation, core directors' duties at general law and under statute, as well as the oppression remedy in the Corporations Act. The provisions of a company code may also provide a basis for liability, when combined with these other sources.

6.2 Definition of Director—Australia

Given that the focus of this chapter is on liability of directors, it is important to briefly outline the persons to whom directors' duties apply. In addition to persons formally appointed as directors, section 9 of the Corporations Act 2001 (Cth) defines the term 'director' to include de facto and shadow directors. Persons acting in the position of director but not formally appointed as directors are therefore included, as are persons in accordance with whose directions or instructions the board is accustomed to act.

It is also important to note that the duties in sections 180–184 of the Corporations Act (discussed below) apply to officers as well as directors and that the duties in sections 182–183 apply to employees. The term 'employee' is not defined in the Corporations Act. The term 'officer' is defined in section 9 of the Corporations Act to include, amongst other categories:

(a) a director or secretary of the corporation; or
(b) a person:
    (i) who makes, or participates in making, decisions that affect the whole, or a substantial part, of the business of the corporation; or
    (ii) who has the capacity to affect significantly the corporation's financial standing; or
    (iii) in accordance with whose instructions or wishes the directors of the corporation are accustomed to act (excluding advice given by the person in the proper performance of functions attaching to the person's professional capacity or their business relationship with the directors or the corporation).

Section 9 then includes various categories of people, such as receivers, administrators and liquidators. The concept of participation requires examination of the person's contribution to the relevant decision and focuses on the person's role in the ultimate act of making a decision, even if the final act of making the decision is taken by someone else.[1] The concern is to identify persons who are involved in the management of the company,[2] as opposed to third parties.[3] The definition of officer has included a director of a holding company of the company in question.[4] In the case of *Shafron v Australian Securities and Investments Commission*[5] the High Court held that the general counsel was an officer, because his role was not confined to providing advice and information to the board; instead, he played a large and active part in the formulation of the proposal approved by the board.[6]

The focus of this chapter is on directors.

6.3 Sources of Directors' Duties—Australia

There are a number of sources of directors' duties and a number of other obligations imposed on directors in Australia. Primary amongst these are the core general law duties (discussed in Sects. 6.4–6.6 below) and the duties in sections 180–184 of the Corporations Act (also discussed below). Legislation may also impose liability on directors directly—for example, statutes regulating environmental protection and occupational health and safety impose liability on directors and officers. This has been a source of concern for directors, and the Australian Institute of Company Directors has repeatedly stated that the extent of liability is too great, thus discouraging potential candidates for directorship and deterring responsible risk-taking.[7]

The recently enacted Treasury Laws Amendment (Enhancing Whistleblower Protections) Act 2019 inserted into the Corporations Act detailed provisions in relation to requisite whistleblower policies,[8] protection of whistleblowers,[9] compensation (and other remedies)[10] and prohibition of victimization.[11] Directors will need to make sure these are implemented and complied with, particularly in light of the requirements of the duty of care outlined in Sect. 6.6 below. This duty would also

---

[1]See *Shafron v Australian Securities and Investments Commission* (2012) 247 CLR 465, 477–80 [22]–[27] ('*Shafron v ASIC*').

[2]See *Australian Securities and Investments Commission v Citigroup Global Markets Australia Pty Ltd [No 4]* (2007) 160 FCR 35; *Buzzle Operations Pty Ltd (in liq) v Apple Computer Australia Pty Ltd* (2010) 238 FLR 384 ('*Buzzle*').

[3]*Buzzle* (n 2).

[4]See *Australian Securities and Investments Commission v Adler* (2002) 168 FLR 253 ('*ASIC v Adler*').

[5](2012) 247 CLR 465.

[6]*Shafron v ASIC* (n 1) 477–80 [22]–[27]. Note that the officer was also company secretary, but argued that the relevant conduct was undertaken in his role as general counsel.

[7]See Australian Institute of Company Directors (2014).

[8]See, e.g., s 1317AI.

[9]See, e.g., ss 1317AA, 1317AAE, 1317AB(1).

[10]See, e.g., ss 1317AD, 1317AE.

[11]See, e.g., ss 1317AC, 1317G(1G).

require directors to take steps to respond to, and address, any problem or issue identified by the whistleblower, quite apart from diligently monitoring and responding to the company's whistleblower system. As demonstrated below, the duty of care requires directors to monitor the company's business, and this would include its whistleblowing arrangements.

The new provisions impose liability on companies and individuals.[12] Directors will therefore need to familiarize themselves with these provisions and take steps to comply. Contravention by the company, particularly if significant financial or reputational loss ensues, may lead to a stepping stones action (discussed in Sect. 6.2.3 below) against a director.

6.4 Outline of Directors' Duties—Australia

Directors are subject to core duties both at general law and under the Corporations Act 2001 (Cth)—it is these duties that are the focus of this chapter. The general law duties imposed on directors include duties to avoid unauthorised conflicts and profits from position, duties to act in good faith in the interests of the company and for proper purposes, a duty of care skill and diligence, and duties to disclose and to retain discretions. The Corporations Act also imposes duties, the central ones being the duty of care and diligence (in s 180), the duties to act in good faith in the interests of the company and for proper purposes (in s 181), the duties to avoid improper use of position or information from position (in ss 182 and 183), duties to disclose material personal interests and, in the case of public companies, to abstain from participation in decision-making (in ss 191 and 195). More specific duties pertain to insolvent trading (in s 588G) and financial benefits to related parties of public companies (in chapter 2E).

The duties in the Corporations Act differ in a number of ways from the general law duties. For example, whilst the general law duties are owed to the company, the statutory duties are not. In addition, it is well-recognised that the statutory duties protect a number of stakeholders in addition to shareholders,[13] although the extent of this public interest element has not yet been clarified.[14] A corollary of these factors is that breach of statutory duty cannot be authorized or ratified by shareholders.[15] Another difference is that the statutory duties pertaining to the conflicts and profits

---

[12]See, e.g., s 1317AE.

[13]For discussion, see, e.g., Harris et al. (2008) and Welsh (2014).

[14]See, e.g., *Australian Securities and Investments Commission v Cassimatis [No 8]* (2016) 336 ALR 209, [453]–[455] ('*ASIC v Cassimatis [No 8]*').

[15]See, e.g., *Forge v Australian Securities and Investments Commission* (2004) 213 ALR 574, 654 [381]; *Angas Law Services Pty Ltd (in liq) v Carabelas* (2005) 226 CLR 507, 523 [32] (Gleeson CJ and Heydon J). See also *Australian Securities and Investments Commission v Australian Investors Forum Pty Ltd [No 2]* (2005) 53 ACSR 305, 315 [33]–[34].

rules are more specific than the equivalent general law duties, which have a broad ambit.[16] Remedies for breach of duty also differ significantly.

It is obviously important for directors to be on guard in cases of conflict or potential personal benefit. An example of a possible conflict in the context of whistleblowing would be the potential benefit to be derived from any whistleblowing payment or use of position to save one's own reputation in the event of any negative reports being brought by whistleblowers. The focus of this chapter is not, however, on the general law and statutory duties regulating conflicts, profits and material personal interests. Instead the chapter analyses the potential application of the duty of care and the duty to act in good faith in the interests of the company in relation to whistleblowing. It also outlines the potential for an oppression action in circumstances in which directors do not comply with the provisions of a company's corporate code relating to whistleblowing. Although oppression is not a duty imposed on directors, it is frequently used by shareholders in circumstances potentially involving a breach of duty by directors.[17]

6.5 Duty to Act in Good Faith in the Interests of the Company—Australia

In Australia, the duty to act in good faith in the interests of the company is imposed both by general law and by section 181(1)(a) of the Corporations Act 2001 (Cth). The duty requires that directors act in good faith in what they believe are the company's interests in exercising their powers and performing their duties. It requires that directors consider the interests of the company and act in what they consider, in good faith, those interests to be. It is not an absolute duty to achieve the best outcome possible for the company. Neither is it simply a duty of good faith. Both elements combine to require directors to act in good faith in the interests of the company.[18]

Particular contexts in which the duty has been applied are group companies (in relation to which directors must consider the interests of the particular company rather than focusing on the interests of the group),[19] companies approaching insolvency (in

---

[16]See Langford (2019), Chap. 3.

[17]See ibid., ch. 12.

[18]In *Re Smith & Fawcett Ltd* [1942] Ch 304, Lord Greene MR said that directors 'must exercise their discretion bona fide in what they consider—not what a court may consider—is in the interests of the company …': at 306. See also *Australian Securities and Investments Commission v Lewski* (2018) 93 ALJR 145, [71].

[19]See, e.g., *Walker v Wimborne* (1976) 137 CLR 1 ('*Walker*'); *Sydlow Pty Ltd (in liq) v Melwren Pty Ltd (in liq)* (1994) 13 ACSR 144; *Maronis Holdings Ltd v Nippon Credit Australia Ltd* (2007) 38 ACSR 404; *Geneva Finance Ltd (recs and mgrs apptd) v Resource & Industry Ltd* (2002) 169 FLR 152; *Australian Securities and Investments Commission v Somerville* (2009) 77 NSWLR 110.

which context directors must also consider the interests of creditors),[20] nominee directors (who must act in good faith in the interests of the company despite any duty—real or perceived—to the nominator)[21] and conflicted directors (who, despite authorisation of a conflict, must act in good faith in the interests of the company and who may also breach the duty to act in good faith in the interests of the company in circumstances of conflict).[22]

6.5.1 Stakeholder Interests

The general law duty is owed to the company. As outlined above, the duty in section 181(1)(a) is not specifically owed to the company and it is well established that the duties in the Corporations Act protect a number of stakeholders. This can be seen in the judgment of Ward J in *International Swimwear Logistics Ltd v Australian Swimwear Company Pty Ltd:*

> The concepts of public interest, public policy and commercial reality in the context of corporate governance encompass considerations of community confidence in the management of commercial businesses by directors. Various indicators point to the fact that there is a public interest in the enforcement of the duties owed by directors to their companies. Indeed, the role of the state (via ASIC) in the enforcement of statutory duties, the existence of civil penalty provisions, and the ability for directors to be held criminally liable for their actions, confirms the recognition of a public interest in the enforcement of directors' duties.[23]

Furious debate has raged, and continues to rage, over what the interests of the company are. The view that the interests of the company consist only of short-term profit maximization is outdated. On the other hand, directors who promote the interests of stakeholders with no regard to benefit to the company are arguably in breach of the duty. The key point for the purposes of this chapter is that stakeholders such as employees do not have standing to bring an action for breach of this duty and the duty is not owed to individual employees. Instead, employees are one group of stakeholders whose interests directors must consider in complying with their duty to act in good faith in the interests of the company. There is of course specific legislation protecting the interests of employees.

---

[20] See, e.g., *Westpac Banking Corporation v Bell Group Ltd (in liq) [No 3]* (2012) 44 WAR 1; *ANZ Executors & Trustee Co Ltd v Qintex Australia Ltd (recs and mgrs apptd)* [1991] 2 Qd R 360; *Kalls Enterprises Pty Ltd (in liq) v Baloglow* (2007) 63 ACSR 557; *Walker* (n 19).

[21] See, e.g., *Bennetts v Board of Fire Commissioners of New South Wales* (1967) 87 WN (Pt 1) (NSW) 307; *Australian Institute of Fitness Pty Ltd v Australian Institute of Fitness (Vic/Tas) Pty Ltd [No 3]* (2015) 109 ACSR 369; *Hawkes v Cuddy* [2009] EWCA Civ 291; *Scottish Co-Operative Wholesale Society Ltd v Meyer* [1959] AC 324.

[22] See, e.g., *Australian Securities and Investments Commission v Warrenmang Ltd* (2007) 63 ACSR 623 ('*ASIC v Warrenmang*'); *Australian Securities and Investments Commission v Sydney Investment House Equities Pty Ltd* (2008) 69 ACSR 1; *Holyoake Industries (Vic) Pty Ltd v V-Flow Pty Ltd* (2011) 86 ACSR 393; *Re Wan Ze Property Development (Aust) Pty Ltd* (2012) 90 ACSR 593.

[23] [2011] NSWSC 488, [106]. See also *ASIC v Cassimatis [No 8]* (n 14) [453]–[455].

6.5.2 *Section 1324*

In terms of potential standing, section 1324 of the Corporations Act provides that '[w]here a person has engaged, is engaging or is proposing to engage in conduct that constituted, constitutes or would constitute' a contravention (or attempted contravention) of the Act, or other involvement in a contravention of the Act,[24] the court may, on the application of ASIC, or of a person whose interests have been, are, or would be affected by the conduct, grant an injunction, on such terms as the court thinks appropriate, restraining the first-mentioned person from engaging in the conduct and, if in the opinion of the court it is desirable to do so, requiring that person to do any act or thing.

The section on first reading appears very broad. It has been held that, in terms of showing that a person's interests have been affected, the 'interests' referred to in the section are those 'of any person (which includes a corporation) which go beyond the mere interest of a member of the public'.[25] It is therefore not necessary 'that personal rights of a proprietary nature or rights analogous thereto are or may be affected nor need it be shown that any special injury arising from a breach of the Act has occurred'.[26] This might suggest that employees as persons affected by a breach of section 181 (or the other statutory directors' duties) would have standing under section 1324. However, the section has been interpreted restrictively to-date. For example, there has been some doubt as to whether section 1324 can be used in cases involving breach of the statutory directors' duties in sections 180–183 of the Corporations Act 2001 (Cth),[27] although the better view is arguably that it can.

Section 1324(10) allows for damages in lieu of an injunction to be granted. However, this provision has been given a narrow interpretation, such that damages will not be granted where there is no prospect that an injunction would be granted. It has also been held that section 1324(10) does not permit damages to be awarded to a creditor for contravention of a civil penalty provision.[28] This may, however,

---

[24]Section 1324 provides that '[w]here a person has engaged, or is engaging or is proposing to engage in conduct that constituted, constitutes or would constitute: (a) a contravention of this Act; or (b) attempting to contravene this Act; or (c) aiding, abetting, counselling or procuring a person to contravene this Act; or (d) inducing or attempting to induce, whether by threats, promises or otherwise, a person to contravene this Act; or (e) being in any way, directly or indirectly, knowingly concerned in, or party to, the contravention by a person to the Act; or (f) conspiring with others to contravene this Act, the Court may, on the application of ASIC, or of a person whose interests have been, are or would be affected by the conduct, grant an injunction, on such terms as the Court thinks appropriate, restraining the first-mentioned person from engaging in the conduct and, if in the opinion of the Court it is desirable to do so, requiring that person to do any act or thing'.

[25]See *Broken Hill Proprietary Co Ltd v Bell Resources Ltd* (1984) 8 ACLR 609, 613.

[26]Ibid.

[27]*Mesenberg v Cord Industrial Recruiters Pty Ltd* (1996) 39 NSWLR 128. Cf *Airpeak Pty Ltd v Jetstream Aircraft Ltd* (1997) 73 FCR 161; *Emlen Pty Ltd v St Barbara Mines Ltd* (1997) 24 ACSR 303, 306; *Re Idylic Solutions Pty Ltd; Australian Securities and Investments Commission v Hobbs* (2013) 93 ACSR 421, 440–6 [58]–[91]; Barnett (2018).

[28]See *McCracken v Phoenix Constructions (Qld) Pty Ltd* [2013] 2 Qd R 27; *Re Colorado Products Pty Ltd (in prov liq)* (2014) 101 ACSR 233, 358–60 [397]–[402].

change in future, given the expansive wording of the section. If this eventuates, then the section may provide standing for employees to bring action in the event that the whistleblowing provisions are breached and this amounts to a breach of the core duties in sections 180–183.

6.5.3 Reputation and Culture

Returning to an analysis of section 181, which incorporates the concept of the company's interests, it is clearly in a company's interests to maintain a good reputation. Correct handling of whistleblowing is important in this regard. As noted by Dixon, wrongdoing that is corrected by the company in a timely manner will avoid external disclosures and potential reputational and financial damage.[29] The importance of a company's reputation was emphasised (albeit in obiter) by Edelman J in *Australian Securities and Investments Commission v Cassimatis [No 8]*. His Honour said:

> Mr and Mrs Cassimatis' duty to consider *Storm's* interests when managing the corporation does not require a narrow construction of Storm's interests which is limited only to the interests of its shareholders ... A corporation has a real and substantial interest in the *lawful* or *legitimate* conduct of its activity independently of whether the illegitimacy of that conduct will be detected or would cause loss. One reason for that interest is the corporation's reputation. Corporations have reputations, independently of any financial concerns, just as individuals do. Another is that the corporation itself exists as a vehicle for lawful activity. For instance, it would be hard to imagine examples where it could be in a corporation's interests for the corporation to engage in serious unlawful conduct even if that serious unlawful conduct was highly profitable and was reasonably considered by the director to be virtually undetectable during a limitation period for liability.[30]

These remarks were made as concerns the application of the duty of care (discussed below), but are equally relevant in considering what a company's interests are for the purposes of the duty to act in good faith in the interests of the company.

The importance of reputation is also noted in the ASX Corporate Governance Principles, which also draw a connection between stakeholder interests and reputation. The fourth edition of the Principles emphasises the need to act lawfully, ethically and responsibly.[31] The commentary to principle 3 states:

> In formulating its values, a listed entity should consider what behaviours are needed from its officers and employees to build long term sustainable value for its security holders. This includes the need for the entity to preserve and protect its reputation and standing in the community and with key stakeholders, such as customers, employees, suppliers, creditors, law makers and regulators.[32]

---

[29] See Dixon (2016, p. 171).

[30] *ASIC v Cassimatis [No 8]* (n 14) [482]–[483]. Note that this decision has been appealed.

[31] For example, Principle 3 of the ASX's Corporate Governance Principles and Recommendations states that '[a] listed entity should instil a culture of acting lawfully, ethically and responsibly': ASX Corporate Governance Council, *Corporate Governance Principles and Recommendations* (4th ed, February 2019) 16 ('ASX Corporate Governance Principles').

[32] Ibid., p. 16. See also commentary to Recommendations 3.4, 7.4 and 8.1.

Although section 181 does not directly incorporate the requirements of the ASX Corporate Governance Principles, the commentary on reputation in those Principles is indirectly relevant to a consideration of the company's interests in maintaining a good reputation. In addition, in terms of the company's interests, the provisions of the ASX Corporate Governance Principles are particularly important for listed companies, given that such companies must comply with these or explain their departure.[33] Directors of listed companies seeking to comply with their duty to act in good faith in the interests of the company should bear these Principles in mind.

Also tied in with these requirements is the increasing emphasis on culture.[34] At one point, the regulator proposed the imposition of liability on management in relation to poor culture, but this was replaced by monitoring of culture by ASIC.[35] The importance of culture—particularly in the sense of treating customers fairly—has been brought to the fore in the proceedings of the Banking Royal Commission.[36] Whistleblowing is intimately tied in with company culture—protection of whistleblowers indicates good corporate culture.

In summary, although the key duty to act in good faith in the interests of the company is owed to the company and cannot be directly enforced by employees, the duty encompasses consideration of stakeholder interests, including those of employees. It is also conducive to a company's reputation, and therefore in its interests, to handle whistleblowing appropriately. This is a factor that should be borne in mind in discharging the duty to act in good faith in the interests of the company.

6.5.4 Comparison with the UK

An interesting comparison can be made with the equivalent duty of directors under the UK Companies Act 2006 (UK). This duty requires directors to act in what they consider, in good faith, would be most likely to promote the success of the company for the benefit of the members as a whole and in so doing have regard to the interests of a number of stakeholders, including employees. Despite the intention of effecting an 'enlightened shareholder value' approach, the section in fact arguably entrenches

---

[33] ASX Corporate Governance Principles (n 31) 2.

[34] See generally Senate Economics References Committee, Parliament of Australia, *Performance of the Australian Securities and Investments Commission* (Final Report, 26 June 2014); Financial System Inquiry Committee, *Financial System Inquiry: Final Report* (Final Report, November 2014). See also Australian Securities and Investments Commission, *Culture, Conduct and Conflicts of Interest in Vertically Integrated Businesses in the Funds-Management Industry* (Report No 474, March 2016); Greg Medcraft, 'Culture Shock' (Speech, ASIC Annual Forum, Sydney, 21 March 2016). Culture is also mentioned multiple times in the fourth edition of the ASX Corporate Governance Principles (n 31): see, in particular, Principle 3.

[35] Liability may be imposed on companies based on corporate culture: see Criminal Code Act 1995 (Cth) s 12.3.

[36] *Royal Commission into Misconduct in the Banking, Superannuation and Financial Services Industry* (Final Report, February 2019).

shareholder primacy more directly than the equivalent general law or statutory duty in Australia. This is because the bottom line is the success of the company for the benefit of the members as a whole.[37] In light of the perception that section 172 has not achieved its purpose, the UK government has recently initiated a suite of reforms. None of these reformulate the duty in section 172 itself—change is instead effected via reporting and via provisions of a new Corporate Governance Code[38] and Guidance on Board Effectiveness.[39]

The striking feature of these provisions is the emphasis on engagement with the workforce. This aspect is the subject of specific provisions in the UK Corporate Governance Code and the Guidance on Board Effectiveness. Principle E of the Code states:

> The board should ensure that workforce policies are consistent with the company's values and support its long-term sustainable success. The workforce should be able to raise any matters of concern.[40]

The Code and Guidance on Board Effectiveness contain provisions protecting employees who raise concerns and recommendations as to whistleblowing policies.[41] Provision 5 of the UK Corporate Governance Code emphasizes the importance of engaging with the workforce and requires premium-listed companies to adopt (on a comply-or-explain basis) one or a combination of a director appointed from the workforce, a formal workforce advisory panel or a designated non-executive director.[42] The Guidance on Board Effectiveness sees workforce broadly, including not only direct employees, but also agency workers, self-employed contractors, and remote workers.[43] In addition, legislation has been introduced to require additional disclosure of corporate governance arrangements.[44]

---

[37] See also GC100, *Guidance on Directors' Duties: Section 172 and Stakeholder Considerations* (October 2018).

[38] See Financial Reporting Council, *UK Corporate Governance Code* (July 2018).

[39] See Financial Reporting Council, *Guidance on Board Effectiveness* (July 2018) ('Guidance on Board Effectiveness').

[40] The Code and Guidance emphasize the importance of this final requirement, with Provision 6 of the Code stating: 'There should be a means for the workforce to raise concerns in confidence and—if they wish—anonymously. The board should routinely review this and the reports arising from its operation. It should ensure that arrangements are in place for the proportionate and independent investigation of such matters and for follow-up action.' Provision 2 of the UK Corporate Governance Code requires the annual report to 'include an explanation of the company's approach to investing in and rewarding its workforce.'

[41] See Guidance on Board Effectiveness (n 39) [57]–[60].

[42] Provision 5 also states: 'If the board has not chosen one or more of these methods, it should explain what alternative arrangements are in place and why it considers that they are effective.' See also Guidance on Board Effectiveness (n 39) [34], [47], [50]–[60], [130].

[43] Guidance on Board Effectiveness (n 39) [50].

[44] See, e.g., Companies *Act* 2006 (UK) ss 414CZA, 426B.

Although the bottom line of the core duty is therefore promoting the success of the company for the benefit of the members as a whole,[45] there is clear emphasis in these other requirements and recommendations on the need to engage with the workforce.

The provisions in the UK Corporate Governance Code on whistleblowing are less detailed than the new provisions in the fourth edition of the ASX Corporate Governance Principles, discussed below. The position in the UK, as in Australia, remains that the duty itself is not owed to employees. Directors who ignore employee concerns—and in the context of this chapter—whistleblowing, may in certain circumstances fail to act in good faith in the interests of the company.

6.6 Duty of Care—Australia

Directors and officers owe a duty of care, skill and diligence, both at general law and under section 180 of the Corporations Act. The duties are alike in content.

6.6.1 Outline of Duty

Section 180(1) of the Corporations Act provides:

(1) A director or other officer of a corporation must exercise their powers and discharge their duties with the degree of care and diligence that a reasonable person would exercise if they:

  a. were a director or officer of a corporation in the corporation's circumstances; and
  b. occupied the office held by, and had the same responsibilities within the corporation as, the director or officer.

Section 180(2) provides a business judgment rule for directors who make a judgment in good faith for a proper purpose; do not have a material personal interest in the subject matter of the judgment; inform themselves about the subject matter of the judgment to the extent they reasonably believe to be appropriate; and rationally believe that the judgment is in the best interests of the corporation.

The Australian duty imposes an objective test, but incorporates subjective elements in that regard is had to the company's circumstances, and the director or officer's position and responsibilities within the company, in assessing whether the

[45]Note, however, the more recent shift to long-term sustainable success: for detail, see Langford (2019), Chap. 10.

director or officer has exercised reasonable care and diligence.[46] The following factors have been found to be relevant in this respect:

(a) the type of company
(b) the provisions of its constitution
(c) the size and nature of the company's business
(d) the composition of the board
(e) the director's position and responsibilities within the company
(f) the particular function the director is performing
(g) the experience or skills of the particular director
(h) the terms on which he or she has undertaken to act as a director
(i) the manner in which responsibility for the business of the company is distributed between its directors and its employees and
(j) the circumstances of the specified case.[47]

The Court considers what an ordinary person with the knowledge and experience of the director in question might be expected to have done in the circumstances, if they were acting on their own behalf.[48]

One of the key emphases of more recent cases, particularly in Australia, concerning the duty of care is the exact duties and responsibilities of the relevant director. The duty of care affixes to these duties and responsibilities—directors who have more extensive duties and responsibilities are subject to increased liability. This can be seen in the cases involving James Hardie.[49] These cases concerned a misleading release to the Australian Securities Exchange regarding the level of funding for asbestosis victims. The executive and non-executive directors were all found to have breached section 180(1) by voting to approve the draft announcement when they ought to have known that it was misleading.[50] However, those directors and officers with more extensive roles and functions were held to have engaged in a number of other contraventions of the duty of care due to their positions and responsibilities.[51]

Courts often assess compliance with the duty of care by balancing the foreseeable risk of harm to the company flowing from the contravention with the potential benefits that could reasonably be expected to have accrued to the company from the

---

[46] See, e.g., *Trilogy Funds Management Ltd v Sullivan [No 2]* (2015) 331 ALR 185, 229 [201] ('*Trilogy*'); *ASIC v Adler* (n 4) [372]; *Australian Securities and Investments Commission v Maxwell* (2006) 59 ACSR 373, [100] ('*ASIC v Maxwell*'); *Australian Securities and Investments Commission v Healey [No 2]* (2011) 196 FCR 430, [165].

[47] See, e.g., *ASIC v Maxwell* (n 46).

[48] *Trilogy* (n 46) 229 [202].

[49] *Australian Securities and Investments Commission v Macdonald [No 11]* (2009) 230 FLR 1 ('*ASIC v Macdonald [No 11]*'); *Morley v Australian Securities and Investments Commission* (2010) 274 ALR 205; *Australian Securities and Investments Commission v Hellicar* (2012) 247 CLR 345; *Shafron v ASIC* (n 1).

[50] *ASIC v Macdonald [No 11]* (n 49) 66–7 [330]–[336] (as concerns non-executive directors), 68–9 [346]–[349] (as concerns the chief executive officer).

[51] Ibid. 68–9 [346]–[349], 75–7 [390]–[406].

conduct.[52] This is done through the lens of the company's circumstances and the director's position and responsibilities. Directors who have significant responsibilities and exercise significant control in circumstances where a breach of the law is likely are therefore more vulnerable to liability.

In this respect, as outlined in Sect. 5.3 above, in *ASIC v Cassimatis [No 8]* Edelman J opined that a company's interests are not limited to merely financial interests[53]—in balancing the risk of harm against the potential benefit of a particular act or omission a court will not, according to Edelman J, balance or weigh these factors as though by a common metric. Thus, an economically justifiable decision to release a large amount of toxic waste based on the fact that the cost of disposing of the waste lawfully outstripped the cost of a penalty could still result in a breach by the director(s) concerned of section 180.[54] This is partly because corporations have interests in their reputations, and also in complying with the law. This should be borne in mind in responding to whistleblowers.

6.6.2 *Application in Relation to Whistleblowing*

There are a number of ways in which the duty of care may be activated in relation to whistleblowing. Firstly, directors must be careful to comply with the requirements of this duty when faced with a report by an employee or other party. This is particularly the case for executive directors tasked with setting up and monitoring a company's whistleblowing policy. Secondly, the duty of care requires directors to implement and ensure the efficacy of a company's whistleblowing policy. Thirdly, any reporting on whistleblowing must be accurate and not misleading. Fourthly, 'stepping stones' liability may be imposed on the basis of failure to properly deal with whistleblowing. Fifthly, a company's reputation is increasingly relevant in the application of the duty of care—the damage to reputation caused by inadequate responses to whistleblowing or failure to protect whistleblowers should be borne in mind in this respect. These points are now discussed.

6.6.2.1 Application in Relation to Whistleblowing Systems

As concerns the first and second points, directors are required to act with care, skill and diligence in exercising their powers and performing their duties. The duty also

---

[52] See, e.g., *Australian Securities and Investments Commission v Mariner Corporation Ltd* (2015) 241 FCR 502, 584 [450]–[451] ('*ASIC v Mariner*'); *ASIC v Cassimatis [No 8]* (n 14) 301–3 [479]–[487]; *Australian Securities and Investments Commission v Rich* (2009) 236 FLR 1, 140 [7238]; *ASIC v Warrenmang* (n 22) 628–9 [22]–[23].

[53] *ASIC v Cassimatis [No 8]* (n 14) [483]. Note that this decision has been appealed.

[54] Ibid. [485].

requires sufficient monitoring.[55] Given the importance of a person's position and responsibilities and the company's circumstances in the application of the duty of care, a company's failure in relation to whistleblowing policies may have different impacts on different directors in terms of the application of the duty of care. Executive directors are likely to bear greater responsibility.

6.6.2.2 Reporting

As concerns the third aspect, reporting is taking on an increasing role in ensuring accountability of directors.[56] Indeed, some commentators see reporting requirements as a key way to make companies more socially responsible and to change corporate behaviour.[57] A focus on reporting (as the impetus for increased corporate social responsibility, including whistleblowing) has a number of advantages. First, it arguably creates a level playing field, allowing investors to choose between companies in light of such disclosure. Secondly, directors' core duties would attach to these requirements in that, as mentioned, a breach of the duty of care, or of the duty to act in good faith in the interests of the company, could potentially be made out in relation to misleading or inadequate disclosure.

Companies are subject to numerous reporting requirements. Investors are also demanding greater reporting, which has associated derivative benefits, such as better relationships with regulators and marketing opportunities. Directors need to comply with reporting obligations and should be wary of misleading or negligent reporting.[58] The duty of care may be breached where reporting is negligent or misleading. Stepping stones liability, as outlined below, could attach to misleading reporting.

In this respect, section 1317AI of the Corporations Act requires public companies, large proprietary companies and proprietary companies that are trustees of registrable superannuation entities to have a policy with information about: the protections available to whistleblowers; how and to whom an individual can make disclosure; how the company will support and protect whistleblowers; how investigations into a disclosure will proceed; how the company will ensure fair treatment of employees who are mentioned in whistleblower disclosures; how the policy will be made available; and any matters prescribed by regulation.[59] Failure to comply with the requirement to have and make available a whistleblower policy will be an offence of strict liability.[60]

---

[55] Although the core focus of a number of cases is the need for directors to monitor the financial situation of the company, this is not exclusively so: see, e.g., *Daniels v Anderson* (1995) 37 NSWLR 438.

[56] For evaluation see North (2015).

[57] See du Plessis (2016a) Disclosure of Non-Financial Information; du Plessis (2016b) Shareholder Primacy and Other Stakeholder Interests.

[58] For a discussion of potential liability see Baxt (2013), du Plessis and Rühmkorf (2015) and Davies and Worthington (2016), 781–3 [21–8]–[21–9].

[59] Note the overlap with the ASX Corporate Governance Principles (n 31).

[60] See s 1317AI(4).

The ASX Corporate Governance Requirements are also relevant in this respect. Currently, under Listing Rule 4.10.3, ASX listed entities are required to measure their corporate governance practices against the ASX Corporate Governance Principles and where they do not conform to disclose the fact and the reasons why. Recommendation 3.2, which relates to codes of conduct, is discussed in Sect. 7 below. Directors of listed companies need to take care in reporting against these principles.

Recommendation 3.3 of the fourth edition of the ASX Corporate Governance Principles states:

A listed entity should:

a. have and disclose a whistleblower policy; and
b. ensure that the board or a committee of the board is informed of any material incidents reported under that policy.[61]

The commentary states:

> In most cases, the best source of information about whether a listed entity is living up to its values are its employees. They should be encouraged to speak up about any unlawful, unethical or irresponsible behavior within the organisation through an appropriate whistleblower policy. The board or a committee of the board should be informed of material incidents reported under the entity's whistleblower policy, as they may be indicative of issues with the culture of the organisation.

Box 3.3 provides suggestions for the content of a whistleblower policy:

- Link the policy to the organisation's statement of values;
- Clearly identify the types of concerns that may be reported under the policy and how and to whom reports may be made (including to senior executives and the board);
- Explain how the confidentiality of the whistleblower's identity is safeguarded and the whistleblower is protected from retaliation or victimisation;
- Outline the processes to follow up and investigate reports made under the policy;
- Provide for the training of employees about the whistleblower policy and their rights and obligations under it;
- Provide for the training of managers and others who may receive whistleblower reports about how to respond to them; and
- Incorporate a periodic audit or review of the policy and related procedures to check if whistleblower reports were appropriately recorded, investigated and responded to and whether any changes are required to the entity's whistleblower policy or procedures...[62]

6.6.2.3 Stepping Stones Liability

As mentioned above, one way in which the application of the duty of care may result in liability for directors as concerns whistleblowing is via the stepping stones model

[61] ASX Corporate Governance Principles (n 31) 17 (footnotes omitted).

[62] Ibid.

of liability.[63] This model, which originated in Keane J's judgment in *Australian Securities and Investments Commission v Fortescue Metals Group Ltd*,[64] could give rise to a breach of the duty of care (or other core duty) by directors in circumstances in which the company breaches, or risks breaching, the law. Stepping stones liability has traditionally consisted of two elements. The first is a breach of the law (whether the Corporations Act or some other law) by the company. In the case of whistleblowing, this may consist in a breach of the new whistleblowing provisions in the Corporations Act or, as mentioned by Dixon, occupational health and safety legislation, anti-discrimination legislation or workers' compensation legislation.[65]

The second 'stepping stone' is a finding that the director has breached the duty of care in allowing, or in failing to prevent, the breach. A number of stepping stones actions have concerned companies failing to comply with disclosure requirements. In *Australian Securities and Investments Commission v Maxwell* ('*ASIC v Maxwell*')[66] certain group companies were found to have contravened various provisions of the Corporations Act in relation to the issue of debentures, which were issued to fund group property development activities. One of the issues was whether the relevant director had breached his duties in sections 180(1), 181(1) and 182(2) of the Corporations Act by permitting, allowing and participating in the various contraventions committed by the companies.

Stepping stones liability is arguably not, however, limited to circumstances in which the company actually breaches the law—a potential breach suffices. Stepping stones liability is in fact in many ways a straightforward application of the duty of care—just as other acts or omissions by a director may result in loss to the company and therefore a finding of breach of the duty of care by the relevant director, so too may a positive action or omission connected with the company's compliance with the law.[67]

Ensuring that the company complies with obligations relating to whistleblowing is therefore something to which directors should be attentive (quite apart from provisions that impose liability on directors)—a company's failure to so comply may found a claim for breach of the duty of care by the director. In addition, as mentioned, in this respect one of the interests directors should bear in mind in seeking to comply with the duty of care is the importance of the company's reputation.

It is, however, important to adopt a balanced perspective as regards stepping stones liability. As stressed by Brereton J in *ASIC v Maxwell:*

---

[63] For discussion and evaluation see Brand (2017), McGregor (2018), Bednall (2018) and Langford (2017).

[64] (2011) 190 FCR 364.

[65] See Dixon (2016, p. 170).

[66] (2006) 59 ACSR 373.

[67] In this respect see also *ASIC v Cassimatis [No 8]* (n 14) 218 [4]–[7], 339 [697]; *Australian Securities and Investments Commission v Drake* [2016] FCA 1552; (2016) 340 ALR 75 [318].

> [Sections] 180, 181 and 182 do not provide a backdoor method for visiting on company directors accessorial civil liability for contraventions of the *Corporations Act* in respect of which provision is not otherwise made.[68]

Courts are reluctant to treat section 180 as a general obligation on the directors to conduct the affairs of the company in accordance with the general law or the Corporations Act. Brereton J made the following comments, which have been repeated in many subsequent cases:

> It is a mistake to think that ss 180, 181 and 182 are concerned with any general obligation owed by directors at large to conduct the affairs of the company in accordance with the law generally or the *Corporations Act* in particular; they are not. They are concerned with duties owed to the company.[69]

These comments highlight the fact that directors are not automatically liable for breach of the duty if the company breaches the law. In other words, it does not flow necessarily from a finding that an entity has contravened the Corporations Act that the officers must have contravened their duty of care to the company. In the case of *Australian Securities and Investments Commission v Mariner,* Beach J stated:

> After all, one expects management including the directors to take *calculated* risks. The very nature of commercial activity necessarily involves uncertainty and risk taking. The pursuit of an activity that might entail a foreseeable risk of harm does not of itself establish a contravention of s 180. Moreover, a failed activity pursued by the directors which causes loss to the company does not of itself establish a contravention of s 180.[70]

In *ASIC v Cassimatis* Edelman J pointed out that the duty in section 180(1) is not a duty of strict liability—'[n]or is it a duty which requires the director to take every possible step to avoid a foreseeable risk of contravention of legislation.'[71] Tying this in with accepted jurisprudence on section 180(1), his Honour noted that the steps that a reasonable director must take for the purposes of section 180(1) 'will always depend on all of the corporation's circumstances.'[72]

6.7 Corporate Codes

Recommendation 3.2 of the fourth edition of the ASX Corporate Governance Principles states that '[a] listed entity should (a) have and disclose a code of conduct

---

[68] *ASIC v Maxwell* (n 46) [110] (Brereton J).

[69] Ibid. [104]. In *ASIC v Mariner* (n 52), Beach J stated that 'The duty owed under s 180 does not impose a wide-ranging obligation on directors to ensure that the affairs of a company are conducted in accordance with law. It is not to be used as a back-door means for visiting accessorial liability on directors. Further, it is not to be used in a contrived way in an attempt to empower the court to make a disqualification order under s 206C by the artificial invocation of s 180 (a civil penalty provision), when such a route is not otherwise available directly.': at [444].

[70] *ASIC v Mariner* (n 52) [452].

[71] *ASIC v Cassimatis [No 8]* (n 14) [529].

[72] Ibid. [530].

for its directors, senior executives and employees; and (b) ensure that the board or a committee of the board is informed of any material breaches of that code.'[73]

Many companies incorporate whistleblowing policies within these corporate codes of conduct. A detailed study of listed companies by Dixon demonstrates that the majority of the ASX 200 listed entities publish a Code that promises protection from retaliation for any employee who reports any act of misconduct in good faith.[74]

However, it is one thing to propound such protections, and another to ensure that they are properly implemented and monitored. Compliance is also emphasised by judges and academics[75] and is particularly important due to provisions in the Criminal Code on culpable corporate culture.[76] The commentary to the current ASX Corporate Governance Principles Recommendation 3.2 states:

> For a code of conduct to be effective, all employees must receive appropriate training on their obligations under the code. Directors and senior executives must speak and act consistently with the code (again, setting the "tone from the top") and reinforce it by taking appropriate and proportionate disciplinary action against those who breach it.[77]

As noted above, depending on a person's position and responsibilities, negligence in implementing and maintaining a company's whistleblowing policies may in some circumstances amount to a breach of the duty of care. Departure from the provisions of a corporate code may also lead to reputational damage. The importance of renewing and monitoring a company's compliance with whistleblowing procedures and protections is therefore evident.

Although corporate codes are voluntary and compliance with such codes is not monitored by ASIC or ASX,[78] it is pertinent to note that in Canada oppression actions have been successful in circumstances in which there has been non-compliance with the provisions of a company's code. It is submitted that this is a real possibility in Australia and that directors should be careful to ensure that the company complies with the provisions of its company code relating to whistleblowing and more

---

[73] ASX Corporate Governance Principles (n 31) 16 (footnotes omitted). The commentary to Recommendation 3.1 of the third edition of the ASX Corporate Governance Principles suggested that the code should '[i]dentify the measures the organisation follows to encourage the reporting of unlawful or unethical behavior. This might include a reference to how the organisation protects "whistleblowers" who report violations in good faith': see ASX Corporate Governance Council, *Corporate Governance Principles and Recommendations* (3rd ed, 27 March 2014) 20.

[74] Dixon (2016) opines that whistleblower protection policies positively influence organizational behavior and culture, and have a regulatory effect through signaling appropriate behavior: p. 172.

[75] See, e.g., *Re Chemeq Ltd; Australian Securities and Investments Commission v Chemeq Ltd* (2006) 234 ALR 511, [84]–[86]; Brand (2017), Baxt (2013) and Lombard and Brand (2018).

[76] See Criminal Code Act 1995 (Cth) ss 12.2, 12.3.

[77] See ASX Corporate Governance Principles (n 31) 17. For further discussion of the legal impact of corporate codes, see Bathurst and Wootton (2018, p. 3).

[78] Dixon (2016) notes that while the ASX requires companies to disclose whether they have a Code, the ASX plays no ongoing role in monitoring or enforcing the Code: p. 203.

generally. The oppression action is briefly outlined in the next section and relevant Canadian jurisprudence is highlighted.[79]

6.8 Oppression

Of the remedies available to shareholders in Australia under the Corporations Act, the oppression remedy has proved successful and popular. The oppression remedy is frequently employed (in Australia and other Commonwealth jurisdictions) in circumstances involving breach (or potential breach) of directors' duties. This is significant, given the often-liberal standing requirements, the absence of a requirement to first obtain leave of the court (which applies to derivative actions), and the broader test that applies as compared to actions for breach of duty.

The oppression remedy in section 232 of the Corporations Act has two limbs. The first is 'contrary to the interests of the members as a whole' and the second is 'oppressive to, unfairly prejudicial to, or unfairly discriminatory against, a member of members whether in that capacity or in any other capacity'. Section 232 states:

The Court may make an order under section 233 if:

(a) the conduct of a company's affairs; or
(b) an actual or proposed act or omission by or on behalf of a company; or
(c) a resolution, or a proposed resolution, of members or a class of members of a company; is either:
(d) contrary to the interests of the members of a whole; or
(e) oppressive to, unfairly prejudicial to, or unfairly discriminatory against, a member or members whether in that capacity or in any other capacity.

The concept of 'the affairs of a corporation' is defined very broadly in section 53.[80] Australian jurisprudence holds that the test of fairness is objective.[81]

In Australia, it will be harder to make out oppression in relation to a decision that is made in good faith by reference to relevant considerations.[82] Courts are, however, reluctant to review business judgments, and mere dissatisfaction with management

---

[79] Corporate codes form part of corporate culture. As noted above, corporate culture has received enormous focus in recent years: see n 34, above. For discussion of corporate culture see Greg Golding's chapter in the present book.

[80] *Australian Securities Commission v Lucas* (1992) 36 FCR 165.

[81] See, e.g., *Wayde v New South Wales Rugby League Ltd* (1985) 180 CLR 459 ('*Wayde*'); *Morgan v 45 Flers Avenue Pty Ltd* (1986) 10 ACLR 692, 704.

[82] See, e.g., *Wayde* (n 81).

is insufficient to constitute oppression.[83] Whilst the oppression remedy is most commonly applied in the context of small companies,[84] it is not limited to this context, although it will rarely apply to listed companies.[85]

Section 234 confers standing on members (and former members in certain circumstances) and persons whom ASIC thinks appropriate having regard to investigations it is conducting or has conducted into the company's affairs or matters connected with the company's affairs.

Section 233(1) gives the court broad discretion to make such order or orders as it thinks appropriate, and courts have shown a willingness to exercise this discretion.[86] Examples given in section 233 include an order that the company be wound up[87]; an order that the company's constitution be modified or repealed[88]; an order for regulating the conduct of the affairs of the company in the future[89]; an order for the purchase of a member's shares by other members or by the company[90]; an order directing the company to institute, defend, or discontinue specified proceedings, or authorizing a member of the company to institute, prosecute, defend, or discontinue specified proceedings in the name and on behalf of the company[91]; an order appointing a receiver (or receiver and manager) of property of the company[92]; an order requiring a person to do a specified act or thing[93]; and an order restraining a person from engaging in specified conduct or from doing a specified act.[94]

There are many examples of the oppression remedy being successfully argued in situations potentially involving breach of directors' duties.[95] It is therefore entirely possible that an oppression action could be brought in situations in which a director

---

[83]See generally *Re G Jeffrey (Mens Store) Pty Ltd* (1984) 9 ACLR 193, 198.

[84]See Austin and Ramsay (2018, p. 808) [10.435].

[85]See ibid. 809 [10.435.3]. See also *Latimer Holdings Ltd v SEA Holdings NZ Ltd* [2005] 2 NZLR 328 345–6 [98]–[111].

[86]See, e.g., *Jenkins v Enterprise Gold Mines NL* (1992) 6 ACSR 539; *Fexuto Pty Ltd v Bosnjak Holdings Pty Ltd* (2001) 37 ACSR 672 ('*Fexuto*'); *LPD Holdings (Aust) Pty Ltd v Phillips* (2013) 281 FLR 227.

[87]Corporations Act 2001 (Cth) s 233(1)(a).

[88]Ibid. s 233(1)(b).

[89]Ibid. s 233(1)(c).

[90]Ibid. ss 233(1)(d), (e).

[91]Ibid. ss 233(1)(f), (g).

[92]Ibid. s 233(1)(h).

[93]Ibid. s 233(1)(j).

[94]Ibid. s 233(1)(l).

[95]See, e.g., *Dwyer v Lippiatt* (2004) 50 ACSR 333; *Vadori v AAV Plumbing* (2010) 77 ACSR 616; *Re Cheal Industries Pty Ltd; Fitzpatrick v Cheal* (2012) 264 FLR 313; *Re B Personal Pty Ltd* [2016] VSC 211; *Exton v Extons Pty Ltd* (2017) 53 VR 520; *Harrington v Sensible Funerals Pty Ltd* (2007) 61 ACSR 359; *Wallington v Kokotovich Constructions Pty Ltd* (1993) 11 ACSR 759; *Sanford v Sanford Courier Service Pty Ltd* (1986) 10 ACLR 549; *Spence v Rigging Rentals WA Pty Ltd* [2015] FCA 1158; *Strategic Management Australia AFL Pty Ltd v Precision Sports & Entertainment Group Pty Ltd* (2016) 114 ACSR 1; *Hannes v MJH Pty Ltd* (1992) 7 ACSR 8; *Western Ventures Pty Ltd v Resource Equities Ltd* (2005) 53 ACSR 568; *Patterson v Humfrey* (2014) 291 FLR 246; *Cowling v Mekken* [2015] VSC 196; *Inform Numbers Australia Pty Ltd v Angelovski* [2014] VSC 537.

breaches their duties in the context of whistleblowing. It is, however, notable that proof of breach of duty alone does not found an oppression action—the circumstances must also constitute one of the two limbs in section 232(d) or (e). Conversely, proof of breach of directors' duty is not necessary in order to found an oppression action, so that if directors' conduct or omissions in responding to whistleblowers satisfies section 232(d) or section 232(e), then an oppression action may be successful.

One of the bases of oppression actions is departure from legitimate (or reasonable) expectations. This term describes an understanding or expectation a member has which, because of equitable considerations, can make it unfair for a party to exercise legal rights. Austin and Ramsay note that Australian courts have continued to use the term 'legitimate expectations' in their consideration of the oppression remedy, although views differ regarding how useful the term is.[96]

In Canada it has been held that 'reasonable expectations' can be created by codes of conduct, particularly where published on a website, as well as by other public documents.[97] In *Firebird Global Master Fund II Ltd v Energem Resources Inc*[98] Fitzpatrick J examined the reasonable expectations of the plaintiff, which in her view included that the company would comply with its legal obligations,[99] that the company's directors and officers were required to abide by relevant statutory and regulatory requirements,[100] that shareholders can rely on written and public pronouncements as to what corporations will do[101] and then said:

> Finally, it is not unusual in this day and age for companies to have codes of conduct. Many publish these codes on their websites, just as Energem did in this case. Again, it is not unreasonable for Firebird to expect that Energem would respect its own code of conduct.[102]

There is no reason why similar reasoning could not be applied in an oppression action in Australia. Companies should therefore take care in framing company codes of conduct and in ensuring compliance with such codes.

---

[96]See Austin and Ramsay (online 2018) [10.450.15] citing *Fexuto* (n 86) 745; *Mopeke Pty Ltd v Airport Fine Foods Pty Ltd* (2007) 61 ACSR 395, [45]; *Ananda Marga Pracaraka Samgha Ltd v Tomar [No 6]* (2013) 94 ACSR 199, [464]; *Wambo Coal Pty Ltd v Sumiseki Materials Co Ltd* (2014) 88 NSWLR 689, [201].

[97]See, e.g., *Firebird Global Master Fund II Ltd v Energem Resources Inc* (2011) 86 BLR (4th) 290 (British Columbia Supreme Court), [102] ('*Firebird*'). See also *Themadel Foundation v Third Canadian General Investment Trust Ltd* (1998) 38 OR (3d) 749; *Deutsche Bank Canada v Oxford Properties Group Inc* (1998) 40 BLR (2d) 302 (Ontario Supreme Court); *BCE Inc v 1976 Debentureholders* [2008] 3 SCR 560, [80].

[98]*Firebird* (n 97).

[99]Ibid. [90].

[100]Ibid. [91].

[101]Ibid. [94]. See also ibid. [100].

[102]Ibid. [102].

6.9 Conclusion

This chapter has provided an overview of the potential application of directors' duties in relation to whistleblowing, with particular focus on Australia. Directors should be particularly mindful of the duty of care and the duty to act in good faith in the interests of the company in ensuring compliance with, and reporting on, such requirements. Compliance with whistleblowing policies and corporate codes should be carefully monitored as part of meeting these core duties.

In providing detailed outline and analysis of directors' core duties, this chapter complements that of Greg Golding, who provides closer detail on the proposed revamped Australian victimisation offence and compensation regimes, as well as on corporate liability and corporate culture.

It has been demonstrated that, as with other important policies and procedures within a corporation, directors may breach their core duties in not properly or adequately responding to, or monitoring, whistleblowing. Such breach is not, however, automatic and depends on the elements of each relevant duty being applied and satisfied. It has been shown that, for the purposes of both the duty of care and the duty to act in good faith in the interests of the company, the company's interests include its reputation. It has also been shown that directors owe their duty to the company and not to employees directly, but that the interests of employees and of other stakeholders need to be considered in considering the interests of the company.

Reporting is taking on a key role for directors and companies, and inadequate or misleading reporting on whistleblowing is something directors should be wary of in seeking to comply with their duties. The oppression remedy, which does not impose a duty on directors as such, is increasingly used in circumstances of breach of directors' duty and has potential application in circumstances of non-compliance with a corporate code. Although the focus of the chapter is on Australian law, the law on directors' duties in other Commonwealth jurisdictions has been referred to and is relevant to the interpretation and development of Australian law. Indeed, given common origins, it is unsurprising that jurisprudence on directors' duties in a number of Commonwealth jurisdictions evinces parallel developments and cross-fertilisation. Thus, the principles outlined in this chapter in relation to whistleblowing and directors' duties could be expected to be of relevance to a range of common law jurisdictions.

References

Austin RP, Ramsay IM (2018) *Ford Austin and Ramsay's Principles of Corporations Law*. LexisNexis Butterworths, Sydney

Austin RP, Ramsay IM (online at July 2018) *LexisNexis, Ford, Austin and Ramsay's Principles of Corporations Law [10.450.15]*

Australian Institute of Company Directors (2014) *The Honest and Reasonable Director Defence*. Policy Paper, 7 August 2014

Barnett K (2018) A Reconsideration of s 1324(10) of the Corporations Act 2001 (Cth): Damages in Lieu of an Injunction. *C & SLJ* 36(4):370
Bathurst TF, Wootton NA (2018) Directors' and Officers' Duties in the Age of Regulation. In: Hanrahan P, Black A (eds) *Contemporary Issues in Corporate and Competition Law: Essays in Honour of Professor Robert Baxt AO*. LexisNexis Butterworths, Sydney
Baxt R (2013) The Importance of a Culture of Compliance *Austl Bus L Rev* 41(2):106
Bednall T (2018) Australian Securities and Investments Commission v Flugge: Section 180 Strikes Again. *C & SLJ* 36(1):61
Brand V (2017) Foreign Bribery Regulation in Australia and "Stepping Stones" Director Liability. *Austl Bus L Rev* 45(3):199
Davies PL, Worthington S (2016) *Gower's Principles of Modern Company Law*. Sweet & Maxwell, London
Dixon O (2016) Honesty Without Fear: Whistleblower Anti-Retaliation Protections in Corporate Codes of Conduct. *Melbourne UL Rev* 40(1):168
du Plessis JJ (2016) Disclosure of Non-Financial Information: A Powerful Corporate Governance Tool. *C & SLJ* 34(1):69
du Plessis J J (2016) Shareholder Primacy and Other Stakeholder Interests. *C & SLJ* 34(3):238
du Plessis JJ and Rühmkorf A (2015) New Trends Regarding Sustainability and Integrated Reporting for Companies: What Protection Do Directors Have? *Co Law* 36(2):51
Harris J, Hargovan A, Austin J (2008) Shareholder Primacy Revisited: Does the Public Interest Have Any Role in Statutory Duties? *C & SLJ* 26(6):355
Langford RT (2017) Stakeholder Interests and the Duty of Care. *C & SLJ* 35(5):342
Langford RT (2019) *Company Directors' Duties and Conflicts of Interest*. Oxford University Press, Oxford
Lombard S, Brand V (2018) Whistleblowing and Corporate Governance: Regulating to Reap the Governance Benefits of "Institutionalised Whistleblowing". *C & SLJ* 36(1):29
McGregor M (2018) Stepping-Stone Liability and the Directors' Statutory Duty of Care and Diligence. *C & SLJ* 36(3):245
North G (2015) *Effective Company Disclosure in the Digital Age*. Wolters Kluwer, Alphen aan den Rijn
Welsh M (2014) Realising the Public Potential of Corporate Law: Twenty Years of Civil Penalty Enforcement in Australia. *F L Rev* 42(1):217

Dr. Rosemary Teele Langford is an Associate Professor with the Melbourne Law School, University of Melbourne, where she teaches a broad range of subjects including Corporations Law and Corporate Governance & Directors' Duties. She has a first class honours degree in Law and a Bachelor of Arts from the University of Melbourne and a Ph.D. from Monash University. Prior to entering academia Rosemary practised with Allens Arthur Robinson (now Allens Linklaters). Rosemary edits the Directors' Duties section of the Company & Securities Law Journal and is on the advisory board of the SSRN eJournal, Fiduciary Law. She is an active member of the Corporations Committee of the Business Law Section of the Law Council of Australia and the Not for Profit Law Committee of the Law Council of Australia.

Part III
Practical Implications of Corporate Whistleblowing Measures

Chapter 7
The United States Securities and Exchange Commission Whistleblower Program: A Long and Winding Road

Daniel J. Hurson

Abstract As a lawyer, I have represented or conferred with dozens of individuals who have wanted to become whistleblowers under the US Securities and Exchange Commission's Whistleblower Program and have represented clients who have received awards. In this chapter, I describe the process of being a whistleblower under this Program from the inside out, including advice on how to decide if one has a viable case which can qualify under the myriad of unforgiving and dense thicket of rules that the SEC carefully crafted to govern the program. The opportunities to fail in this process are many, the time periods can be quite long (into the years) and the process from the whistleblower's perspective can be very frustrating. On the other hand, the prospect that your information can bring down the awesome power and expertise of the SEC on your target after providing the initial information and otherwise qualifying as a whistleblower, can be downright thrilling, and supremely satisfying as you see the "bad guys" getting their due. By describing my practice and cases, if even in a somewhat generic outline, I can give some guidance to readers who may be considering what will become one of the most important decisions of their lives—to "tell truth to power" and become a whistleblower in aid of the U.S. government's worldwide enforcement of its powerful securities laws.

Keywords Whistleblower program · Dodd frank · Office of the whistleblower · Qui tam · Foreign corrupt practices act · Whistleblower award

7.1 Introduction

Since its inception in 2011, the United States Securities and Exchange Commission (SEC) Whistleblower Program (the "Program"), created as part of the Dodd-Frank

[1]Dodd-Frank Wall Street Reform and Consumer Protection Act, Pub. L. No. 11-203 § 922(a), 121 Stat 1894 (2010), 5 U.S.C. Sec. 78u-6(h).

D. J. Hurson (✉)
The Law Offices of Daniel J. Hurson, Annapolis, MD, USA
e-mail: dhurson@comcast.net
URL: https://www.hursonlaw.com

S. Lombard et al. (eds.), *Corporate Whistleblowing Regulation*,
https://doi.org/10.1007/978-981-15-0259-0_7

Act,[1] has received more than 28,000 tips and has distributed (as of March 2019) more than $376 million in awards to 61 whistleblowers.[2] In FY 2018 alone, the Program received more than 5200 tips.[3] Although none of the whistleblowers' names have ever been disclosed by the SEC, and the cases they cause to be brought by the SEC remain largely unidentified, the program has clearly had a significant impact on the SEC's and the U.S. Department of Justice (DOJ) enforcement programs, and has become feared in corporate suites around the globe. In fact, over the life of the program, the SEC states that more than $2 billion in total monetary sanctions has been recovered in cases brought with information from whistleblowers, of which over $450 million has been returned to harmed investors.[4] A few of the awards have been in the multi-millions, and are widely reported.[5]

Nevertheless, as can be readily seen by the numbers, 28,000 tips since 2011 funneling down to about 70 whistleblower awards to date, the odds of an individual tipster getting an award are rather small, but hope springs eternal and the tips keep coming. I will endeavor in this chapter to describe the process from start to finish, including advice on how to decide if one has a viable case which can qualify under the dense thicket of rules that the SEC crafted to govern the program. Some of these observations are most relevant to potential whistleblowers themselves, and to their lawyers (if they choose to employ one, which I highly recommend). Frankly, the chances to fail in this process are considerable, and the time periods leading up to an award can be quite long (five years or more in some cases). This process, from the whistleblower and the lawyer's, perspective, can be most frustrating, as we will explore. Hopefully, by describing what I have learned in my practice representing whistleblowers, I can provide some guidance to readers who may be considering what will become one of the most important decisions of their lives: whether to become a whistleblower in aid of the U.S. government's worldwide enforcement of its powerful securities laws.[6]

The beauty of this Program is that one whistleblower's information, when properly documented and presented, is the essence of "speaking truth to power." It can bring down the awesome might and expertise of the SEC and DOJ on the corporate target. This process, albeit painfully slow, can be downright thrilling and supremely satisfying as one eventually sees the "bad guys" getting their due as the result of one lowly whistleblower speaking up. And, as noted, the awards can be very large–in

---

[2]Securities and Exchange Commission (2018).

[3]Ibid, p. 20.

[4]Ibid, p. 1.

[5]Ibid. In 2018 the SEC awarded $83 million (shared by three individuals), and an award of almost $54 million (shared by two individuals). In March 2019, awards totaling over $50 million were given to two whistleblowers.

[6]The U.S. Commodity Futures Trading Commission (CFTC) has a whistleblower program nearly identical to that of the SEC. It has as of early 2019 made 9 awards to whistleblowers, totaling $87 million. The largest award, $30 million, was made in July 2018. The program had a modest start but appears to be picking up steam. See Commodity Futures Trading Commission (2019). In many respects, my observations will be applicable as well to that program.

2018 $168 million was awarded to 13 whistleblowers.[7] Yet I continually find that, for all of my clients, it is that personal satisfaction that propels them, "that desire to do the right thing," much more so than the potential award.

One of the most impressive statistics put out by the SEC, little-noted but very impressive, stated in the SEC's Office of the Whistleblower (OWB) 2018 Report, is that the "OWB currently is tracking over 900 matters in which a whistleblower's tip has caused an [SEC] Matter Under Inquiry or investigation to open, or has been forwarded to Enforcement staff for review and consideration in connection with an ongoing investigation."[8] These are the matters that may, or may not, flower into serious enforcement investigations, which can end in a settlement with a corporate respondent generally in the millions, and for which the whistleblower can be awarded from 10–30% of the penalties. Many of these matters are in various states of gestation, not all will result in settlements, and most will take from 2–4 years or more to resolve themselves. But the important fact here is that all these 900 or so started or were assisted by a whistleblower tip, and more than a few are destined to produce large settlements (very few SEC cases are litigated). The SEC's pipeline is long, to be sure, but it is full of potential awards, and the SEC has $300 million in the pot (a number which must be replenished if it falls below that amount) with which to pay out awards.[9]

I will also discuss the issue of retaliation, and how the SEC rules and enforcement actions are designed to protect whistleblowers and sanctioning those who would try to interfere with the Program. I will also touch on how the whistleblower process may consider reporting internally as well as or in lieu of becoming a whistleblower. In the process, I will impart some "practice tips" for the would-be whistleblower and his or her lawyer.

7.2 My Practice Representing Whistleblowers

First a word on my background. By 2010, I had been practicing law in the US for nearly four decades, in private practice in law firms and as a sole practitioner, and as both a DOJ federal prosecutor and later as an SEC trial lawyer. When the SEC program was born as part of the Dodd-Frank Act in 2011, I decided that my background could be well-suited for being a lawyer for whistleblowers. I knew the territory, so to speak, as both a former prosecutor and securities enforcement lawyer. I reasoned that I had some credibility with the DOJ and SEC staff, as I had worked in both agencies (this can be a factor in the success of the effort, and should be considered in selecting counsel).

Moreover, with this background I figured I might attract clients (always a primary consideration for a lawyer), be in a position to give them good counsel, and take

[7] Securities and Exchange Commission (2018, p. 1).

[8] Ibid, p. 24.

[9] Ibid, p. 30, and section 21F(g)(3) of the Exchange Act, 15 U.S.C. § 78-6(g)(3).

quality clients and their information when they came my way, but also be experienced enough to decline matters that, however tempting they appeared at first blush, were ultimately in all likelihood to be unsuccessful. I owe potential whistleblowers such candid advice, for becoming a whistleblower is an enormous gamble, which may risk one's career or in some cases their personal safety. Moreover, it is an endeavor not too different from buying a lottery ticket.[10] Over the years, I have represented or conferred with dozens of individuals who were considering becoming SEC whistleblowers. Some became my clients, some did not, and some I discouraged from even starting this difficult process. Several have even received substantial multi-million dollar awards, and others among these clients may (hopefully) follow.

As a practitioner in this field, I believe my most meaningful contribution herein would be to educate readers who are actually considering becoming a whistleblower, but who know little of the complexities involved in formally starting and succeeding in the Program. I also hope to help lawyers unfamiliar with this area of practice to be able to competently represent their clients amid the myriad of complex rules laid down by the SEC (in several hundred dense pages of regulations). Other chapters in this book consider the theory of whistleblowing, its "morality," the hardships endured by whistleblowers, the impact of their actions, and the process from the perspective of the corporations and employers who are on the receiving end of a whistleblower case. However, what is largely absent is the voice of the whistleblowers and their experiences. Given the small number of largely anonymous members in the relatively exclusive club of successful SEC whistleblowers, the likelihood is that very few will ever publicly disclose their identify or the specifics of their cases, much less how they went about becoming a successful SEC whistleblower. Perhaps I can provide some insight into the operation of the Program and in a sense, speak for them.

7.3 Where to Start: Make Sure You Really Want to Be a Whistleblower

There are many unhappy, frustrated, angry, or simply disgusted corporate managers, executives, employees (former or current), compliance officers, auditors, and others who possess information they believe might prove securities fraud by their current or former employer. Maybe you are a mid-level manager who sees accounting fraud taking place in your division. Maybe you are aware of payments to a foreign official to get or keep your company's business. Maybe you observe earnings reports or public filings being made which are materially false. Maybe you have participated in or condoned such activity in the past and want it stopped. Hopefully you have no

[10]Ibid., p. 1. In FY 2018, the SEC awarded three individuals in the same matter a total of $83 million, and an award of almost $54 million to two individuals.

exposure or involvement in the activity, but even those who do can still qualify in some circumstances to become SEC whistleblowers.[11]

Most people who learn such information will, especially in tough economic times, stay silent, for fear of rocking the boat and potentially facing demotion or dismissal, or worse. It's only human, and nothing to be ashamed about, despite what your company Code of Ethics may decree. Some may complain about it to superiors, and are told to mind their own business, or are just ignored. We are all familiar with what can happen to those who become seen as "troublemakers." Their duties shrivel, they get transferred to the Nome, Alaska branch, and their career suddenly leads to nowhere.

Others, however, being well-motivated or interested in the reward, or both, consider "blowing the whistle." Under the SEC process, one can, using an attorney, remain anonymous, at least until the case goes to trial (which very few do).[12] While SEC whistleblowers are required to reveal their identities at the time of applying for an award, the SEC is required by law to keep confidential the name of the whistleblower when it announces the award, and thereafter.[13]

Nevertheless, as the title of this chapter suggests, being a whistleblower can be a lonely, long and winding road. Life can become very difficult for a whistleblower, even a successful one. Of course, if the case succeeds, and you qualify, you might eventually earn enough to make it financially worthwhile. But there are no guarantees and many things have to fall into place before getting a whistleblower award.

Many whistleblowers have already complained internally within the company to no avail. While retaliation is always a possibility, the SEC has issued strong retaliation provisions that can be enforced by the Commission itself[14] or by a lawsuit filed by the whistleblower.[15] The corporate world, including the lawyers, is increasingly sensitive to treating whistleblowers gingerly. The SEC whistleblower office treats retaliation cases as a top priority, and has over the years brought and settled a number of them.[16] But one has to report first to the SEC to utilize the retaliation protections.[17] While the environment may be improving for whistleblowers, human nature being what it is, you will still be pretty much on your own if you pick up that whistle. If you can

---

[11]SEC Rules, 17 C.F.R. (2011), § 240.21F-6(b)(1). The most up to date version of these SEC whistleblower rules should be able to be accessed via the Google search "Regulation 21F-SEC.gov". See also www.sec.gov/whistleblower, then go to "Resources" then to "Statutes and Regulations" then to "Section 922 of the Dodd-Frank Act.".

[12]Ibid, § 240.21F-7(3)(b).

[13]Ibid, § 240.21F-7(a).

[14]Securities and Exchange Commission (2018, p. 7).

[15]Securities Exchange Act of 1934, 15 U.S.C. § 78u-6(h)(1)(B).

[16]Securities and Exchange Commission (2018, p. 7).

[17]In the major case of *Digital Realty Trust, Inc. v. Sommers*, 138 S.Ct. 767 (2018), the U.S. Supreme Court held that the whistleblower protections of the Dodd-Frank Act require that a person report a possible securities law violation to the SEC initially to qualify as a whistleblower protected from retaliation under Section 21F(h) of the act. Thus, reporting to the employer alone, or going to the SEC only after suffering retaliation, will not protect the whistleblower under the generous provisions of that law.

sleep with that, and your family can as well, and you are the kind of person who just feels better about doing the right thing, then you should consider becoming an SEC whistleblower.

7.4 You Must Present the SEC with "Original Information" to Qualify for an Award

Maybe you are aware of accounting fraud at your company, maybe insider trading, false or inadequate, maybe the payoff of a foreign official. You want to tell the SEC. Is it as simple as picking up the phone and dialing the main number in Washington? Unfortunately not. First, you have to have "original information." The SEC defines (on its "Office of the Whistleblower" webpage) "Original information" to be that "derived from your independent knowledge (facts known to you that are not derived from publicly available sources) or independent analysis (evaluation of information that may be publicly available but which reveals information that is not generally known) that is not already known by [the SEC]."[18] You don't have to be an insider—you can be a customer, an outside advisor, or someone who hears about the illegal activity secondhand. The information cannot violate the company's attorney-client privilege or come from an auditor or compliance officer, with some important exceptions.[19] Don't assume the SEC knows about or is acting on the information already. You would be surprised about what they don't know (I can speak from experience—I used to work there). You may have the information that could bring a major enforcement action by the SEC or another government agency. About two thirds of whistleblowers who have received awards provided information that caused the staff to open an investigation.[20]

Even if the SEC already knows something, or there has been publicity, or a Congressional hearing, or something on the Internet, and the SEC is already investigating it, you can still qualify if your information "significantly contributes to the success of [the SEC's] resulting enforcement action."[21] One third of award recipients to date assisted an existing investigation.[22] Likewise, as long as your tip is not exclusively derived from public sources, you can still qualify. If you see something in the media, but it does not tell the whole story, or it has it wrong in some respect, or you are aware that your company has claimed to be "cooperating in an SEC investigation" but is secretly withholding or providing false information, do not hesitate to make the submission. Demonstrate to the SEC that the information that has been given to it by the company, disclosed in filings, or reported in the media up to that point

[18] Securities and Exchange Commission (29 October 2018).

[19] See Hurson (2015).

[20] Securities and Exchange Commission (2018, p. 16).

[21] SEC Rules, 17 C.F.R. (2011), § 240.21F-4(c)(2).

[22] Securities and Exchange Commission (2018, p. 16).

is incomplete, inaccurate, or untruthful. Whistleblowers may be current or former employees, but do not have to have any particular connection with the company.

The information has to relate to a violation of the US securities laws. Those laws are quite broad, and cover just about every aspect of finance, markets, corporate governance, financial reports to the SEC and the public, insider trading, keeping of accurate books and records, and even, somewhat surprisingly, payment of bribes to foreign officials–the infamous Foreign Corrupt Practices Act (FCPA), which has generated massive monetary fines and numerous prison terms over the years, and sits tucked within the securities laws.[23]

7.5 Would-Be Whistleblowers Must Be Creative, and Investigate Cases Previously Brought by the SEC

Potential whistleblowers tend to focus on one specific transaction or practice they feel is wrong or dishonest. Sometimes this activity is a violation of the securities laws, sometimes it is not. The US securities laws are very broad, cover corporate activity worldwide, and are continually being expanded by the SEC to new business practices and legal theories. For example, there has recently been scrutiny of companies who hire the children of public officials to gain influence with their parents as a potential violation of the FCPA.[24] Some very substantial fines have resulted against prominent US Firms. Likewise, the SEC conducted an insider trading investigation involving law firms and consultants who allegedly were informing their clients about impending government and U.S. congressional actions that could affect their business, and presumably their stock prices. This is standard fare in Washington, and no one has yet figured out where the line should be drawn as to what might be insider

[23]A useful guide to US securities law is Wake Forest Professor Palmiter (2017). The SEC website contains descriptions of most enforcement actions, called "Litigation Releases." It may aid a prospective whistleblower to review cases involving other entities in the same or a related business or industry to see if similar conduct has been prosecuted. A very good FCPA primer is the DOJ and SEC's, Resource Guide to the U.S. Foreign Corrupt Practices Act [Department of Justice and Securities and Exchange Commission (2012)], available on their respective websites or Google "FCPA Resource Guide".

[24]In November 2016, JPMorgan Chase settled an FCPA case with the SEC, DOJ and the US Federal Reserve, paying total penalties and fines of more than $264 million. Over a seven-year period, the firm had hired approximately 100 interns and full-time employees at the request of foreign government officials. As the SEC announced it: "JP Morgan engaged in a systematic bribery scheme by hiring children of government officials and other favored referrals who were typically unqualified for the positions on their own merit." This was done to enable the firm to win or retain business resulting in more than $100 million in revenues to JP Morgan. This case could have resulted in a whistleblower (if there was one) award of almost $80 million, see Securities and Exchange Commission (2016). The SEC settled a similar case with Deutsche Bank in August 2019, in which the bank paid $16 million in penalties for making such hires. A valuable source of information on SEC enforcement cases, including FCPA cases, is found in the quarterly and annual summaries compiled by the Gibson Dunn law firm, available on its website, https://www.gibsondunn.com/.

trading in these situations. Thus, there is no harm in filing a whistleblower report about activity which may turn out to be of doubtful legality.

The best guide to the general nature of most whistleblower tips is found in the Annual Report of the Office of the Whistleblower. In FY 2018, out of the 5282 tips "Corporate Disclosures and Financials" and "Offering Fraud" accounted for about 20% (1000 tips each), "Manipulation" of stock 12%, Insider Trading 5% (262), "Trading and Pricing" 6% (333), "Unregistered Offerings" 5% (252), FCPA 202 (4%), with "Market Events" Municipal Securities and Public Pensions, and miscellaneous others (1210) making up the rest.[25] These categories have remained fairly stable over the eight years the program has been reporting (through November 2018), although the number of tips has grown by 76%.[26] However, in FY 2018 some 39 tips were received involving "Initial Coin Offerings and Cryptocurrencies," an area to which the SEC has devoted considerable attention recently.[27]

Would-be whistleblowers are emerging all over the world. In FY 2018, tips came from every state, led by California (554), New York (345), Florida (276) and Texas (251).[28] Tips from 119 countries outside the United States have been received over the life of the program, with tips from 72 countries in FY 2018 alone, the largest numbers being Canada, the United Kingdom, Australia and China.[29] The international contingent may reflect the fact that few jurisdictions outside the United States provide substantial awards, and some place excessive restrictions and obligations upon the whistleblowers.[30]

7.6 Building a Successful Whistleblower Case—The Process and the Need for Patience

My experience suggests that some potential whistleblowers see or hear of some activity that appears to be illegal, go to the SEC website, and then type-in a disjointed complaint on the SEC's TCR form that is a somewhat stream-of-consciousness download of a lot of information, attaching dozens of documents, many irrelevant. It then comes as a surprise and disappointment to them when they never hear a word from the SEC. The fact that 28,000 tips have resulted in only about 70 awards over the nine years of the Program indicates that the vast majority of tips are not resulting in SEC investigations. Even when the whistleblower has a lawyer, as do my clients, good tips oftentimes produce no action by the SEC, and even when investigations are instituted and clients are interviewed by SEC counsel, sometimes, for presumably valid reasons not disclosed to the whistleblower, the cases are never brought. No

[25] Securities and Exchange Commission (2018, p. 21).

[26] Ibid, p. 20.

[27] Ibid, p. 22.

[28] Ibid, p. 34.

[29] Ibid, p. 23.

[30] This is discussed further in part 21.

SEC lawyer who wants to keep their job would give out any information about a matter that has not been acted on to a whistleblower or his or her attorney.

While you need to be the first to report this "original information" to the SEC to qualify as a whistleblower, the key is to make your submission the one that kicks off an investigation, and you can do some of your own analysis and investigation. Read the company's annual and quarterly reports. Scrutinize its press releases and analyst conference calls. If you hear the widget division in Singapore is having a bad year, see if those results show up in the financial statements. If the company has huge potential environmental liabilities it is not disclosing, you may have a case. If the company is winning overseas business using shady middlemen or is entertaining government officials lavishly, there is probably an FCPA bribery case in progress (despite all the education and compliance programs, I suspect the FCPA continues to be violated around the globe, in ever more creative ways). Watch carefully for signs of insider trading, and failures to report material negative information. Large sales or purchases of stock by insiders can be tracked, and "water cooler rumors" about large transactions by senior managers may be true.

In fact, while the FCPA foreign bribery cases grab the headlines, historically the accounting provisions of that act relating to bookkeeping and internal controls have been far more likely to form the basis of an SEC case. These provisions are intended to protect the general integrity of financial statements, and apply equally to U.S. and non-U.S. operations of companies required to file reports with the SEC. They also apply to majority-owned foreign subsidiaries. Sometimes an FCPA case that falls short of enough evidence to assert bribes can be settled on a "books and records" violation, by alleging failures in the company's internal controls over the handling of foreign agents or vendors. The penalties can still run into the millions. My sense is that, across the entire spectrum of business activity subject to these provisions, there are untold violations of these provisions being committed every day, many of which would be of great interest to the SEC staff if only someone informed them where to look. Whistleblowers often have access to documents that would be very hard for the SEC to obtain, such as foreign records beyond the SEC's subpoena power. This makes the help and contribution of the whistleblower much more valuable, to both the SEC and the whistleblower.

Likewise, the Sarbanes-Oxley Act requires officers to certify the integrity of their companies' financial statements and review the adequacy of their internal controls.[31] Find a mid-level manager who is unhappy about a false certification he was pressured to make and you may have a case. Look for period-ending account adjustments that tend to enhance results or depress revenue in an effort to "smooth out" results. While more accounting provision violations are being uncovered, many (but surely not all) are being reported to the SEC. This too can be a fertile ground for whistleblowers. The SEC announces a settled case in detail in an "Order" published on its website. It also publishes a summary of the case in what is called a "Litigation Release." You may easily review these documents periodically to see if another company in your business sector has been caught by the SEC doing something that is also done in

[31] Sarbanes-Oxley Act, 15 U.S.C. § 7241(a).

your own firm, perhaps known to many others in the workforce but never viewed as truly illegal, but maybe just treated as a routine business practice, i.e. "we have always been doing it this way."

7.7 Make the Submission Succinct and Persuasive; Consider Carefully Which Documents to Submit

Your submission should get to the point quickly, and be specific without overwhelming the staff with details, which can be added later if they decide to follow-up on the matter. You can tell of a bribe to a foreign official in a paragraph ("My company has been paying off the Minister of Finance of Guatador by sending cash to his sister"). You can describe a complex accounting fraud in a page or so ("My company cooks the books each quarter by using cookie-jar reserves, as shown in the attached accounting records"). You should attach a few "smoking gun" documents if you have them, and tell the SEC you have more documents, if that is the case. Don't send them a box full of dog-eared paper and expect a harried staff lawyer to spend much time trying to sort them out. If you can name individuals at the company that you know or have good reason to know are aware of the activity, or participants in it, don't hesitate to name them and their positions. Be specific. If you simply have suspicions but no direct proof, tell the SEC that too. Don't hype, puff, or over-promise. You don't have to present a clear cut and overwhelming case, they have the resources to find all that out. Tell them about yourself, your position and background, how you came about the information, and why you believe it to be true. If you have reported internally (even a verbal complaint to your manager) describe that in some detail, and what, if anything, happened to the matter afterward.

If your information relates to an event already made public in any respect, indicate that but show how you are adding to the information, or perhaps correcting falsehoods put out by the company. You can even make a submission based entirely on publicly available information if your examination and evaluation of it reveals information that is not generally known or available to the public.[32] If you have chosen not to retain counsel but have someone you trust to keep your information confidential (and perhaps knows something about the issues you are raising), you might ask them to read a draft of your submission before submitting it to the SEC. Do not confide in anyone at the office. You simply can't be sure they won't out you somehow, particularly if your tip leads to an SEC investigation of the company.

In selecting documents to submit, be aware that you may be violating company policies against disclosing confidential or proprietary information. This risk is pretty much part of the life of a whistleblower. However, if the matter ever went to court, perhaps in an employment dispute, the need to reveal illegal acts should normally trump routine confidentiality language in an employment agreement or employee

[32] Securities and Exchange Commission (29 October 2018).

manual. There are legal protections in U.S. for whistleblowers who turn over evidence to law enforcement authorities.[33] Nevertheless, if you have documents which are highly sensitive, and might involve serious breaches of the law on your part to disclose (e.g. "national security" matters) or trade secrets, it may be best to hold them back until you are certain the SEC is interested in your submission, and then discuss with the staff how to handle such information.[34] Likewise, the SEC staff is extremely sensitive to using documents or information which may violate the company's attorney client privilege. If you have any documents which involve attorney advice (such as emails to or from inside or outside company counsel) it is advisable not to include them in your initial submission, or clearly segregate them among your attachments. They can be addressed later when and if the SEC responds to your information. The SEC has knowledgeable teams of lawyers called "taint teams" to review such documents before any are disclosed to the enforcement lawyers who will investigate the matter.

7.8 To Report up or not, and When: Important Decisions Which Can Help or Hurt Your Case

Unless it seems risky, or useless, and if you are a current employee, you should consider reporting your information internally in a well-documented written submission to the responsible corporate officials, such as the general counsel or chief compliance officer, or their top subordinates. When the SEC issued proposed whistleblower rules for public comment, there was considerable concern expressed in the corporate community that the SEC whistleblower program would seriously undermine internal reporting through compliance programs.[35] This has not happened.[36] Most whistleblowers still report internally first in some fashion, but get frustrated, discouraged, or punished, before they go to the SEC. However, the SEC, in an effort to acknowledge the value of internal compliance programs, and encourage internal whistleblowing, has stated that it will consider an increase in the percentage of the award closer to the 30% limit if the information was reported first internally.

Having said that, in the wake of the *Digital Reality* decision (discussed in Footnote 17 above), to qualify as a legal "whistleblower" under Dodd-Frank and be protected from retaliation, one first has to report information regarding a securities law violation directly to the SEC, not just to the employer. A Dodd-Frank retaliation claim for actions taken against the whistleblower by the company before he or she has reported to the SEC will fail (as some recently have in the wake of *Digital Realty*). One tactic would be to report to the SEC first and then report to the company promptly. You

[33] See Hurson (2016).

[34] The Defend Trade Secrets Act of 2016, 18 U.S.C. Sec. 1836, has strong whistleblower protection provisions.

[35] Securities and Exchange Commission (2011, p. 95).

[36] Securities and Exchange Commission (2018, p. 17).

do not have to tell them you have gone to the SEC first but under the circumstances, including the *Digital Realty* decision, the company (or at least its lawyers) should understand why you went to the SEC first. The company would not be happy with you, but, probably would not attempt any retaliation. Even if you never report internally, and the company does not know you are a bona fide SEC whistleblower, it still would be subject to SEC retaliation provisions (see below) and a private suit by you under the Dodd-Frank Act, if it retaliated against you after your report to the SEC.

7.9 Reporting up Internally—The Right Way, and the Wrong Way

If you choose to report internally, do it right. Don't just leave a message on a company hotline, or mumble something in a random conversation to a supervisor. It may be hard later to prove you gave the information, and exactly what you reported and when. Proof of providing a timely internal report can be an important factor to be considered by the SEC in getting a large award (although it is not required by the SEC). Such proof can also be critical evidence in a retaliation action. If you decide to report internally, put together a written report of your information. Sign and date it, and present it (preferably in person) to a superior you trust, and one who has the responsibility to report up the chain of command. It may be an internal auditor, a member of the legal department, an HR or compliance officer. Start as high up the chain as you can. You do not have to go directly to your immediate superior, especially if that person is part of the problem, likely to bury the information or make your life difficult thereafter.

The important thing is to make the information as comprehensive, detailed, and authenticated as possible. If you have documents or emails, provide them. If you are not supposed to have such materials, it might be wise to consult your own counsel before showing them to company officials. If you do report through a hotline, make a record of it. If the Hotline is run through an internal message system, save and copy the messages back and forth. This will be hard evidence that the company was on notice by you, and when. If you report via phone hotlines, insist on talking to someone, and ask his or her permission to tape the conversation (they are probably taping it as well). Often these report lines are staffed by third-party firms, and you need to be clear you want to get the information to, or be connected with someone inside the company. If you are asked to come into speak to others, including company lawyers, consider getting your own counsel to accompany you. In any event, do a memo to the file afterwards to document when and to whom you gave the information, and exactly what you told them.

7.10 When Good Intentions Can Go Awry—The Case Against Reporting Up Internally

There are some reasons *not* to report internally: if you are convinced it will do no good, or that superiors were already aware of the activity (often the case) or if there is a high likelihood of retaliation by the company against you, or if you simply do not want to identify yourself publicly as a whistleblower. If you are going to provide the SEC with confidential company documents, as many whistleblowers do, it would be very dangerous to show them first to the company and then turn them over to the SEC. The SEC reports that something like 80% of whistleblowers claim they have reported internally before coming to the SEC,[37] but what constitutes such reporting may fall far short of making a formal complaint.

In the case of a smaller company whose top management is deeply involved in the wrongdoing, or if the wrongdoing is clearly already known to superiors in the management, or if others who have reported it have been punished, or for any of the other reasons just mentioned, then the whistleblower should go directly to the SEC, or employ counsel to make an anonymous report to the SEC. As the Program has developed, my sense is the SEC no longer views failure to report internally as a detriment to receiving a healthy award, particularly after the decision in *Digital Realty*. Likewise, if you have any reasonable basis to believe that your safety, or that of your family, may be jeopardized if you report internally, then go directly to, and only to, the SEC. In many parts of the world, such risks are real, and the SEC will certainly understand if you choose to come to them first under the circumstances.[38]

If you are a former employee, the decision to report "internally" may have less significance. You can certainly contact the company and inform it of your information, and disclose if you choose that you intend to contact the SEC as well. If you essentially reported the issue at the time you were an employee (and can prove it somehow) but nothing was done as far as you know, you basically have satisfied the internal reporting suggestion in any event. If you are concerned about retaliation, such as blacklisting by your former employer (it happens) or efforts to alert your current employer that you are a troublemaker, or other forms of retaliation, then it may be best not to call the former employer and perhaps explain to the SEC in your submission why you did not do so. In the case of former employers, my sense is that the SEC does not really expect you to contact them in any event.

---

[37] Securities and Exchange Commission (2018, p. 17).

[38] See Hurson (2017), in which I have set forth a number of these considerations for whistleblowers and their lawyers.

7.11 Timing Is Everything—The 120 Day Rules

Under SEC rules, even if you had reported internally first, you may still report to the SEC within 120 days in order to insure you get credit as the original source (as of the first day you reported it internally).[39] This is necessary to preserve your claim if the company decides to report it to the SEC as well, or if someone else reports it to the SEC before you do. In this case, the SEC will consider your place in line for determining whether your information is 'original information' to be the date you reported it internally. If you do report internally first, do not wait around to see what the company does with the information, even if someone is advising you to "keep this confidential." You may even want to inform the company you have already provided your information to the SEC, but of course this will identify you as the whistleblower. The rules on this are rather confusing, for example, high-level officers, auditors and compliance officials in certain circumstances, should *wait* 120 days before reporting to the SEC.[40]

If you do report internally, the company will be under considerable pressure to "self-report" to the SEC once it knows the SEC has your information. Also, in the wake of *Digital Realty,* most companies will assume you have or soon will be going to the SEC, and they have at no more than 120 days at the most to inform the SEC of the issue and initiate an internal investigation. Another plus to reporting to the company is that your information may trigger a wider investigation when conducted by outside company counsel and reported to the SEC, for which you should get the credit, whereas your independent tip to the SEC without reporting internally might not get a similar priority by the agency, or there may be considerable delay before the SEC decides to open an investigation, or your tip may be ignored entirely. But normally if you give the information to the SEC only, and it is serious enough to warrant follow-up, the agency will probably ask the company to open an internal investigation anyway. In any event, it is important to remember that you can report to the SEC before reporting internally, or not report internally at all, and still be eligible for a whistleblower award.

7.12 Submitting Your Tip—Not Just Another Form to Fill Out

The SEC process for reporting information has recently become more user-friendly. You go to the SEC website, then to the Office of the Whistleblower tab, then to "Submit a Tip." You will see FORM TCR (which stands for Tips, Complaints and Referrals). You (or your lawyer if you are proceeding anonymously) will have to

---

[39]SEC Rules, 17 C.F.R. (2011), § 240.21F-4(b)(7).

[40]SEC Rules, 17 C.F.R. (2011).

answer a battery of questions regarding your eligibility and then describe your information. Hit submit to file the form, at which point you should receive back a "TCR Number" indicating your claim has been filed. Retain that response as proof you filed the information and the date on which you submitted it. The SEC now recommends filing electronically, as opposed to mailing in the form.[41]

When I make an electronic whistleblower submission for a client, I do not try to set out details of the matter on the TCR form but rather I write a detailed cover letter explaining the submission, possibly including a statement directly from the whistleblower. I believe it important for the lawyer to make clear the information is coming directly from the whistleblower, not from the lawyer interpreting or expanding upon the whistleblower's knowledge (nor does the lawyer want to be in the position of making representations to the SEC which may turn out to be inaccurate). I do not try to overwhelm the SEC staff with a phone book of exhibits or try to tell every aspect of the story. I indicate my client is willing and ready to be interviewed by the SEC staff. I attach the statement and the exhibits in pdf format on the TCR form.

7.13 The Long Wait—Do the Best You Can to Help the SEC

After that, a long period of "radio silence" may begin. If you are very lucky, your lawyer will get a call from an SEC enforcement staff lawyer, most likely seeking to talk to the client whistleblower (over the phone, in person as possible, and in limited instances via the SEC's video conference facilities in major cities). This may take several months as the tip is initially sent to the OWB which turns it over to the SEC's Office of Market Intelligence to determine which SEC office (home or regional) gets the tip. You might well receive a call from an SEC attorney in a regional office on the other side of the country. At first, the SEC lawyer may just have a few questions for the lawyer or the client. In other cases, your lawyer may hear nothing, for months or even years (in one of my cases, we heard nothing from the SEC for several years. Eventually, a case was brought by the SEC).

The review process at the agency is something akin to a "black hole" in which no one outside the SEC knows whether anyone is looking at the submission or if it has been rejected, or buried among the thousands of other tips. Or, it may be that the SEC is vigorously investigating the matter. If the whistleblower is still with the company, he may in some manner hear "around the water cooler" that something is happening, or if he has left may hear something from friends still with the company. Or the company itself may disclose the SEC investigation in an SEC filing (often buried deep in a footnote) not saying much beyond the fact of an investigation in which the company is invariably "giving its full cooperation." If the lawyer tries, as I have, to inquire about the submission, a staff lawyer at the OWB will probably not say much more than they have received the submission and it has been forwarded to

---

[41] Securities and Exchange Commission (29 October 2018).

the appropriate enforcement branch, but can give no further information as to what if anything is happening with it.

SEC cases can take literally years to go through the entire enforcement process to get to a final judgment against the company, and then more time to decide whether there will be a whistleblower award made and how much it will be. With a small staff at the OWB and the large number of claims (many of questionable merit) which must be reviewed in turn, the time frame for getting a decision on an award claim has been approaching two years of more. The SEC says it is making a real effort to speed this process up,[42] and will introduce new rules to streamline the process, but for now I have been advising prospective clients that this process from start to finish (filing of the tip to receipt of an award) may take 5 years or more.

Thus, in the lengthy investigation stage, and after that the award stage, the whistleblower must be patient and understand that neither he or she nor their lawyer will be getting much if any information while the case is under investigation, or review for an award. The SEC views whistleblowers as a valued source and strives to protect their anonymity. But the whistleblower is in no way a "partner" in the process. Normally, the lawyer for the whistleblower is not briefed on the progress of the investigation, except for an occasional call from the staff attorney. The lawyer should call the SEC if the whistleblower obtains additional information, and can perhaps get some sense as to whether the case is moving or not. Throughout this process, the whistleblower is viewed as a source of valuable information, and respected as the person who may have brought a major fraud to the attention of the government. But the outcome, for him or her, will not reveal itself for a long, long time. Hopefully, on one fine day somewhere in the future, often without warning, an SEC Order will be released announcing the settlement of the case, and the lawyer and client will learn if the tip they submitted so long before has borne fruit and led to a major SEC enforcement action.[43] Then the second wait—to learn of any award—will begin. As suggested in the caption above, the whistleblower has to be courageous at the start of the process, and very patient thereafter.

[42] Securities and Exchange Commission (28 June 2018a).

[43] I have been told, on good authority, that the lawyer can ask SEC staff if the investigation has been closed, and the staff is authorized to answer yes or no. I recently did just that, and the Whistleblower Office called to inform me about the status of the case. But the fact the case is not closed only means it is not formally closed, but that may only mean that it is technically still open but not being actively investigated. Many investigations stall out, lawyers leave the agency, witnesses fade away, priorities change, or they just get stale, e.g. meaning the statute of limitations is approaching or has been passed. A recent U.S. Supreme Court case, *Kokesh v. SEC*, 137 S.Ct. 1635 (2017), held that disgorgement (repayment of unlawfully gained monies) in securities enforcement cases is covered by the general five-year statute of limitations on penalties. Thus, any activity over five years old cannot be the basis for a substantial SEC settlement with disgorgement. In real terms, and given the time it takes to get most SEC investigations off the ground, I would be concerned that any fact pattern involving activity more than three to four years old and not ongoing presently will probably not attract the attention of SEC enforcement staff regardless of its venality. You could also face a substantial award reduction for failure to come to the SEC sooner.

7.14 Before Going to the Company, or to the SEC, Assess Your Personal Exposure

There is considerable risk to the whistleblower, whether reporting up internally or to the SEC alone, if he or she has had any involvement in the illegal activity. In the complex world of securities fraud, many individuals may not realize they have personal legal exposure for their action or inaction. Other situations, of course, are more obvious. But the SEC Program permits such individuals to still qualify as a whistleblower, if they have not been convicted of a crime or are already the "subject or target" of a criminal investigation in connection with the information being provided to the SEC.[44] If you have any concern about such issues, you definitely need to consult with an experienced securities enforcement attorney before contacting the SEC, or reporting internally. There are ways that counsel can work with the SEC to enter into a "cooperation agreement" to convey the information and protect you from civil or criminal liability, while keeping you eligible for an award (perhaps with a larger reduction factor). But until a qualified lawyer hears your story, you should not be talking to the SEC, which can do with it what it may wish, including referring it to the DOJ for criminal investigation. Of course, if you had nothing to do with the illegal activity other than learning about it, you are free to go to the SEC without concern.

Reporting to the company if you may have personal exposure, including any violation of corporate ethics rules, is also very risky. You will be describing conduct that the company may consider privileged as far as turning it over to the government is concerned, but it will be their privilege, not yours. Some companies, especially US based, may use *Upjohn* warnings (named after a well-known case[45]) given to the employee, which should include the warning that the information you are giving could be turned over to the government by the company, and often is, since the company will want to appear to the government to be fully cooperating. You may also be providing emails or other documents which you might not be entitled to possess. What you may think is very tangential involvement may be considered by the company to be very serious, and you could find yourself terminated and benefits revoked, etc. This may not be considered retaliation in every instance.

No matter what you tell the company, the first question a company lawyer may ask is "how long have you known about this" followed by "why didn't you tell us sooner?" The company may be looking for scapegoats. If the company contacts you first, as sometimes happens in internal investigations, you should also consult your own attorney before meeting with company managers or lawyers. You could also still go to the SEC at that point, as long as the SEC has not directly contacted you first. As noted earlier, if you can afford one, you should hire your own attorney, not one hired by the company. Under these circumstances, an attorney might advise you to let him or her first approach the SEC to work on a cooperation agreement, and if

[44]SEC Rules, 17 C.F.R. (2011), § 240.21F-8(c)(3).

[45]Upjohn Company v United States [449 U.S. 383 (1981)].

that is ironed out you can inform the SEC first, after which you and your counsel determine how to handle the request from the company.

7.15 Construct Your Submission with the Goal of Qualifying Under the Complex Rules and Making a Strong Case that Attracts the Attention of the SEC Staff

As I have made all too clear up to this point, there is nothing certain about getting a whistleblower award, even if the SEC decides to pursue a case based on your information. You may end up dealing with one or more attorneys at the SEC and possibly the DOJ over an extended period of time. You may be asked to repeat information to the DOJ that you have already given to the SEC (they have rules preventing them from sharing certain information). You may see the case brought and settled, and a large fine or disgorgement ordered, and assume you are assured of a large award. The decision to make an award is very subjective, and a number of SEC enforcement attorneys will have a major say or what happens to your claim, and as to what recommendation they will make to the full Commission (see discussion below). You have to assume that the staff may have disagreements over the many legal requirements built into the rules for getting an award, and the staff and the SEC members may have differing views of the value of your contribution.

There are a number of criteria the SEC has to review under the law to determine if an award is allowed and the amount of any award. The first hurdle to overcome is whether your information was "sufficiently specific, credible, and timely to cause the staff to commence an examination, open an investigation, reopen an investigation that the Commission had closed, or to inquire concerning different conduct as part of a current examination or investigation, and the Commission brought a successful judicial or administrative action based in whole or in part on conduct that was the subject of your original information."[46]

That is a mouthful of legalese, but it is critically important to pass this test. For example, your tip may have related to the same company, or the same enforcement action, but was not the information that led to the specific action settled by the SEC. This requirement has led to considerable delays in making awards, as every settlement may draw claims that are either bogus or do not deserve an award, even though the whistleblower thinks they may. Other cases have a number of whistleblowers who contributed to the matter, in varying degrees, and the staff has to sort out who will get the awards, and how much. The SEC has issued a number of Orders in which it denies claims by some whistleblowers and grants others.

Likewise, the whistleblower gives "original information" about conduct "that was already under investigation by the Commission, the [U.S.] Congress" or a number of

---

[46]SEC Rules, 17 C.F.R. (2011) § 240.21F-4(c)(1).

other specified regulatory or law enforcement organizations, and "your submission significantly contributed to the success of the action," the whistleblower is eligible for an award.[47] This requirement is also highly subjective, and has been the subject of dispute in some cases. The problem is that, since all decisions of the Commission are heavily redacted to protect the identity of the whistleblower, there is no record or guidance as to how each award, and its amount, was determined.[48]

7.16 The Award Amount Factors: Increases and Decreases

Even after eligibility is established, there are a number of other factors which can increase or decrease as award. For example, the SEC is entitled to consider whether the "reliability and completeness" of your information "resulted in the conservation of Commission resources."[49] This means, as I read it, that if you give them speculative information that forces them to spend time tracking down dead ends, or if you give them some but not all of what you know (and they figure that out), your award may be reduced. The Commission staff (a 5-person group of senior SEC staffers known as the "Claims Review Committee") will also consider whether you provided "ongoing, extensive and timely cooperation and assistance by, for example, helping to explain complex transactions, interpreting key evidence, or identifying new and productive lines of inquiry."[50]

As we have noted, SEC staff will also consider the "timeliness" of your report to the SEC or to internal compliance or similar authorities at your company. The staff has recently indicated that it may consider a delay of over six months in reporting information to be considered "unreasonable" that could lead to an award reduction, depending on the length of delay and the reason for it.[51] As noted above, SEC staff will consider as well whether you did report internally, and the extent of your help in any internal investigation. Again, the recent *Digital Realty* decision may make this consideration less relevant, and in fact the number of tips coming to the SEC has increased since that decision.[52]

---

[47] SEC Rules, 17 C.F.R. (2011) § 240.21F-4(c)(2).

[48] These criteria are set forth in the SEC Rules, 17 C.F.R. (2011) § 240.21F-4(1) and (2). For suggestions as to how to access these rules, see note 11, above.

[49] SEC Rules, 17 C.F.R. (2011) § 240.21F-6(a)(1)(i).

[50] SEC Rules, 17 C.F.R. (2011) § 240.21F-6(b)(2)(i). For a more detailed explanation as to how the claim review process works, see Securities and Exchange Commission (2011) pp. 6, 12–15, 24–25.

[51] Securities and Exchange Commission (28 June 2018b, p. 56).

[52] Securities and Exchange Commission (2018).

7.17 Consider Hiring a Qualified Lawyer to Assist You in Reporting to the SEC

We have already discussed the need for an attorney if the whistleblower may have personal involvement in the potentially illegal activity being reported. But even for the "honest whistleblower" (the vast majority) the complex process for becoming eligible for a whistleblower award, and the many pitfalls for qualifying, strongly suggest the need for counsel. Indeed, if the whistleblower wishes to remain anonymous, he or she has to report to the SEC through counsel.[53]

An attorney, particularly one experienced with the SEC and with the securities laws, can help frame your information in a way that will be more likely to get the SEC's attention. A whistleblower submission that is a jumbled narrative of complicated events could be overlooked, ignored, or shelved in the SEC review process. Likewise, you are more likely to get your information reviewed and acted upon if you have a lawyer advocating for you with the agency. Some cases sell themselves, others may need some help from your own lawyer. Unlike the typical enforcement case, in whistleblower situations I believe the staff are more comfortable dealing through an attorney, who obviously wants to help them make the case and can help the client tell the story in a coherent fashion and locate documents that may be relevant.

As the investigation proceeds, the attorney should also be making a record of the degree of cooperation the client whistleblower is providing. If the client speaks to SEC counsel, or meets with them, the attorney should be taking copious notes of the meeting or conversations. I have added copies of my notes made at SEC staff interviews of my clients when I submit claims for clients. The attorney can help the whistleblower select documents to present to the SEC, and screen out improper documents, such as attorney-client privileged documents the SEC does not want to see and the whistleblower should not retain in any event. If the employee remains with the company after his or her tip has started an SEC investigation, the whistleblower, with help from the attorney, can continue to supply relevant non-privileged information to the SEC. This can be very effective when the whistleblower is privy to the response (or lack of same) the company is making to SEC inquiries or subpoenas. If the whistleblower learns that the company is misleading the SEC, either in selective witness testimony or dragging its heels in the production of documents, this information can cause the SEC to come down much harder on the company when it comes to settling the case.

It is also to the whistleblower's advantage to have counsel when the whistleblower is still employed by the company and becomes in effect a "mole" aiding the SEC surreptitiously during an investigation. Both the SEC, the whistleblower and counsel have to remain very careful not to expose the whistleblower or draw attention to him or her. A rather bizarre situation that may arise is when the whistleblower is still employed by the company which is conducting an internal investigation for the SEC and, not aware the employee is the whistleblower, company counsel contacts the

---

[53]SEC Rules, 17 C.F.R. (2011) § 240.21F-7(a)(3)(b).

whistleblower to ask for an interview. It may be best to allow the whistleblower to take the interview, tell the truth, but not disclose he or she is working with the SEC. These are the kinds of decisions the SEC staff cannot make for the whistleblower, but advice from the whistleblower's own counsel could be very valuable.

Over the years the Program has been in existence, there has developed a relatively small bar of experienced lawyers who take on whistleblower cases, typically on a contingent fee basis. These attorneys tend to have prior SEC or DOJ enforcement experience, or experience with whistleblowers in false claims act cases or class action securities cases. Is in not difficult to locate such attorneys on the Internet or through consultation with attorneys familiar with lawyers who practice in this area.

7.18 Proceeding Toward an Award After the Company Settles with the SEC

About a month after the SEC settles with the company it will post on its website (on the last day of every month) a list of cases which are eligible for whistleblower awards.[54] This "Notice of Covered Actions" list will show that a given case is now eligible for an award claim. It does not indicate whether there was a whistleblower involved and in many settled cases that may well be the case. These are the cases where the enforcement action results in monetary sanctions exceeding $1 million, the minimum amount required to seek an award. But if the settled case is clearly one that was initiated or supported by you as a whistleblower, you will have 90 days to apply for an award.[55] This is done by filing SEC form WB-APP.[56] Normally, if a given whistleblower is, in the view of the staff at the OWB, likely to be entitled to an award, the staff attorney who handled the case will contact the lawyer for the whistleblower, or the whistleblower herself, to urge them to file the award claim. But the SEC is not required to give such notice, and it is always best to be on the alert yourself for the settlement of the case and the Notice of Covered Action which sets the clock running for the claim to be filed.

In the form, the whistleblower is given an open-ended opportunity to put in writing the exact extent and importance of their contribution to the successful SEC proceeding. Comparing the whistleblower's information to the detailed explanation of the case usually provided in the SEC Order settling the case can be very important to making the case for a large award. Every occasion on which the whistleblower assisted the SEC should be detailed. Do not assume that the staff will provide or recall all such information. This claim filing is critical to the whistleblower's chances for an award because neither the whistleblower or his or her lawyer will have any other opportunity to appear before the Claims Review Staff. There is no meeting before

---

[54] SEC Rules, 17 C.F.R. (2011) § 240.21F-10.

[55] Ibid.

[56] Ibid. The form is available at https://www.sec.gov/about/forms/formwb-app.pdf. Accessed 16 April 2019.

the panel which will decide the claim application. It is also important to ask the staff attorney who handled the case to provide to the OWB a statement as to the assistance provided during the investigation by the whistleblower. This should be in writing if at all possible, perhaps in the form of an email sent to the OWB with a copy to the whistleblower or the attorney, which can then be submitted with the claim. The claims award line is long, and several years may pass between the settlement of the case and the award review. Some staff attorneys may leave the agency. As the most recent SEC Report puts it: "In keeping with OWB's goal of processing meritorious claims, claims that appear to be eligible for an award are prioritized for processing."[57]

7.19 Understanding, and Surviving, the SEC Process for Reviewing Awards

The OWB puts the claim through a thorough analysis, what it describes as "a multi-tiered, robust review process, including review and comment by [the Enforcement Division's] Office of Chief Counsel and the Commission's Office of General Counsel."[58] The OWB makes a recommendation to The Claims Review Staff, which issues a Preliminary Determination. It considers various positive and negative factors, some of which are described above.[59]

If the Claims Review Staff recommends an award less that the 30% maximum, or no award at all, the whistleblower has the right to ask to meet with the OWB staff and ask for the record of the matter from the SEC[60] (which will not disclose the SEC's deliberations). The claimant whistleblower can ask for reconsideration of the Preliminary Determination, which if it stands will go to the Commission for final review (as do all award claim decisions).[61] If no member of the Commission asks for review within 30 days, the Preliminary Determination becomes the Final Order of the SEC.[62] If still unsatisfied, the whistleblower can take an appeal to the federal court of appeals.[63] Frankly, there is little chance that under US law the court will overrule the judgement of the SEC on a matter within its discretion (and to date this has never happened). The best way to get a substantial award is to take the time and effort to present a comprehensive, professional award application that will speak persuasively for the whistleblower.[64]

---

[57] Securities and Exchange Commission (2018, p. 13).

[58] Ibid, p. 14.

[59] Ibid, p. 17 (for a description of the factors).

[60] SEC Rules, 17 C.F.R. (2011) § 240.21F-10(e)(1)(i).

[61] Ibid § 240.21F-10(e)(2).

[62] Ibid § 240.21F-10(g)-(h).

[63] Ibid § 240.21F-13.

[64] As noted, currently (2019) the time for the award decision from the time of the claim has been running two years or more in some cases. The SEC proposed in 2018 some new rules [see Securities and Exchange Commission (28 June 2018b)] to streamline the review process. The OWB has

7.20 Retaliation and Whistleblowing—Frequent Warring Bedfellows

The old adage "no good deed goes unpunished" is quite apt in the whistleblowing arena. Despite the routine pronouncements of corporate managements that they encourage whistleblowing and expect loyal employees to internally report wrongdoing, retaliation against whistleblowers is a recurring result of "doing the right thing." That retaliation takes many forms, some subtle, others direct and career-ending. A whistleblower is routinely ostracized by co-workers, suffers any number of insults and slights at work and elsewhere, may be reassigned to less favorable tasks or locations, receive negative evaluations, reductions in compensation, or may be terminated outright, usually for pre-textual reasons allegedly having nothing to do with their whistleblowing. Some companies go to great lengths to paint the whistleblower as a "disgruntled" or problem employee against whom the negative company actions were deserved and unrelated to the whistleblowing.

The SEC Program has made a vigorous effort to combat retaliation. The Dodd-Frank Act itself contains protection for whistleblowers and expanded rules against retaliation.[65] The SEC has also prohibited anyone from preventing a whistleblower from contacting the SEC directly to report a possible securities violation.[66] As of early 2019, the SEC has taken some twelve enforcement actions against various corporations based on retaliatory conduct or actions taken to impede reporting.[67] For example, in 2015 the SEC settled a case with engineering firm KBR which had required employees to sign confidentiality agreements threatening them with termination and other discipline if they disclosed wrongdoing to anyone outside KBR without prior approval of the legal department.[68] Similar cases came down on companies trying to prevent employees from reporting to the SEC after signing severance agreements, or from receiving any monetary awards for reporting wrongdoing to the SEC. But, as noted above, the *Digital Realty* case held that these Dodd-Frank protections apply only to those persons who provide information relating to a violation of the securities laws to the SEC first, not just internally.

Under US law, employees have a separate private right of action under Dodd-Frank to file a retaliation complaint in federal court.[69] The employee can seek double back pay reinstatement, attorney fees, and reimbursement for certain costs.[70] The statute of

stated: "We anticipate increased efficiencies in the claims review process if certain proposed rule amendments are adopted by the Commission." (see Securities and Exchange Commission (2018, p. 15).

[65] Securities Exchange Act of 1934, 15 U.S.C. § 78u—6(h).

[66] SEC Rules, 17 C.F.R. (2011) § 240.21F-17.

[67] Securities and Exchange Commission (25 July 2018).

[68] Securities and Exchange Commission (2015).

[69] Securities and Exchange Commission Act of 1934, 15. U.S.C. § 78u—6(h)(1)(B)(i).

[70] Ibid., § 78u—6(h)(1)(C).

limitations for such action is a generous 6 years.[71] Under an earlier law, the Sarbanes-Oxley Act,[72] a US employee can sue for retaliation against employees who report wrongdoing either internally or to the SEC. The various provisions and restrictions under both laws should be reviewed by a lawyer to see which statute (or both) is appropriate for a given whistleblower.[73]

7.21 The Keys to Successful Whistleblowing—Why the SEC and CFTC Programs Are the World's Best

In spite of these protections, it remains the case that the best retaliation protection provided under US law is twofold, first, the ability to be an SEC whistleblower and remain anonymous, provided an attorney is used to file the tip; second, the absence of any requirement to report internally, which obviously carries the risk of retaliation, overt or subtle. In every case I have handled, the whistleblower remained anonymous. This does not guarantee protection from retaliation (particularly when the employer may have suspected an individual of being a whistleblower) but it does reduce the likelihood of overt retaliation, which the company would have to fear would be reported by the whistleblower to the SEC, to the obvious detriment of the company. In most other whistleblower regimes around the globe, one or both of these protections are missing. In my view, these programs, of which most, but not all, have no provisions for an award, will never reach the degree of success achieved by the SEC Program if they continue to reject or restrict these incentives and protections for the whistleblower.[74]

---

[71] Ibid., § 78u—6(h)(1)(B)(iii).

[72] Section 806 of the Sarbanes-Oxley Act, 18 U.S.C. § 1541 A.

[73] The SEC OWB website contains an extensive discussion of retaliation protections (https://www.sec.gov/whistleblower/retaliation). A good description of the two statutes and a comparison of their provisions is found in Zuckerman and Stock (2018). One unfortunate development in US law is a decision from an influential lower US appellate court holding that overseas whistleblowers are not protected by retaliation provisions. That court, which covers federal cases arising from New York and several other states, has held that traditional extraterritoriality doctrines of US law compel that such laws are not enforceable outside the United States, at least in cases where the events in question take place outside the country. *Liu Meng-Lin v. Siemens AG,* 763 F. 3d 175 (2 Cir. 2014) [see *Morrison v. Nat'l Austl. Bank, Ltd.,* 561 U.S. 247 (2010)]. Despite the *Liu* holding, the SEC has continued to pay *awards* to foreign nationals when there is a "sufficient U.S. territorial nexus" such as a violation of U.S. securities laws. Nevertheless, this restriction on retaliation jurisdiction strongly suggests that overseas whistleblowers should use an attorney and report anonymously, and forgo reporting up internally.

[74] The Ontario Securities Commission (OSC) in Canada created a whistleblower law in 2016 modeled after the SEC Program and gives awards of 5–15% of monetary sanctions up to $5 million [see Ontario Securities Commission (2016)]. The AMF program in Quebec does not pay an award (see Autorité des marchés financiers (2016). The new Australian law does not give awards [see Treasury Laws Amendment (Enhancing Whistleblower Protections) Act 2019 (Cth)]. Chinese whistleblowing laws allow payment of up to about $73,000 for "significant contributions" to anti-corruption enforcement, (see China Daily 8 April 2016). European countries have not given awards. In April

7.22 Conclusion

The SEC and CFTC whistleblower programs roll on, bringing in thousands of tips and churning out more rewards, a few very large. Hopefully there are many more awards in the pipeline. In the meantime, I feel confident that more whistleblowers will step up to reach out for that brass ring. They will have the courage to begin, and the patience to endure, the long trek to become a successful whistleblower. Along the way, they will continue to instill fear among the many companies against whom they blow the whistle. That threat may continue be the best worldwide deterrent to corporate wrongdoing that exists, more so than any government investigative or regulatory agency could achieve. I hope the observations and suggestions set forth here will help those future whistleblowers to continue to bring "truth to power" and obtain suitable, and just, rewards, at the end of that road.

References

Autorité des marchés financiers (18 February 2016) *No Rewards for Whistleblowers.* https://lautorite.qc.ca/en/general-public/media-centre/news/fiche-dactualites/no-rewards-for-whistleblowers-1/. Accessed 6 Apr 2019

China Daily (8 April 2016) *China Regulates to Protect Whistleblowers on Official Crimes.* http://www.chinadaily.com.cn/china/2016-04/08/content_24385723.htm. Accessed 6 Apr 2019

Commodity Futures Trading Commission (2019) *The Whistleblower Program.* www.whisleblower.gov. Accessed 11 Apr 2019

Department of Justice and Securities and Exchange Commission (2012) *A Resource Guide to the U.S. Foreign Corrupt Practices Act.* https://www.sec.gov/spotlight/fcpa/fcpa-resource-guide.pdf. Accessed 5 Apr 2019

European Parliament (2019) *Directive (EU) 2019/…of the European Parliament and of the Council of…on the Protection of Persons Reporting on Breaches of Union Law.* http://www.europarl.europa.eu/doceo/document/A-8-2018-0398-AM-155-155_EN.pdf. Accessed 17 Apr 2019

Hurson DJ (2015) *When Should Auditors and Compliance Officers Become SEC Whistleblowers?* Mondaq. http://www.mondaq.com/unitedstates/x/654192/Compliance/An+Emerging+Risk+Compliance+Officer+Liability. Accessed 5 Apr 2019

Hurson DJ (2016) *The Whistleblower Protections of the Defend Trade Secrets Act Could Have a Broad Impact—But Only If Employees Are Told About Them.* Mondaq. http://www.mondaq.com/unitedstates/x/526468/Whistleblowing/The+Whistleblower+Protections+Of+The+Defend+

2019, the European Parliament passed a Whistleblower Directive [see European Parliament (2019)] however this does not contain provisions for rewards. In July 2018, the National Whistleblower Center in Washington wrote to the President of the European Parliament and President of the European Commission regarding that Directive Regarding the lack of awards for whistleblowers in the proposal, the NWC stated:

> We strongly urge the EU to establish reward laws, modeled on the successful U.S. Programs. Without these laws, whistleblowers will never be fully and properly compensated for the risks they take, and the overwhelming majority of persons who may otherwise blow the whistle will remain silent.
>
> [see National Whistleblower Centre (2018, p. 15)].

Trade+Secrets+Act+Could+Have+A+Broad+ImpactBut+Only+If+Employees+Are+Told+About+Them. Accessed 5 Apr 2019

Hurson DJ (2017) Sarbanes Oxley, Dodd-Frank, Retaliation and Reward. *ABA J Labor Employment L* 32(3):381

National Whistleblower Centre (2018) *Letter to the President of the European Parliament.* https://www.whistleblowers.org/wp-content/uploads/2018/11/nwc-eu-whistleblower-directive-feedback.pdf. Accessed 17 Apr 2019

Ontario Securities Commission Policy 15-601 (2016) *Whistleblower Program.* http://www.osc.gov.on.ca/documents/en/Securities-Category1/20160714_15-601_policy-whistleblower-program.pdf. Accessed 17 Apr 2019

Palmiter A (2017) *Securities Regulation, Wolters Kluwer (7th Ed) Securities and Exchange Commission (2011) Whistleblowers Incentive and Protections Final Rules* [Release No. 34-64545; File No. S7-33-10]. https://www.sec.gov/rules/final/2011/34-64545.pdf. Accessed 12 Apr 2019

Securities and Exchange Commission (2015) *In the Matter of KBR, Inc., Respondent* [Release No. 74619; File No. 3-16466]. https://www.sec.gov/litigation/admin/2015/34-74619.pdf. Accessed 6 Apr 2019

Securities and Exchange Commission (2016) *Press Release 2016-241: JPMorgan Chase Paying $264 Million to Settle FCPA Charges.* https://www.sec.gov/news/pressrelease/2016-241.html. Accessed 5 Apr 2019

Securities and Exchange Commission (2018) *Annual Report to Congress Whistleblower Program.* https://www.sec.gov/files/sec-2018-annual-report-whistleblower-program.pdf. Accessed 5 Apr 2019

Securities and Exchange Commission (28 June 2018a) *Press Release 2018-120: SEC Proposes Whistleblower Rule Amendments.* https://www.sec.gov/news/press-release/2018-120. Accessed 5 Apr 2019

Securities and Exchange Commission (28 June 2018b) *Proposed Rule.* https://www.sec.gov/rules/proposed/2018/34-83557.pdf. Accessed 16 Apr 2019

Securities and Exchange Commission (25 July 2018) *Office of the Whistleblower: SEC Enforcement Actions.* https://www.sec.gov/whistleblower/retaliation. Accessed 5 April 2019

Securities and Exchange Commission (29 October 2018) *Office of the Whistleblower: Frequently Asked Questions.* https://www.sec.gov/whistleblower/frequently-asked-questions. Accessed 5 Apr 2019

Zuckerman JM, Stock M (2018) *Dodd-Frank Whistleblower Protection Post-Digital Realty.* National Employment Lawyers Association Exchange. http://exchange.nela.org/blogs/nela-hq/2018/12/04/dodd-frank-whistleblower-post-digital-realty. Accessed 6 Apr 2019

Daniel J. Hurson has been a practicing attorney for over 45 years. He is a graduate of Georgetown University in Washington, D.C. and Harvard Law School. Over his career, he served as an Assistant United States Attorney in Maryland (a U.S. federal prosecutor) and as an Assistant Chief Litigation Counsel for the U.S. Securities and Exchange Commission. In private practice, he has represented many clients in investigations before the SEC and U.S. Department of Justice. After the passage of the Dodd-Frank Act in 2010, he began representing SEC whistleblowers. His clients have assisted the SEC and DOJ in a number of investigations, and some have obtained substantial awards under the SEC program. He has written numerous articles on whistleblowing, spoken on the subject on various professional panels, and appeared on television networks and national news publications.

Chapter 8
Directors Dealing with Whistleblowing

Greg Golding

Abstract Increased regulatory focus on the role performed by corporate whistleblowers and how Australian laws should better protect and encourage whistleblowing represents one of the most significant developments in Australian corporate law in recent years, and offers insight into the evolving area of corporate whistleblowing regulation more broadly. Recent wide-ranging reforms to better protect private sector whistleblowing are designed to rewrite the way in which whistleblowing allegations are handled in the corporate context. A revamped victimisation offence, as well as the related compensation right, have significantly complicated the handling of whistleblower complaints and the role played by Australian directors in dealing with such matters. The question arises as to the approach Australian directors should now take in dealing with whistleblowing complaints. In the past it could have been expected that many examples of whistleblower complaints did not reach the boards of major Australian corporations. Key questions to be considered in light of the new regime include whether directors should make changes so that all complaints of material breaches of law made by whistleblowers are notified to the board, and the responsibility of directors for whistleblowing within the context of corporate culture. These issues have potential implications for corporate governance elsewhere, as attitudes to corporate whistleblowing and its management continue to evolve.

Keywords Board accountability for internal whistleblowing processes · Corporate culture · Director liability

8.1 Introduction

The Australian reforms to whistleblowing should be on the agenda of all directors, as the implications for corporate governance are likely to be significant.

This chapter considers the issues that directors should be cognisant of when confronted with whistleblower claims, assessed by reference to the Australian legal

G. Golding (✉)
Level 11, 5 Martin Place, Sydney, NSW 2000, Australia
e-mail: greg.golding@ashurst.com

S. Lombard et al. (eds.), *Corporate Whistleblowing Regulation*,
https://doi.org/10.1007/978-981-15-0259-0_8

environment and contemporary community expectations of whistleblower protections.

One of the key policy objectives of the whistleblower reforms in 2017 and 2018 was to improve governance and integrity practices within Australian business.[1] For the reasons that follow, that policy objective may not have been well implemented in a number of respects.

Nevertheless, the relationship of the reforms to good corporate culture and contemporary expectations of whistleblower protections mean that all directors need to be attuned to both the corporate and personal consequences of failing to show leadership in dealing with whistleblowing.

8.2 The Need for a Strong Functioning Policy

The amended Corporations Act[2] requires that all public companies and large proprietary companies must have a formal whistleblowing policy compliant with the requirements of the Corporations Act by no later than 1 January 2020.[3] That policy must be made available to officers and employees of the relevant company.[4]

The whistleblowing policy must set out information about the protections available to whistleblowers, how whistleblowing can take place, how the company will support whistleblowers, how it will investigate whistleblowing disclosures and how it will ensure fair treatment of employees who are mentioned in disclosures made by whistleblowers.[5]

For Australian Stock Exchange listed entities this reform should also be seen in the context of relevant listing requirements. Under the ASX listing rules, listed entities must benchmark their corporate governance practices against the ASX Corporate Governance Council's Corporate Governance Principles and Recommendations[6] by

---

[1]Second reading speech 7 December 2017, Treasury Laws Amendment (Enhancing Whistleblower Protections) Bill 2017, Senate Hansard at 10098 (Senator Cormann).

[2]As amended by the Treasury Laws Amendment (Enhancing Whistleblower Protections) Act 2019 No. 10, 2019, effective 1 July 2019.

[3]S 1317AI(1)(a),(2)(b). That obligation begins to apply 6 months after the section commenced—s 1644(3).

The application to all public companies is too broad. Many public companies will have no employees. Many public companies may be small businesses or small mutuals. A better approach would have been to apply the requirement to any public company (or group of related bodies corporate that includes a public company) that has, say, more than 50 employees (note that ASIC has a class order exemption power—s 1317AJ).

A large proprietary company is a company that has revenue or gross assets over a monetary threshold or more than 50 employees—Corporations Act s 45A(3). The imposition of this requirement on large proprietary companies seems reasonable. The obligation to comply arises within 6 months of becoming a large proprietary company—s 1317AI(2).

[4]S 1317AI(1)(b), (2)(b).

[5]S 1317AF(5).

[6]Fourth Edition (February 2019), effective for financial years commencing 1 January 2020.

including in its annual report a corporate governance statement.[7] The corporate governance statement must disclose on an 'if not why not' basis the extent to which the entity has followed the recommendations contained in those principles.

From the financial year commencing 1 January 2020 a listed entity should[8]:

- Have and disclose a whistleblower policy.
- Ensure that the board or a committee of the board is informed of any material incidents reported under that policy.

Clearly these developments mean that it is imperative Australian listed entities have in place effective up-to-date whistleblowing policies that specifically address the issues required by the regulations.

Anecdotally it would seem that most major Australian listed companies have had formal whistleblowing policies for some time,[9] particularly following a number of corporate scandals involving whistleblowing and government inquiries in recent years.[10] However, it would seem that there is variable adoption of whistleblowing processes across Australia's business and government sectors and scope for better standards and guidance.

In 2016 a benchmarking survey was conducted across a range of public and private businesses by researchers co-ordinated through Griffith University.[11] The results of that survey suggested that[12]:

- While most organisations reported having systems for recording and tracking wrongdoing concerns, almost a quarter of organisations (22.5%) reported they had no particular system in place.
- While almost all organisations (96.2%) reported the availability of at least one nominated type of support for staff who raise wrongdoing concerns, most support types related to the provision of information or advice rather than more active or concrete support (less than half of organisations (46.2%) reported that staff had access to management-designated support persons in the organisation).
- Three quarters (77.2%) of organisations reported that they would respond to reprisals or detrimental impacts through management intervention, and less than a fifth of organisations (16.4%) reported having mechanisms for ensuring adequate compensation or restitution.
- A composite score for the overall strength of the processes adopted to deal with whistleblowing matters was reported as a mean score of 5.66 out of 10.

---

[7] ASX Listing Rule 4.10.

[8] Recommendation 3.3.

[9] A 2010 survey of ASX200 companies had suggested only about one third of surveyed companies then had robust whistleblowing programs—Pascoe and Welsh (2011).

[10] See by way of example Senate Economics References Committee (June 2014) ch 14 ("Corporate whistleblowing; ASIC's performance and issues with the current protections").

[11] The Whistling While They Work research project. 634 organisations were surveyed across 18 industry groups in the public, private and not-for-profit sectors. See http://www.whistlingwhiletheywork.edu.au.

[12] Brown and Lawrence (2017).

The pressure on Australian business to improve standards has been ongoing, as now illustrated by the policy requirements referenced above. Clearly, there is much that can be done to upgrade whistleblowing processes from those traditionally in place for Australian corporations.[13]

It is not clear how much involvement directors have had in the governance processes involving whistleblowing in the past. The amended Corporations Act does not explicitly require escalation of whistleblowing reports to the board—either as a component of the required whistleblowing policy or generally. On the other hand, the ASX Corporate Governance Principles suggest that material incidents should be reported to the board or a board committee. The commentary to the ASX recommendations suggests that the reporting of material incidents may be indicative of issues within the culture of the organisation.[14]

It is therefore recommended that the general areas of potential focus for directors in considering the development of enhanced whistleblowing policies should be to[15]:

- take an active interest in the development of new policies having regard to the issues discussed below;
- focus on growing a culture of internal scrutiny of reports of wrongdoing[16];
- become more active in participating in investigations where reports of wrongdoing are made; and
- ensure that a comprehensive suite of internal compliance tools is in place.

Effective whistleblowing arrangements require a much greater commitment than a checklist mentality of propagating a written policy without giving it life and relevance in the governance of the organisation. The policy needs to be implemented within the organisation through leadership promotion and through training programs.

Further, a policy that looks good on paper but is not embraced throughout the organisation, particularly at senior levels, is most unlikely to create the required compliance culture in the organisation or lead to changes in employee attitudes.[17] Employees take their cues from the actual behaviour and values they see in those above them in the organisation. Directors can, and should, therefore take an active role in promoting these values and attitudes if they want to facilitate change.

---

[13]An Australian Standard had previously been available, although that standard has been withdrawn—see Standards Australia (2003).

A further source of guidance is the International Chamber of Commerce ICC Guidelines on Whistleblowing.

[14]Recommendation 3.3, Commentary.

[15]For more detailed discussion of active steps that directors should consider see Ashcroft et al. (2011).

[16]For discussion of the challenges in developing a compliant culture around whistleblowing see Pascoe (2009).

[17]For discussion see Kaptein and Schwartz (2008).

If a policy is not embraced throughout the organisation, the policy is not likely to deter wrongdoing in practice.[18] Furthermore, ineffectively adopted policies add to red tape, bureaucracy and business costs without providing corporate benefit.

In addition to the practical necessity of embracing the values reflected in the policy, paying lip service to corporate policies may well have legal consequences under common law employment contracts, industrial awards or legislation where an employee relies on the terms of that policy and suffers detriment.[19] The policy may create an independent cause of action available to an employee who has suffered detriment in circumstances where a policy expressing the approach the organisation has stated it intends to adopt has not subsequently been followed.

Having regard to the developments outlined above and the factors considered in this chapter, what would a good functioning whistleblowing policy look like?[20] Such a policy should be assessed by reference to the following checklist of issues that might be considered in policy design.

Policy issue	Areas to be addressed
Corporate culture	Corporate commitment to proper review of whistleblowing disclosures Corporate commitment to protect whistleblowers and prevent retaliation Commitment/planning/internal presentations showing right tone at the top Plan for instilling trust in the integrity of the whistleblowing review process Availability of the policy[a] Training programs for employees and other potential whistleblowers[b] Training programs for managers and others who may receive whistleblower disclosures[c] Impact of the policy on employment agreements Impact of the policy on board and board committee charters
Making protected disclosures	Expectation that disclosure of reportable conduct will be made Persons who may make protected disclosures Facilitation of anonymous disclosures What is reportable conduct[d] What is not reportable conduct Relationship of policy to personal employee grievances Interaction with other corporate policies Internal resources available to facilitate disclosure Internal points of first contact[e] External points of first contact[f] External resources available to facilitate disclosure Method of making disclosures—written, email, phonelines, other Recognition of the right of whistleblowers to disclose to regulatory bodies

(continued)

[18]For a contrarian view that many corporations pay lip service to corporate compliance programs see Kraweic (2003).

[19]For discussion see Dixon (2016).

[20]Having regard to the matters specified in s 317AI(5) and the suggestions for the content of a whistleblowing policy (Box 3.3) in the ASX Corporate Governance Principles.

(continued)

Policy issue	Areas to be addressed
Internal review processes	How disclosures will be investigated[g] Chain of escalation within the organisation Circumstances where escalation to the board or a committee of the board should be made and relationship between the board and committees in considering such referrals[h] Functions of persons and bodies involved in the review process Independence of the review procedure Reporting to the whistleblower on progress and outcome of review Escalation rights available to the whistleblower if dissatisfied with review outcome Obligation of employees to report protected disclosures made to them by whistleblowers How the corporation will protect the whistleblower from detriment[i] Disciplinary consequences of engaging in retaliation Fair treatment and due process to persons who may be mentioned in protected disclosures or to whom the protected disclosures relate[j] Need-to-know disclosure of protected disclosures within the organisation Protection and confidentiality of the identity of the whistleblower[k] Protection and confidentiality of protected disclosures and review materials generated Reporting to and role of senior management in the review process Reporting to the board Role of board committees Governance and board charter recognition of whistleblowing issues Regulatory self-reporting procedures
Resources available to whistleblowers	Information about the protections available to whistleblowers[l] Information about how whistleblowers will be supported[m] Availability of internal support services outside the review process Access to independent legal advice Access to independent support services Discretionary support and benefits that may be made available to whistleblowers Availability of compensation when protected disclosures are made and process to access that compensation Rewards offered for disclosure of valuable information Possible immunity to the whistleblower from disciplinary proceedings where the whistleblower has been involved in conduct that is the subject of protected disclosure

(continued)

(continued)

Policy issue	Areas to be addressed
Other	Policy review processes[n] Amendment procedure

[a]Compliance with s 1317AI(5)(f)
[b]Box 3.3 (item 5) of ASX Corporate Governance Principles
[c]Box 3.3 (item 6) of ASX Corporate Governance Principles
[d]Box 3.3 (item 2) of ASX Corporate Governance Principles
[e]Including specification of persons authorised by the corporation to receive protected disclosures for purposes of s 1317AAC(1)(d) and compliance with s 1317AI(5)(b). See also suggestion Box 3.3 (item 2) of ASX Corporate Governance Principles
[f]Ibid
[g]S 1317IJ(5)(a) and Box 3.3 (item 6) of ASX Corporate Governance Principles
[h]Recommendation 3.3 of ASX Corporate Governance Principles
[i]Compliance with s 1317AI(5)(c) and Box 3.3 (item 3) of ASX Corporate Governance Principles. The potential implications of this requirement are discussed below
[j]Compliance with s 1317AI(5)(e)
[k]Including compliance with s 1317AAE(1) and (4) and Box 3.3 (item 3) of ASX Corporate Governance Principles
[l]Compliance with s 1317AI(5)(a)
[m]Compliance with s 1317AI(5)(c)
[n]Box 3.3 (item 7) of ASX Corporate Governance Principles

To be sure, a number of the items referred to above may seem at odds with the way Australian companies have traditionally dealt with whistleblowing issues. Further, recognition of these issues could be seen to be inflammatory in dealing with employees who have employment-related grievance claims, or may generally undermine the ability of the company to deal with performance management issues involving employees.

However, to instil genuine cultural change around the phenomena of whistleblowing, a strong corporate commitment to embrace the benefits of internal rectification of corporate issues should be illustrated by a whistleblowing policy.

In addition to an internal commitment to set the right tone at the top concerning whistleblowing, a good way to reinforce expectations might be by way of periodic external reporting to investors and the community generally of how the corporation has dealt with whistleblowing complaints. In its annual governance statement, there would be nothing to prevent an ASX listed company reporting details of its whistleblowing policy, the number of protected disclosures that have been received and the general outcomes that resulted from the review of disclosures that were made. Disclosure of such general nature could be made without compromising confidentiality surrounding the identity of whistleblowers or the exact steps taken in response to disclosures made. Such an approach would be consistent with espousing best corporate practice in dealing with whistleblowing issues.

8.3 Directors Investigating Whistleblowing Claims

The question arises as to the approach Australian directors should take in personally dealing with and seeking to investigate whistleblowing claims. In the past it could have been expected that many whistleblower claims did not reach the boards of major Australian corporations.

As noted above, the ASX Corporate Governance Principles now suggest it will be appropriate for the review of any material issues raised by whistleblowers to become an area addressed by boards or board committees.

The confidentiality obligations under the Corporations Act may complicate the manner in which details of whistleblower claims are handled within a corporation and can be escalated internally so as to be properly considered by the board and senior management.

While the list of persons to whom a whistleblower may make a protected disclosure is relatively broad,[21] those persons are not explicitly permitted to then share details of the whistleblower among themselves or within the organisation in then investigating the whistleblowing claim.

The Corporations Act provides that it is both an offence and a civil penalty provision for a person to disclose the identity of the whistleblower or information likely to lead to the identity of the whistleblower being disclosed.[22] This obligation arises when the person obtained those details of the whistleblower directly or indirectly because of the protected disclosure made by the whistleblower.

The prohibition is limited to matters concerning the identity of the whistleblower, and not other aspects of a protected disclosure. There is nothing to prevent the sharing of information concerning the conduct disclosed by the whistleblower, provided that does not risk disclosure of their identity. That is made clear by explicit recognition that the prohibition on disclosure does not apply if the disclosure is not of the identity of the whistleblower, is reasonably necessary to investigate the complaint, and all reasonable steps are taken to reduce the risk of whistleblower identification.[23]

There is also an explicit exception for onward disclosure of the identity of the whistleblower to ASIC, APRA and the AFP.[24] As such, there is no difficulty for the corporation self-reporting misconduct uncovered through whistleblowing at any stage, including by self-reporting details of the identity of the whistleblower.[25]

There is a further explicit exception for disclosure to a legal practitioner for the purpose of obtaining legal advice or legal representation in relation to the operation

---

[21] The Eligible Recipients referred to in s 1317AAC in the corporate context are an officer or senior manager, an auditor and a person authorised by the corporation to receive whistleblower disclosures.

[22] S 1317AAE(1).

[23] S 1317AAE(4).

[24] Ss 1317AAE(2)(a), (b), (c).

[25] ASIC, APRA and the AFP can also disclose the identity of the whistleblower to other federal and state government bodies to assist that body to perform their functions or duties—s 1317AAE(3).

of the whistleblowing provisions of the Corporations Act.[26] As a matter of statutory interpretation, it appears unclear whether the exception permits to disclose the identity of the whistleblower to a legal practitioner in the general investigation of the complaint made in the whistleblowing disclosure, or just in relation to legal representation concerning how the whistleblowing provisions of the Corporations Act apply. There is a risk that the latter narrower restriction may be the case. The preferred view should be, of course, that there ought to be no impediment to a corporation seeking legal advice on the conduct disclosed by a whistleblower, and to disclosing to the legal advisor the identity of the whistleblower as part of that legal advice.[27]

Finally, there is an explicit exception for disclosure made with the consent of the whistleblower.[28]

This disclosure restriction should therefore be assessed in the context of a typical corporate environment. A typical whistleblowing policy would encourage a whistleblowing disclosure to be made in the first instance to a compliance officer or an external reporting service. The policy would typically then provide for an investigation of the conduct disclosed and contemplate the escalation of material issues through the organisation in order for decision-making to be undertaken as to what response the corporation should make in relation to the whistleblowing claim.

From a director's perspective, in many situations it would be desirable that the escalation involve disclosure of the identity of the whistleblower on a need-to-know basis so that the context of the disclosure could be better understood. However, the legislation does not facilitate such disclosure, and therefore whistleblowing policies should explicitly provide for the masking of the identity of the whistleblower and any disclosure that could reveal it.

The practical ability to mask details that may lead to identification of a whistleblower may also be an issue. For example, there may only be a small number of persons familiar with the issues that have been disclosed by the whistleblower, or there may only be a small number of people working in the relevant part of the organisation, meaning that it is relatively easy to speculate who the whistleblower is. As such, the ability of the organisation to make decisions at senior levels may be hampered by the disclosure restriction.

Clearly from a policy perspective, the inclusion of a specific exception to allow disclosure of a whistleblower's identity within an organisation to persons who otherwise meet the definition of eligible recipient on a need-to-know and confidential

---

[26] S 1317AAE(2)(d).

[27] Of course, from a policy perspective the legislation would be improved by deleting the words "in relation to the operation of this Part," on the basis that there should be nothing objectionable in a corporation disclosing the identity of a whistleblower to a legal advisor who is subject to ethical and confidentiality duties in connection with their retainer.

A possible work around to this technical concern is to explicitly provide that the retainer arrangements for the legal advisor extends to both the corporation's obligations in dealing with the whistleblower under the Corporations Act, and in investigating the conduct disclosed by the whistleblower. The restriction does not state that the disclosure to the legal advisor must be solely for purposes of legal advice on the operation of the whistleblowing provisions of the Corporations Act.

[28] S 1317AAE(2)(f).

basis would be a preferred approach. A regulatory structure that facilitates a corporation properly assessing whistleblowing disclosures and internally dealing with them without the need to involve external regulatory bodies is the preferred outcome that should be encouraged and facilitated by the legislation.

Of course, this impediment does not arise if the whistleblower consents to the internal disclosure of their identity. A whistleblowing policy that encourages the giving of such a consent is desirable. In part, that will require the existence of a corporate culture that causes the whistleblower to believe that their concerns will be taken seriously, and that they will not be the subject of retaliation. The obtaining of whistleblower consent may be facilitated by robust internal processes that protect the interests of whistleblowers, including, for example, by way of allowing relatively free access to independent legal advice.[29]

A further issue concerning the confidentiality of whistleblowers arises in connection with disclosure of their identity before a court or tribunal. Again, disclosure of the identity of a whistleblower or information that is likely to lead to their identification cannot be required before a court or tribunal—or in a document required to be produced to a court or tribunal—except where it is necessary to give effect to the whistleblowing provisions of the Corporations Act or where the court or tribunal thinks it necessary in the interests of justice.[30]

Corporations will need to be cognisant of this further restriction in dealing with steps that may subsequently be taken to address the consequences of whistleblowing disclosures—for example, in pursuing enforcement actions that may arise from the whistleblowing claim.

8.4 Directors Dealing with Retaliation Issues

It can be expected that a revamped victimisation offence will also significantly complicate the handling of whistleblower complaints and the role played by directors in dealing with such matters. Directors will need to consider both their own liability position and the liability position of the corporation in dealing with whistleblowers and in considering whistleblower disclosures.

A person faces potential liability if:

- they engage in conduct that causes detriment to another person;
- the person engaging in the conduct believes or suspects the other person may have, proposes to or could make a protected whistleblower disclosure; and
- that belief or suspicion is the reason or part of the reason for this conduct.[31]

[29]Noting that disclosure by a whistleblower to a legal practitioner for the purpose of obtaining legal advice or legal representation in relation to the operation of the whistleblowing provisions of the Corporations Act is itself a protected disclosure—s 1317AA(3).

[30]S 1317AG.

[31]S 1317AC(1).

A person also faces potential liability if:

- a person makes a threat to cause detriment to another person;
- the person making the threat intends for the threat to be carried out or is reckless as to the risk the other person will fear the threat being carried out; and
- the person makes or may make a protected whistleblower disclosure.[32]

A person also faces potential liability if a corporation contravenes the victimisation offence and they are involved in that contravention as an officer or employee of the corporation.[33]

Engaging in such prohibited conduct is both a criminal offence and can be enforced by ASIC under the civil penalty regime of the Corporations Act.[34]

The civil penalty regime contained in the Corporations Act has proven a very effective enforcement mechanism for ASIC since its introduction in the early 1990s.[35] A declaration of contravention of a civil penalty provision is determined on the civil burden of proof rather than the criminal burden. Where a court orders a declaration of contravention, a pecuniary penalty order can then be imposed, which since 2019 can be very substantial in amount.[36]

It should be noted that the person suffering victimisation does not have to be a protected whistleblower. It is sufficient that there be belief, suspicion, intention or recklessness (as the case may be) that the victim may or could be a protected whistleblower. As such, a person who suffers detriment through being mistakenly treated as a whistleblower will be protected through the victimisation offence, whether or not they are in fact a whistleblower.

In addition, the possibility that a person may become a whistleblower in the future is sufficient to protect the person under the legislation.

[32] S 1317AC(2). The threat may be express or implied—s 1317AC(4).

[33] S 1317AC(3).

[34] Footnotes to ss 1317AC(1), (2) and (3).

The criminal offence is 120 penalty units (currently $25,000), or imprisonment for 2 years or both.

The civil penalty regime is contained in Corporations Act Part 9.4B. The legislation makes it clear that civil penalty proceedings can be brought even if a criminal prosecution has not been brought or could not be brought—s 1017AF.

[35] See Comino (2007), Welsh (2004) and Welsh (2009).

[36] S 1317G(1H), (1J). Following the enactment of the Treasury Laws Amendment (Strengthening Corporate and Financial Sector Penalties) Act 2019 No. 17, 2019 (effective 13 March 2019), those maximum pecuniary penalties are 5000 penalty units (currently $1,050,000) or 3 times the benefit derived or detriment avoided for an individual (up from $200,000) and 50,000 penalty units (currently $10,500,000) or 3 times the benefit derived or detriment avoided or 10% of annual turnover to 2.5 million penalty units (currently $525 million) for a corporation (up from $1,000,000).

8.4.1 *What Is Detriment?*

Detriment is very broadly defined for purposes of these provisions, with a detailed non-exclusive list of nine types of detriment specified and a final sweeping reference to "any other damage" to a person.[37]

Employment-related detriment includes changes in employment terms, dismissal as an employee, a change in employee duties or position to an employee's disadvantage and discrimination between an employee as compared to other employees.[38]

Detriment is also expressed to apply to various traditional forms of physical and economic damage—with injury, property damage and business or financial damage referenced.[39] More intangible forms of harm are also listed—with harassment, intimidation, physiological harm and damage to reputation referenced.[40]

It should be noted that there is a carve-out from protected whistleblowing for personal work-related grievances that needs to be considered.[41] Under this provision, disclosed information that concerns a personal work-related grievance of the discloser and does not concern an actual or alleged contravention of the victimisation offence is not a protected disclosure under the legislation.[42] A work-related grievance is defined as information concerning a grievance about the discloser's employment or prior employment having or tending to have implications for the discloser personally that does not have significant implications for the corporation to which it relates and does not involve actual or alleged conduct explicitly listed as matters giving rise to protected disclosure.[43]

The note to the section gives four examples of personal work-related grievances—an interpersonal conflict between employees, a decision concerning engagement transfer or promotion, a decision concerning terms and conditions of engagement and a decision to suspend or terminate an engagement or to discipline.

It can be expected that in many instances management of a corporation will argue that a whistleblower has come forward with a disclosure consequent on a perceived slight that has occurred to the whistleblower in the workplace, and the issue

[37] S 1317ADA.

[38] Ss 1317ADA(a), (c) and (d).

[39] Ss 1317ADA(b), (g) and (i).

[40] Ss 1317ADA(e), (f) and (h).

[41] S 1317AADA. This section implements a recommendation of Moss (2016)—see paragraph 1.16 of the Supplementary Explanatory Memorandum: Amendments to be moved on behalf of the Government—Treasury Laws Amendment (Whistleblowers) Bill, December 2018. The Moss Report had noted that Commonwealth agencies had submitted that in the first two years of the Public Interest Disclosure Act the overwhelming majority of public sector whistleblowing disclosures related to issues like workplace bullying, disrespect and minor allegations of wrongdoing—Moss (2016, para 67).

[42] S 1317AADA(1).

[43] S 1317AADA(2). The explicit matters are various contraventions of specific Commonwealth legislation (including the Corporations Act), offences under Commonwealth law punishable by imprisonment of 12 months or more, or that are a danger to the public or the financial system (ss 1317AA(5)(c)–(f)).

is therefore a personal work-related grievance rather than a protected whistleblower disclosure. Further, where an employee anticipates that they may suffer employment detriment through performance management, they may seek to counter that threat by making a whistleblowing complaint.

Previously the Corporations Act required that a protected whistleblowing disclosure be made by the whistleblower in "good faith". It was felt that the good faith requirement meant that whistleblower claims made for collateral purposes could be disregarded. Now the motives of the whistleblower are irrelevant to whether or not the whistleblower is protected.

There are difficulties with the work-related grievances carve-out in the corporate context, as the circumstances that can be characterised to constitute a personal work-related grievance will also involve detriment to the whistleblower. If the whistleblower claims that they have suffered detriment that gives rise to a right to compensation, the personal work-related grievance carve-out ceases to apply. As such, the application of the carve-out could be easily circumvented by a whistleblower claiming detriment.[44]

In the corporate context this difficulty should be managed by focusing on whether or not the additional limbs of the victimisation offence beyond the existence of detriment are present—i.e. suspicion of a protected disclosure that is the reason (or part of the reason) for the detrimental conduct. Provided there is a clear delineation and due process around dealing with a performance management issue involving the whistleblower that could be considered both a personal work-related grievance as well as detriment under the victimisation offence, no victimisation issues should arise.

As such, whether or not the information is a personal work-related grievance should not affect how a corporation deals with performance management issues concerning a whistleblower. That being said, the task of navigating a claim of detriment where whistleblowing may be claimed while also performance-managing an employee—or where there is a work-related grievance—can be expected to be an extremely sensitive matter.

8.4.2 *Individual Culpability*

The circumstances in which an individual will be liable for conduct that constitutes victimisation in a corporate context are fairly clear. That will be when that individual engaged in proscribed conduct and had the relevant belief, suspicion, intent or recklessness (as the case may be).

[44]The operation of the section is also different from that proposed by the Moss Report for public sector whistleblowing. The Recommendation provided that the authorised officer considering the disclosure should have discretion to treat the matter as a protected disclosure involving a systemic issue (see Recommendation 5 proviso to the Moss Report).

Officers and employees should therefore be extremely circumspect about engaging in conduct that could be considered detrimental if they wish to avoid potential personal criminal or civil liability for that conduct. Clearly, the amended Corporations Act means that the stakes will significantly increase for individual officers and employees who engage in conduct that prejudices persons who have made whistleblower disclosures.

Officers who are required to deal with a whistleblowing disclosure will need to take great care to ensure that any action taken in dealing with the whistleblower cannot be characterised as detriment to the whistleblower arising from the disclosure.

From a director's perspective, there is little to be gained (and much to be lost) in inserting themselves in the decision-making process where a whistleblower may be considered to suffer detriment as part of the review that is undertaken of the disclosed conduct.

8.4.3 Corporate Culpability

It is clear from the structure of the Corporations Act that a primary objective of the legislation is to encourage greater focus by corporations on the correct handling of whistleblower disclosures and protection of whistleblowers. It is unfortunate that the legislation does not explicitly deal with the manner in which culpability for the acts of its officers and employees will be imposed on a corporation.

The Corporations Act proceeds on the basis a corporation is a person that can commit the victimisation offence.[45] How then will the conduct of officers and employees be attributed to a corporation in this context?

The starting point of that analysis is by reference to traditional general law theories of attributing direct liability to a corporation.[46] Traditionally, culpability would only be imposed on a corporation for conduct engaged in by relatively senior officers or employees of the corporation.

At its most basic level, corporate liability will generally only be attributed to a corporation if the preconditions to the commission of the offence can be traced to a person who is the directing mind and will of the corporation and who exercises control of the activities of the corporation so as to be considered as acting as the corporation for these purposes.[47] This is the so-called identification principle of corporate culpability.

For most corporations that power will derive from the constitution, whereby the powers of management are vested in the board. However, those powers may also

---

[45] See the penalties and the reference to a company contravention in s 1317AC(3).

[46] At general law, a corporation, as principal of its officers and employees, could have vicarious liability imposed on it in contract and tort. The focus here is to identify when a corporation has direct liability as a legal person under the Corporations Act provisions.

[47] *Tesco Supermarkets Ltd v Nattrass* [1972] AC 153; *Hamilton v Whitehead* (1989) 63 ALJR 80 (HC, Mason CJ, Wilson & Toohey JJ).

be conferred by the board on the managing director or a senior officer, with direct delegated management power from the board or managing director to act on behalf of the corporation without being subject to the oversight and instruction of the board.[48]

In this context, the distinction between an officer or employee acting in the performance of their duties and an officer or employee acting as the corporation can be ambiguous. The distinction properly lies in the officer and employee having the delegated authority to act entirely independently of the board so as to have the power to speak and act as the company in relation to the relevant issue. An employee with delegated power to implement the instructions of the board (directly or through the management structure of the corporation) does not have this unrestrained freedom of action and will not be considered to be acting as the corporation.

However, to define corporate attribution so narrowly in the context of a large business organisation would be extremely restrictive, and allow large corporations to enjoy plausible deniability of its obligations in complying with legal obligations by having the board and senior management insulated from the officers and employees who are charged with ensuring legal compliance. For that reason, the courts have clarified that in the statutory context it is also necessary to engage in statutory interpretation to determine how a corporation can be considered to have direct liability through the acts of its officers and employees by considering the nature of the statutory offence and the policy and objectives of the statute. Officers and employees who have corporate authority to make decisions and undertake the relevant conduct in the name and with the authority of the corporation to ensure legal compliance will therefore generally have their conduct attributed to the corporation.[49]

Again, the effect of this secondary rule of corporate attribution is not to provide that the conduct of all officers and employees undertaking corporate activities is considered the act of the corporation. As a general rule, it is only officers and employees responsible for determining actions of the corporation—as distinct from officers and employees charged with implementing its decisions—who will have their conduct attributed to the corporation.

The victimisation offence focuses on the person engaging in detrimental conduct and an intention that the conduct cause detriment. The Courts have noted that the rules relating to attribution are of particular importance where the statutory provision turns on a state of mind.[50] On the other hand, the amended Corporations Act clearly enunciates a policy objective that corporations have strong procedures to ensure that whistleblowers not be subjected to detriment at any level of the organisation.

---

[48] See for example the analysis in Grantham (2001) and Overland (2010, p. 275).

[49] *Meridian Global Funds Management Asia Limited v The Securities Commission* [1995] 2 AC 500 (chief investment officer was considered the directing mind and will of a funds management company for the purposes of preparing and lodging substantial shareholding notice disclosure obligations as he had authority within the company to make decisions concerning compliance with those notices). See also the application of this expanded principle in *Director General, Department of Education and Training v MT* [2006] NSWCA 270 (Spigelman CJ, Ipp JA, Hunt AJA).

[50] *R v Commercial Industrial Construction Group* [2006] VSCA 181 (Maxwell P, Buchanan and Redlich JJA) at 32.

It can be concluded from this analysis that conduct engaged in by directors and senior officers charged with implementing whistleblowing review procedures or human resources decisions concerning whistleblowers will likely have their conduct attributed to the corporation. It is less clear that peers of the whistleblower or persons not directly in a superior position to the whistleblower will have their conduct attributed to the corporation if they cause detriment to the whistleblower.

In relation to criminal liability for contravening the victimisation offence, the Commonwealth Criminal Code provides for a unique alternative regime that seeks to extend the scope of corporate culpability from the general law identification principles of attribution discussed above.[51] That will only be relevant to a criminal prosecution for corporate victimisation. If a civil penalty action is brought by ASIC against a corporation (the most likely action), the general law attribution principles discussed above will apply.[52]

The Criminal Code clearly distinguishes between the physical and fault elements of a criminal offence.[53]

For the physical elements of a criminal prosecution, corporate liability will be established if the conduct is undertaken by an employee, agent or officer of the corporation acting within the actual or apparent scope of his or her employment or within his or her actual or apparent authority.[54] As such, for the victimisation offence, an employee, agent or officer must engage in the relevant conduct while acting within his or her actual or apparent scope of authority.[55] Unlike the common law identification principle, there is no requirement that the relevant employee, agent or officer be the directing mind of the corporation to satisfy the physical element; merely that the person act within the actual or apparent scope of their authority.

The fault element of a criminal prosecution is established differently. In the case of a corporation, if intention, knowledge or recklessness is the fault element of an offence (as is the case with the victimisation offence), that fault element will be attributed to the corporation if it expressly, tacitly or impliedly authorised or

---

[51] Criminal Code Part 2.5. The regime applies to all offences provided for in the Criminal Code, unless expressly excluded. This provision derives from Model Criminal Code Chapters 1 and 2—Criminal Law Officers Committee of the Standing Committee of Attorneys-General (1992).

[52] *ASIC, in the matter of Whitebox Trading Pty Ltd v Whitebox Trading Pty Ltd* [2017] FCAFC 100 (Allsop CJ, Middleton & Bromwich JJ) is authority for the proposition that principles of the Criminal Code do not apply to civil penalty proceedings initiated by ASIC.

[53] Criminal Code s 3.1. These are the required elements for criminal conduct at general law now codified by the Criminal Code (corresponding to the general law elements of *actus rea* and *mens rea*).

[54] Criminal Code s 12.2. A question arises as to whether the employee, agent or officer who performs the physical element of the offence must also have the required fault element of the offence—see Davids and Schubert (2011, pp. 107–8).

[55] It therefore follows that if the person is not an employee, agent or officer of the company, the physical element will not be satisfied. For example, conduct of an employee, agent or officer of a subsidiary of a parent entity might not be attributed to the parent entity because of basic principles of separate corporate identity between the parent and its subsidiary—see the principles enunciated in *Briggs v James Hardie & Co Pty Ltd* (1989) 16 NSWLR 549 (Hope & Meagher JJA, Rogers AJA).

permitted the commission of the offence.[56] Authorisation or permission for these purposes may be established where[57]:

- the board of directors[58] has intentionally, knowingly or recklessly (as the case may be) carried out the conduct, or expressly, tacitly or impliedly authorised or permitted the commission of the offence;
- a "high managerial agent"[59] has intentionally, knowingly or recklessly (as the case may be) engaged in the conduct, or expressly, tacitly or impliedly authorised or permitted the commission of the offence;
- a corporate culture existed within the body corporate that directed, encouraged, tolerated or led to non-compliance with the provision; or
- the body corporate failed to create and maintain a corporate culture that required compliance with the provision.

The third and fourth limbs direct attention to a corporate culture that directed or encouraged non-compliance or that failed to create and maintain a compliant culture. Although the introduction of the "corporate culture" limbs of criminal culpability for corporations was generally positively received in Australia at the time the Criminal Code test was formulated, it was said at the time of its adoption that the term's ambiguity could cause problems for prosecutions, and the practical workability of the concept was subject to question.[60] In the years that have now passed since this standard was introduced this has yet to be tested.[61] The paucity of active enforcement means that the practical usefulness of the regime continues to remain unclear.

For these purposes, a "corporate culture" is an attitude, policy, course of conduct or practice existing in the body corporate generally or the part of the body corporate where the conduct occurred.[62] It can be expected that there may be challenges in pursuing a corporate conviction based on proof of attitudes or practices within a corporate entity.[63] The concept of a prevailing attitude or practice within a large and complex commercial organisation operating through many employees and agents may be very difficult to pin down. The larger the organisation, the more difficult it could be expected to prove a poor corporate culture.

---

[56] Criminal Code s 12.3(1).

[57] Criminal Code s 12.3(2).

[58] Defined as the body exercising the executive authority of the body corporate (Criminal Code s 12.3(b) definition).

[59] Defined as an employee, agent or officer with duties of such responsibility that his or her conduct may fairly be presumed to represent the body's policy (Criminal Code s 12.3(6) definition).

[60] Criminal Law Officers Committee of the Standing Committee of the Attorneys-General (1992); Criminal Law Officers Committee of the Standing Committee of Attorneys-General (1993, p. 1073).

[61] It has been said that the provisions "remain largely of academic interest through lack of use"—Clough and Mulhern (2002, p. 148).

[62] Criminal Code s 12.3(6) definition.

[63] It has been said that culture is an inherently slippery and legally imprecise concept—for discussion of the ambiguities associated with the term and the factors listed in the s 12.3(6) definition see Colvin and Argent (2016, pp. 36–39) and the materials referred to there.

The background materials to the legislation make it clear that policies requiring compliance alone will not be sufficient if non-compliance is encouraged or tolerated in practice.[64]

The legislation further provides that factors relevant to assessing corporate culture include whether approval to commit the same or a similar offence has been given by a high managerial agent or whether the relevant person believed on reasonable grounds that a high managerial agent would have authorised or permitted the commission of the offence.[65]

In addition to the paucity of an enforcement history of the Criminal Code provisions, there has been little Australian case law that considers issues surrounding corporate culture. A notable exception is *Re Chemeq Ltd*,[66] a case involving the determination of a pecuniary civil penalty for an agreed violation of continuous disclosure obligations. French J stated that it was relevant to consider the entity's compliance procedures in assessing the appropriate pecuniary penalty and made the following general observations[67]:

- The court will consider both the form and content of the policies as well as the measures adopted to ensure that they are understood and applied.
- The court will consider the training measures adopted for officers (including directors) and whether refresher training has been undertaken.[68]
- A proper culture of compliance does not require a risk-averse mentality in the conduct of the company's business, but a kind of inbuilt mental checklist as a background to decision-making.
- Proper risk management requires a conservative approach that errs on the side of avoiding the possibility of contravention.
- Those who play calculated risk games in the shadow of legal rules cannot expect indulgence from the courts if their judgement as to compliance is found to be incorrect.

The consequence of this Criminal Code analysis from a director's perspective is therefore fairly clear. To ensure that there is reduced responsibility for victimisation from a corporation's perspective:

- The necessary whistleblowing policy should be clear in the directions it gives.
- The requirements of the whistleblowing policy should be clearly enunciated in the organisation.
- The board and senior management should foster a commitment in the organisation to the prevention of victimisation.

As noted above, the Criminal Code analysis does not apply to a civil penalty proceeding that may be pursued by ASIC. As the offence contains a mental element

---

[64]Explanatory Memorandum to Criminal Code Bill 1994 at 44.

[65]Criminal Code s 12.3(4). It has been suggested that these factors could be construed as necessary elements to establish corporate culture—see Brand (2000, pp. 480–1).

[66]*ASIC, Re Chemeq v Chemeq Ltd* [2006] FCA 936 (French J).

[67]Ibid at 84–89.

[68]In *Chemeq* the judge was critical that there was no clear evidence of refresher training.

of intent or recklessness, this means that corporate attribution for a civil penalty proceeding will be tested by the narrower identification theory of corporate culpability. The general law principles of corporate attribution will therefore not encourage the reporting of poor behaviour towards whistleblowers to the board and senior management of a corporation. That is unfortunate from a policy perspective.

8.4.4 Director Culpability

Having regard to the above analysis, the question arises as to whether the director of a corporation (particularly a non-executive director) can have liability for victimisation when prohibited conduct has occurred within the organisation.

Clearly, where the director is directly involved in the relevant conduct, they can have individual liability (see above).

In addition to imposing liability for directly engaging in victimisation, the Corporations Act also provides that if a company contravenes the victimisation prohibition, any officer or employee of the company involved in the contravention also contrives the prohibition.[69] This liability therefore requires it to be established that the corporation engaged in the prohibited conduct.

The relevant case law establishes that accessory liability requires evidence of the following matters:

- that the accessory helped, encouraged or induced the principle offender to commit the offence[70]; and
- that the accessory knew the essential matters that constituted the offence.[71]

The first element of the offence is a requirement for participation in the offence. It has long been a feature of the law of accessory liability that the accessory must perform an act which in some way assists the contravention of the offence in question.[72] Failure to supervise or make inquiries cannot constitute participation.

The second element of accessory liability might have greater relevance to director liability if the participation requirement could be established. The requirement that the accessory know of the essential matters that constitute the offence was clearly established by the High Court in the *Yorke v Lucas* and *Giorgianni* cases.[73] It is

[69]S 1317AC(3). Involvement in a contravention is defined in Corporations Act s 79 in terms of aiding, abetting, counselling, procuring, inducing, being knowingly concerned in, or conspiring. This offence is also a criminal and civil penalty provision (see notes).

[70]See *National Coal Board v Gamble* [1959] 1 QB 11 (Lord Goddard, Slade & Devlin JJ).

[71]*Johnson v Youden* [1950] 1KB 544 (Lord Goddard, Humphreys & Lynsky JJ); *Giorgianni v The Queen* (1985) 156 CLR 473; *Yorke v Lucas* (1985) 158 CLR 661.

[72]In *Giorgianni v The Queen* Gibbs CJ said that the accessory must *"in some sort to associate himself with the venture, that he participate in it as something that he wishes to bring about, that he seek by his action to make it succeed"* [citing *United States v Peoni* 100 F 2d 401 (2nd Cir, 1938)].

[73]*"A person will be guilty of the offences of aiding and abetting or counselling and procuring the commission of an offence only if he intentionally participates in it. To form the requisite intention*

not necessary to prove that it was known that the facts in question constitute a contravention of law—merely that all the facts required to establish the offence are known by the defendant.[74]

The requirement of a degree of participation in most cases will make the separate accessory offence superfluous, as in many cases it could be expected that it would also constitute direct conduct within the meaning of the offence (see above).

The Corporations Act therefore creates a high bar in imposing liability on directors removed from day-to-day activities for victimisation conduct that occurs in their organisation. Again, that will discourage directors from seeking to become directly involved in decision-making where a whistleblower might be considered to suffer detriment when a protected disclosure is being investigated.

8.5 Directors Dealing with Compensation and Related Claims

Linked to the victimisation offence is a broad civil liability regime of remedies that are available to a person who suffers whistleblower victimisation.[75]

The Corporations Act provides that a Court may make orders if:

- a person engages in conduct that causes detriment or is a threat of detriment;
- in circumstances where they believe or suspect that a person has made or could make a protected whistleblowing disclosure; and
- the belief or suspicion is the reason or part of the reason for the conduct.[76]

The orders the court can make are extremely broad-ranging, and include financial compensation, injunction, apology, reinstatement of an employment position and exemplary damages.[77] Where the detriment involves loss of employment, the Court must consider the period of time the person is likely to be without employment as a result of the conduct.[78]

---

he must have knowledge of the essential matters which go to make up the offence whether or not he knows that the matters amount to a crime".

Yorke v Lucas above, 667 (Mason ACJ, Wilson J, Deane J, Dawson J). See also *Giorgianni v The Queen* above, 505 (Wilson, Deane, Dawson JJ).

[74]See *Rural Press Ltd & Ors v ACCC & Ors* [2003] HCA 75, 48 (Gummow J, Hayne J, Heydon J): "*In order to know the essential facts ... it is not necessary to know that those facts are capable of characterisation in the language of the statute.*"

[75]It is clear that the right to compensation arises independently of whether action is taken in relation to the victimisation—s 1317AF. The background material also makes it clear that criminal victimisation need not be established to access compensation rights caused by detriment—see paragraph 1.35 of Supplementary Explanatory Memorandum: Amendments to be moved on behalf of the Government—Treasury Laws Amendment (Whistleblowers) Bill, December 2018.

[76]S 1317AD(i). A threat is very broadly defined for these purposes—ss 1317AD(3), (4).

[77]S 1317AE(1).

[78]S 1317AE(2). This section links the period to the conduct rather than other factors such as social ostracisation (although the section is not expressed to limit the matters the Court may consider).

Under this regime there is a reversal of the onus of proof so that if the whistleblower can adduce or point to evidence that suggests a reasonable possibility that they have suffered detriment or have received a threat of detriment, the defendant then bears the onus of proving the other elements of the claim are not made out.[79]

In bringing an action, the claimant will not be susceptible to a costs order being made against them if they lose the case unless the Court is satisfied the case was initiated vexatiously or without reasonable cause, or the Court is satisfied the claimant's unreasonable act or omission caused the costs.[80]

This reversal of the onus of proof and protection from costs orders are obviously significant factors (subject to the point made below) that are likely to encourage whistleblowers to use litigation where they believe they have suffered detriment through whistleblowing.

It can also be expected to encourage plaintiff law firms and litigation funders to seek out whistleblowing claims.

8.5.1 Individual Culpability

The circumstances in which an individual will be liable to compensation or other orders being made against them in relation to whistleblower disclosures in a corporate context are therefore fairly clear. That will be when that individual engaged in proscribed conduct, had the relevant belief or suspicion and that belief or suspicion at least partly motivated the conduct in question.

Officers and employees should therefore be extremely circumspect in engaging in conduct that could be considered detrimental if they wish to avoid potential personal civil liability for that conduct.

Again, there will be little incentive for a director to become involved in decision-making concerning a whistleblowing disclosure if detriment to the whistleblower can be alleged.

8.5.2 Corporate Culpability

In terms of corporate culpability, the Corporations Act provides for a complicated regime of liability.

The starting point of analysis is where the corporation itself is considered to have engaged in proscribed conduct. The general law identification theory of corporate liability will apply in determining whether or not the conduct was engaged in with

[79] S 1317AD(2B).

[80] S 1317AH.

the required intent in connection with the statutory liability regime.[81] As such, the potential difficulties associated with establishing that the directing mind and will has exercised control over the activities of the corporation in causing that detriment will arise.

In the same way as discussed above, it will be necessary to undertake a process of statutory interpretation to assess the terms of the statutory provision and the policy objectives of the statute to attribute direct culpability to a corporation.

As a general rule, the principles of attribution for imposing civil liability on a corporation are likely to be less stringent than for criminal liability.[82] Again it can be expected that a Court would consider that the amended Corporations Act expects that a corporation should be responsible for the conduct of its officers and employees if they engage in detrimental conduct towards a whistleblower. Whistleblower policies should reinforce that expectation broadly across the organisation.

The reversal of the burden of proof may also assist a person who has suffered damage in this context. As noted above, the plaintiff need only establish that there is a reasonable possibility the corporation has engaged in detrimental conduct. This seems a reasonably low hurdle if the conduct has been engaged in through an employee or officer acting within their delegated authority. The more difficult challenge would be for the required intent to be established based on identification principles, but that is for the corporation to rebut.

In addition, two further bases of corporate culpability arise under the legislation.

First, where an employee engages in conduct in connection with their position as an employee that causes detriment to a whistleblower, compensation orders can be made against the employer on a vicarious liability basis.[83] The order against the employing corporation can relate to part of the loss, the full loss or be joint with the employee engaging in the conduct. Corporate liability under this head is limited to compensation for loss, damage or injury—not the other remedies referenced in the section. It follows that the corporate culpability regime applicable to a corporation is straightforward under this head—every employing entity has presumptive liability for compensation in relation to the conduct of its employees.

This head of liability will only impose liability on an entity that is an employer in relation to conduct engaged in by its employees. The relevant employment relationship is to the person engaging in the detrimental conduct, not the whistleblower. The whistleblower need not be an employee to seek compensation under this head.

For these purposes, only a corporate entity in a common law employment relationship would be liable.[84] Based on fundamental principles of separate corporate

---

[81] For examples of the imposition of the general law test of corporate culpability onto a statutory liability regime see the analysis in *Nationwide News Pty Ltd v Naidu & Anor* [2007] NSWCA 377 (Spigelman CJ, Beazley JA, Basten JA) and *Christian Youth Camps Ltd v Cobaw Community Health Services Ltd* [2014] VSCA 75 (Maxwell P, Neave, Redlich JJA). Again, corporate attribution should be assessed by reference to the particular legislation in question, taking into account the language of the statute and its content and policy.

[82] *North Sydney Council v Roman* [2007] NSWCA 27 (McColl JA, Brysen JA, Basten JA) at 41.

[83] S 1317AE(1)(b).

[84] See for example the approach in *McClusky v Karagiozis* [2002] FCA 1137.

identity, other entities in a corporate group will generally not have liability under this head.[85]

Second, a body corporate may be responsible for the conduct of third persons where the corporation is under a duty to prevent the third person engaging in that detrimental conduct or a duty to take reasonable steps to ensure the third person does not engage in that detrimental conduct, and that duty is not fulfilled in whole or in part.[86]

It is odd from a policy perspective to impose corporate liability based on the existence of a duty to prevent conduct. It begs the general question of when a Court will impose a duty on a corporation to protect whistleblowers from suffering detriment.

The Corporations Act itself imposes no express duty of this nature on corporations, including employing corporations. The explanatory materials to the amending legislation suggest that duty may arise under employment law or state law.[87]

At general law an employer owes its employees a duty of care both in contract and tort to take reasonable care to avoid exposing them to unnecessary risks of injury.[88] The duty is also commonly expressed as a duty to create a safe workplace or to adopt safe systems where there is a real risk of injury.[89] In this context, the relevant risk of injury extends beyond the risk of physical harm.[90] The common law duty is supported by workplace and safety legislation[91] that imposes a primary duty of care on employers to ensure so far as is reasonably practicable that the health and safety of workers are protected while at work.[92]

It would not be a very adventurous application of these general principles to conclude that when the Corporations Act is considered in the context of growing community expectations around the protection of whistleblowers, a duty to prevent detrimental conduct might be considered a component of this general law and statutory duty.[93] That being said, from a policy perspective it would have been much more desirable to impose corporate liability in a clearer fashion than by reference to relatively vague obligations of general employment law duty.

---

[85] See the principles enunciated in *Briggs v James Hardie & Co Pty Ltd* (1989) 16 NSWLR 549 (Hope & Meagher JJA, Rogers AJA).

[86] S 1317AD(2A). The whistleblower has the burden of proof in establishing the existence of the duty.

[87] See for example the second reading speech, Hansard House of Representatives, 14 February 2019 at 13439 (Angus Taylor MP).

[88] *Hamilton v Nuroof (WA) Pty Ltd* (1956) 96 CLR 18; *Czartyrko v Edith Cowan University* [2005] HCA 15.

[89] *Smith v The Broken Hill Pty Ltd* (1957) 97 CLR 337.

[90] See *Koehler v Cerebos Australia* [2005] HCA 15; *Nationwide News Pty Ltd v Naidu & Anor* [2007] NSWCA 377 (Spigelman CJ, Beazley JA, Basten JA) (both cases relating to mental health injury where that that type of harm is a reasonably foreseeable form of injury).

[91] *Work Health and Safety Act* 2011 (Cwth). Each State and Territory has similar legislation.

[92] S 19. See the inclusive definition of health and safety issues in s 19(3).

[93] See also the unreported whistleblowing case of *Wheadon v New South Wales* (District Court of NSW, Cooper J, 2 February 2001) described in Dixon (2016, p. 180).

In addition, this analysis does not take the position very far in many instances of workplace behaviour, as an employing corporation already has vicarious liability for the acts of its employees engaging in detrimental conduct against a whistleblower under the first limb of corporate culpability discussed above.[94]

It should be noted that a whistleblower seeking to impose liability on a corporation bears the burden of adducing or pointing to evidence that suggests a reasonable possibility that the duty exists before the overall burden of proof is reversed as described above.[95] The uncertainties created by the analysis above may therefore be problematic for a whistleblower pursuing compensation and other remedies against a corporation.

It is unfortunate that the amended Corporations Act did not offer greater simplicity and clarity on these important issues of corporate culpability.

In imposing liability on an employer the Court may have regard to whether the employer took reasonable precautions and exercised due diligence to avoid the victimising conduct, the extent to which it gave effect to its whistleblowing policy and any duty that it had to prevent the detrimental conduct or to take reasonable steps to ensure the detrimental conduct was not engaged in.[96] This represents a softening of the initial drafts of legislation that instructed the Court not to impose liability where appropriate due diligence was exercised. The listed matters are not intended to limit the matters the Court may take into account.[97]

The Explanatory Memorandum notes that consistent with this power it would be appropriate for the Court to consider applicable industry standards relating to whistleblower support, international or Australian standards or guidance published by ASIC or other regulatory agencies.[98]

It should be noted that the defence is only explicitly expressed to apply to the corporate culpability of an employer under the vicarious liability limb referred to above. However, it would be reasonable for a Court to also consider these matters to be relevant to corporate culpability based on duty as discussed above if that corporation is also an employer.[99]

The standard of an employer taking reasonable precautions and exercising due diligence is a readily understood legal standard and represents the converse of negligent conduct.[100] It should be noted that equating due diligence with a statutory

[94] Although the existence of a duty on the part of the employer is a matter that may bear on exculpation from liability, as discussed below.

[95] S 1317AD(2B)(a)(iii).

[96] S 1317AE(3).

[97] Paragraph 1.28 and 1.29 to Supplementary Explanatory Memorandum: Amendments to be moved on behalf of the Government—Treasury Laws Amendment (Whistleblowers) Bill, December 2018.

[98] Ibid. As noted above, the Australian Standard that was previously available has been withdrawn.

[99] Under s 1317AD(2A) a Court "may" make an order in these circumstances.

[100] See *Tesco Supermarkets Limited v Natrass* [1972] AC 153. Also note the comments of the United States Supreme Court in *Ernst & Ernst v Hochfelder* 425 US 185 (1976) and compare *Australian Iron & Steel Pty Limited v Environmental Protection Authority* (1992) 29 NSWLR 497 (Court of Criminal Appeal) at 510 (Abadee J).

negligence standard also intrudes on the discussion of a more general duty concerning the protection of whistleblowers as discussed above in the context of broader corporate culpability.

The second matter of giving effect to a policy can be readily understood. The comments of the Court in *Re Chemeq* referenced above are particularly apposite in considering how a Court should approach the task of judging whether a whistleblowing policy has been properly implemented and appropriately executed upon receipt of a whistleblowing disclosure.

The third matter of having regard to whether a duty existed seems subordinate in relevance to the two preceding points, as relief from liability would be tested by reference to the measures taken to act appropriately in dealing with a whistleblowing disclosure, rather than being determined by reference to the nature of any duty that existed. The relatively vague nature of a duty to take reasonable care to avoid exposing employees to risk in the context of whistleblowing has been noted above.

When these factors bearing on exculpation for corporate culpability are weighed up, it can be concluded that the desirability of having a robust whistleblowing policy that is properly embedded in the organisation and properly applied is clear.

8.5.3 Director Culpability

Again the question arises as to whether the director of a corporation (particularly a non-executive director) can have liability for victimisation when prohibited conduct has occurred within the organisation. Liability in this connection follows the same path as for the victimisation offence discussed above (albeit in the civil context).

Where a person is an officer or employee of a corporation that engages in victimising conduct and the officer is an accessory to the conduct, the Court may also make orders against the accessory officer or employee.[101] As with the victimisation offence, this liability requires it to be first established the corporation engaged in the conduct.

Consistent with the analysis above, that accessory liability requires evidence of the following matters:

- that the accessory helped, encouraged or induced the principle offender to commit the offence; and
- that the accessory knew the essential matters that constituted the offence.[102]

Again, in most cases it can be expected that the accessory liability extension will be superfluous, as the requirement of participation may likely lead to direct liability.

---

[101] S 1317AD(2). Accessary liability is based on the relatively standard formulation used in the Corporations Act (see for example section 79) of aiding, abetting, procuring, counselling, being knowingly concerned in or conspiracy.

[102] The civil and criminal principles for imposing accessory liability are the same—*Yorke v Lucas* (1985) 158 CLR 661.

8.6 So Should Directors Get Involved?

Having considered the legal analysis outlined above, the key issue that therefore arises for directors under the Corporations Act is to what extent should internal whistleblowing policies dictate disclosure of whistleblowing claims to boards of directors, and whether directors should get involved in the investigation of whistleblowing claims.

8.6.1 Direct Liability

The analysis above suggests that from a technical legal perspective:

- Corporation liability for victimisation in a criminal proceeding relies, in part, on nebulous and unused considerations of corporate culture.
- Corporation liability for victimisation in a civil penalty proceeding is determined by the somewhat ambiguous general law identification principles discussed above.
- Each of these considerations suggests it is in the interests of the corporation that the board and senior management distance themselves from conduct that may involve victimisation of a whistleblower.
- Corporation liability for compensation is relatively complicated, albeit likely to be reasonably effective in imposing liability on an employing corporation.
- If a director gets involved in issues involving whistleblowing claims, that would significantly increase the risk of direct liability (or accessory liability), both for purposes of the victimisation offence and the compensation regime.

This seems an unfortunate result from a public policy perspective.

However, what is clear from the discussion above is that the amended Corporations Act creates a much stronger regime—compared to the existing law around victimisation and compensation—that may have real teeth against individuals involved in that type of conduct. As such, the stakes where corporations and their employees behave badly towards whistleblowers are significantly higher than was previously the case.

Even with the ambiguity that surrounds corporation and director liability, for the corporation and its board reputational issues will loom large in any event, particularly as community expectations shift towards greater sympathy to the position of whistleblowers.

An advantage that a non-executive director can bring to a consideration of a whistleblowing claim is a more independent approach, compared to that of management who may work day-to-day with a whistleblower and may be implicated in some way in the behaviour which is the subject of the complaint.

In some cases, the whistleblower may have been motivated to come forward by virtue of a grievance. The good faith requirement that existed in the Corporations Act before 2019 for protected whistleblowing is no longer a relevant consideration in determining whether a disclosure made by a whistleblower is protected. As such, it is the nature of the complaint, rather than the reasons as to why the whistleblower has come forward, that should be the only relevant consideration. The motivations of the individual coming forward should not be a factor that influences how the complaint is dealt with.

All this suggests that strict independence from the management structure of the organisation should be mandated when whistleblowing complaints are received.

However, will that necessarily mandate involvement of the directors? As discussed above, the legal regime does not encourage that involvement.

8.6.2 Stepping Stones Liability as a Further Consideration for Directors

Where a director has been put on notice of a possible serious contravention of law through whistleblowing, director duty considerations will also arise. This potential additional head of liability may also influence the decision of a director to get involved in whistleblowing claims.

At common law a director owes a duty of care, skill and diligence.[103] In Australia this duty has also been codified as the obligation of a director or other officer to exercise their powers and discharge their duties with the degree of care and diligence that a reasonable person would exercise in the circumstances if they were an officer in the corporation and occupied the office held and had the same responsibilities as the officer.[104] The officer has available a business judgement defence based on establishing a rational belief that a business judgement is in the best interests of the corporation.[105] Contravention of the statutory duty may be enforced by ASIC pursuant to the civil penalty regime of the Corporations Act.[106]

Traditionally, the duty of care, skill and diligence had been assessed by reference to the subjective knowledge and skills of the particular director, a legal standard that was pitched particularly low.[107] However, the statutory formulation in the Corporations Act imposes a much more objective standard of conduct that is more reflective of the concept of negligence at general law.

---

[103] For more detailed discussion of the duty of care, skill and diligence see Golding (2012, pp. 267–8).

[104] Corporations Act s 180. For these provisions, an officer is, among other persons, a director, secretary, a person who makes or participates in the making of decisions that affect the whole or a substantial part of the business of a corporation, a person who has the capacity to affect significantly the financial standing of the corporation, and a person in accordance with whose instructions or wishes the directors are accustomed to act (s 9 definition). As to the scope of the term officer, see *Shafron v ASIC* [2012] HCA 18 (company secretary and general counsel held to be an officer).

[105] Corporations Act s 180(2).

[106] Corporations Act s 1317E(1).

[107] For discussion see Golding (2012, pp. 268–72).

Some of the basic elements of the duty of care, skill and diligence as enunciated by Australian Courts can be summarised as follows[108]:

- There is a core irreducible requirement that a director or officer be involved in the management of the company and guide and monitor the activities of the company, tested by what a reasonable person of ordinary prudence would do.[109]
- From that core irreducible requirement any additional skills and expertise that a director or officer has should be factored in,[110] and the role that the director or officer performs in the governance structure must also be assessed.[111]
- A director must acquire an understanding of the business of the company and become familiar with its fundamentals.[112]
- A director must remain informed about the activities of the company and monitor those activities.[113]
- In determining whether the duty has been breached, the foreseeable risk of harm must be balanced against the potential benefits that could reasonably be expected to accrue from the conduct.

Basing a breach of duty on the possibility the corporation exposed itself to liability through a breach of law is known as the "stepping stones" approach to imposing liability on an officer.[114]

Not every contravention of law by a corporation will impose such a liability on its officers. Liability will only arise where the corporation's interests were jeopardised in a way that the risks assumed by the director outweighed the potential benefits and the directors could have taken reasonable steps to avoid those risks.[115]

---

[108]This summary is taken from Golding (2012, pp. 270–1).

[109]*Deputy Commissioner of Taxation v Clark* (2003) 57 NSWLR 113 at 140 (Spigelman CJ, Handley & Hodgson JA).

[110]*Daniels v Anderson* (1995) 37 NSWLR 438 at 505 (Clarke, Sheller & Powell JJA).

[111]Most notably illustrated by the characterisation of the role performed by a chairman with deep experience in a company's development, as described in *Australian Securities and Investments Commission v Rich* [2003] NSWSC 85 (Austin J) (the *Greaves* decision). The *Greaves* decision was technically only a ruling on ASIC's statement of claim rather than a liability finding. The defendant ultimately consented to civil penalty orders being made, and as part of the making of those orders the judge applied the analysis of the *Greaves* decision: see *ASIC v Rich* [2004] NSWSC 836 at 37–41 (White J). See also the characterisation of a director who is also chief executive officer: *Australian Securities and Investments Commission v Vines* [2005] NSWSC 738 at 1057–1059 (Austin J). In *Shafron v ASIC* [2012] HCA 18 at 20 the High Court again adopted a specific characterisation for a company secretary who also acted as general counsel.

[112]*Daniels v Anderson* (1995) 37 NSWLR 438 at 503–4 (Clarke, Sheller & Powell JJA) referring to *Francis v United Jersey Bank*, 432 A 2d 814 (NJ, 1981).

[113]Ibid. This was described in *Statewide Tobacco Services Ltd v Morley* (1990) 2 ACSR 405 at 431 (SC Vic Ormiston J) as a 'diligent and intelligent interest' in the information available to the director or which the directors might request from management and advisors.

[114]See Herzberg and Anderson (2012).

[115]See discussion in *ASIC v Maxwell* [2006] NSWSC 1052 (Brereton J); *ASIC v Mariner Corporation Limited* [2015] FCA (Beach J); *ASIC v Cassimatis* (No. 8) [2016] FCA 1023 (Edelman J).

While the Courts have stressed that the theory is not to be used as a back-door method of imposing liability on directors where an officer has not been put on notice of a serious matter, ASIC has enjoyed a remarkable success rate in bringing actions against directors using the argument.

8.6.3 The AWB Case Study

The potential application of the duty of care, skill and diligence to corporate officers who might not be sufficiently diligent in addressing whistleblower concerns is well illustrated by ASIC's civil penalty enforcement record in relation to AWB Limited (previously the Australian Wheat Board). It is worth recounting that litigation as a case study as to how failure to follow up whistleblowing claims can expose a director to liability.

In 2006 a Royal Commission found AWB had made disguised payments to the government of Iraq (unusual transport charges paid for the trucking of wheat sold to Iraq) that circumvented sanctions imposed by the United Nations on Iraq.[116]

Following damning findings of the Royal Commission against AWB and its officers, ASIC commenced civil penalty proceedings against a number of the officers of AWB, which played out over a very protracted period.

The Chief Executive Officer and the Chief Financial Officer each settled the claims against them and consented to civil penalty orders being made against them.[117] In making findings against the Chief Executive Officer, the Court found that while the contraventions of duty did not involve deliberate wrongful acts or dishonesty, he was essentially negligent in managing the risks associated with undertaking business in Iraq.[118]

The claims made against the Chairman and another senior executive officer ultimately went to trial.[119] Orders of contravention were made against the Chairman.[120] Again the Court did not consider that the Chairman had been dishonest in his dealings or that he had actual knowledge that the payments made by AWB were contrary

---

[116]See Cole (2006).

[117]*ASIC v Lindberg* [2012] VSC 332 (Robson J) and *ASIC v Ingleby* [2012] VSC 339 (Robson J). In the proceedings against the Chief Executive Officer the Court affirmed an agreed pecuniary penalty of $100,000 and a 3-year disqualification period from managing corporations in relation to the contraventions. In the proceedings against the Chief Financial Officer on appeal by ASIC the penalties finally imposed were a pecuniary penalty of $40,000 and a 15-month disqualification period—*ASIC v Ingleby* [2013] VSCA 49 (Weinberg & Harper AJA, Hargrave AJA).

[118][2012] VSC 332, at 73 and 121.

[119]*ASIC v Flugge; ASIC v Geary* [2016] VSC 779.

[120]*ASIC v Flugge (No 2)* [2017] VSC 117. A pecuniary penalty of $50,000 and a 5-year disqualification period from managing corporations was imposed. ASIC appealed the decision concerning the senior executive officer. The ASIC appeal was dismissed—*ASIC v Geary* [2018] VSCA 103 (Ferguson CJ, Weinberg JA, Sifris AJA).

to the United Nation sanctions.[121] Instead the Chairman had been put on notice at a meeting with United Nations officials that another wheat-exporting country had complained that AWB was making improper payments in Iraq. Having become aware of this whistleblowing-type complaint, it was the ongoing failure of the Chairman to make reasonable inquiries into the proprietary of the payments that constituted a breach of the duty of care, skill and diligence.[122]

One response to the analysis illustrated by the AWB case might be to suggest that it is better for a director not to be made aware of a whistleblowing complaint so that no duty to investigate the red flag is raised.

As noted above, that is not the end of the matter. Whether or not a red flag is raised, the director has a duty to become familiar with the fundamentals of the business of the company and must remain informed and monitor the activities of the company.

It therefore follows that it would be unsafe to consider that a director can be perfectly insulated by keeping allegations of serious contraventions of law made by a whistleblower from the board. Being put on notice of a whistleblowing claim can clearly cause a red flag to arise that should be investigated by the board. Permitting an organisational structure to exist that prevents important issues getting through to the board risks a claim of inadequate supervision.

8.7 A Concluding Comment

The work of whistleblower reform is not done in Australia, and that may have further significant implications for corporations and directors.[123]

This chapter has illustrated that it is unfortunate that the amended Corporations Act did not offer greater policy clarity on the important issues of corporate and director liability concerning whistleblowing. That being said, there is much to be learned by all directors from the debate being had in Australia and the lessons it offers for contemporary whistleblower regulation.

References

Ashcroft J, Hanaway C, Griem C (2011) Whistleblowers Cash in, Unwary Corporations Pay. *Hofstra L Rev* 40:367

Australian Labor Party (2019) *Media Release—Labor Will Protect and Reward Banking Whistleblowers*. https://www.billshorten.com.au/labor_will_protect_and_reward_banking_whistleblowers_sunday_3_february_2019. Accessed 10 May 2019

---

[121] [2016] VSC 1890-1.

[122] [2016] VSC at 1287-8; at 1902-3.

[123] As part of its platform for the 18 May 2019 federal election, the Australian Labor Party promised to enact a unified whistleblower law, establish a whistleblower protection authority, fund a special prosecutor and introduce a whistleblower rewards scheme—see Australian Labor Party (2019).

Brand V (2000) Legislating for Moral Propriety in Corporations? The Criminal Code Amendment (Bribery of Foreign Public Officials) Act 1999. *C&S Law J* 18:476

Brown AJ, Lawrence SA (2017) *Strength of Organisational Whistleblowing Processes: Analysis from Australia. Further Results from the Whistling While They Work 2 Project.* Griffith University, Brisbane

Clough J, Mulhern C (2002) *The Prosecution of Corporations.* Oxford University Press, Oxford

Cole T (2006) *Report of the Inquiry into Certain Australian Companies in Relation to the UN Oil for Food Program.* http://www.oilforfoodinquiry.gov.au/agd/WWW/unoilforfoodinquiry.nsf/Page/Report.html. Accessed 10 May 2019

Colvin J, Argent J (2016) Corporate and Personal Liability for 'Culture' in Corporations. *C&S Law J* 34:30

Comino V (2007) The Enforcement Record of ASIC Since the Introduction of the Civil Penalty Regime. *Austl J Corp L* 20:183

Criminal Law Officers Committee of the Standing Committee of Attorneys-General (1992) *Model Criminal Code Chapters 1 and 2—General Principles of Criminal Responsibility.* Australian Government Printing Service

Criminal Law Officers Committee of the Standing Committee of Attorneys-General (1993) *Final Report—General Principles of Criminal Responsibility.* Australian Government Printing Service

Davids C, Schubert G (2011) Criminalising Roreign Bribery: Is Australia's Bark Louder than Its Bite? *Crim Law J* 35:98

Dixon O (2016) Honesty Without Fear? Whistleblower Anti-Retaliation Protections in Corporate Codes of Conduct. *Melbourne U L Rev* 40:168

Golding G (2012) Tightening the Screws on Directors: Care, Delegation and Reliance. *UNSWLJ* 266

Grantham R (2001) Attributing Responsibility to Corporate Entities: A Doctrinal Approach. *C&S Law J* 19:168

Herzberg A, Anderson H (2012) Stepping Stones: From Corporate Fault to Director's Personal Liability. *Fed Law Rev* 40:181

Kaptein M, Schwartz M (2008) The Effectiveness of Business Codes: A Critical Examination of Existing Studies and the Development of an Integrated Research Model. *J Bus Ethics* 77:111

Kraweic K (2003) Cosmetic Compliance and the Failure of Negotiated Governance. *Wash ULQ* 81:487

Moss P (2016) *Review of the Public Interest Disclosure Act 2013: An Independent Statutory Review Conducted by Philip Moss AM.* https://www.pmc.gov.au/sites/default/files/publications/pid-act-2013-review-report.pdf. Accessed 10 May 2019

Overland J (2010) Corporate Liability for Insider Trading: How Does a Company Have the Necessary 'Mens Rea'. *Am J Comp L* 24:266 at 275

Pascoe J (2009) Corporate Sector Whistleblowing in Australia; Ethics and Corporate Culture. *C&S Law J* 27:524

Pascoe G, Welsh M (2011) Whistleblowing, Ethics and Corporate Culture: Theory and Practice in Australia. *Comm L World Rev* 40:144

Senate Economics References Committee (2014) *Performance of the Australian Securities and Investments Commission.* https://www.aph.gov.au/Parliamentary_Business/Committees/Senate/Economics/ASIC/Final_Report/index. Accessed 10 May 2019

Standards Australia (2003) *AS 8004-2003 Corporate Governance—Whistleblower Protection Programs for Entities*

Welsh M (2004) Eleven Years on—An Examination of ASIC's Use of an Expanding Civil Penalty Regime. *Aust J Corp Law* 17:175

Welsh M (2009) The Regulatory Dilemma: The Choice Between Overlapping Criminal Sanctions and Civil Penalties for Contraventions of the Directors' Duty Provisions. *C&S Law J* 27:370

Greg Golding is a partner in leading multinational law firm Ashurst, specialising in corporate transactions in the areas of listed company takeovers, reconstructions and capital raisings. Greg has a market leading practice having been involved in many of Australia's most significant mergers and acquisition transactions; he also publishes in academic outlets on corporate law matters and chairs whistleblowing and foreign bribery sub-committees of the Law Council of Australia's Business Law Division.

The manufacturer's authorised representative in the EU is Springer Nature Customer Service Centre GmbH, Europaplatz 3, 69115 Heidelberg, Germany. If you have any concerns regarding our products, please contact ProductSafety@springernature.com

Printed and bound by CPI Group (UK) Ltd, Croydon, CR0 4YY

30/09/2026

02225508-0003